WARREN BUFFETT

Biography

Investing in the Values of Life

TABLE OF CONTENTS

PART ONE / The Bubble

PART TWO / The Inner Scorecard

PART THREE / The Racetrack

PART FOUR / Susie Sings

PART FIVE / The King of Wall Street

THE BUBBLE

THE LESS FLATTERING VERSION

Omaha, June 2003

Warren Buffett leans back in his chair, his long legs crossing at the knees behind his father Howard's plain wooden desk. His pricey Zegna suit jacket hangs around his shoulders like an untailored version from the rack. The jacket remains on all day, every day, regardless of how casually the other fifteen employees at Berkshire Hathaway headquarters dress. His usual white shirt rests low on his neck, its undersized collar bursting away from his tie, as if he hadn't checked his neck size in forty years. His hands are laced behind his head amid strands of white hair. One particularly huge and untidy finger-combed chunk flies over his skull like a ski jump, soaring upward at the knoll of his right ear. His shaggy right brow raises above the tortoiseshell glasses. This brow lends him a skeptical, smart, or bewitching expression at different moments. He is currently wearing a slight smile, which gives the wandering brow a compelling appearance. Nonetheless, his pale blue eyes are fixed and earnest.

He sits surrounded by icons and memorabilia from the previous fifty years. In the corridors outside his office, there are Nebraska Cornhuskers football photos, his salary from a soap opera performance, an offer letter (never accepted) to buy a hedge fund named Long-Term Capital Management, and Coca-Cola paraphernalia everywhere. A traditional Coca-Cola bottle can be found on the coffee table in the office. A baseball glove covered in Lucite. A certificate indicating that he completed Dale Carnegie's public-speaking course in January 1952 hangs over the sofa. On top of a bookcase, the Wells Fargo stagecoach travels westbound. His financial partnership controlled Sun Newspapers of Omaha, which earned a Pulitzer Prize in 1973. Books and newspapers are scattered over the room. Photographs of his family and friends cover the credenza and a side table. Instead of a computer, they rest beneath the hutch opposite his desk. A big portrait of Buffett's father sits above his head on the wall behind his desk. It confronts every visitor that enters the room.

Although a late-spring Omaha morning beckons outside the windows, the brown wooden shutters remain closed, obscuring the vista. The television aimed at his workstation is tuned to CNBC. The sound is muffled, but the crawl at the bottom of the screen provides him with

news updates throughout the day. Th
him throughout the years, which he ha
Only a few individuals know him wel
starting when I was a financial analyst covering Berkshire Hathaway
stock. Our friendship has become more amicable over time, and I hope
to get to know him even better today. We're sitting in Warren's office
because he's not going to write any books. His bushy brows accent his
words as he repeats, "You'll do a better job than I would, Alice." I am
delighted you are writing this book, not me." Why he would say that
will become clearer in time. Meanwhile, let us begin with the issue
that is most important to him.

"Warren, where did it originate from? "Do you care so much about
making money?"

His eyes drift away for a few seconds as his thoughts journey inward:
flick, flip, flip through the mental files. Warren begins telling his story:
"Balzac once stated that behind every great fortune lurks a crime.
"That is not true at Berkshire." He leaps out of his chair to convey the
message, crossing the room in a few strides. He leans forward in a
mustardy-gold brocade couch, more like a teenager talking about his
first relationship than a 72-year-old businessman. How to interpret the
tale, who else to interview, and what to write? The book is entirely up
to me. He talks extensively about human nature and memory's
weakness before saying, "Whenever my version differs from someone
else's, Alice, use the less flattering version."

Some of the most valuable lessons can be learned simply by observing
him. Here's the first. Humility disarms.

In the end, there won't be many reasons to go with the less favorable
version—but when I do, it's usually due to human nature rather than
memory's weakness. One of these incidents occurred in Sun Valley in
1999.

SUN VALLEY

Idaho, July 1999

Warren Buffett got out of his car and took his suitcase out of the trunk.
He stepped through the chain-link gate onto the airport's tarmac, where
a shining white Gulfstream IV jet—the size of a regional commercial
airliner and the world's largest private aircraft in 1999—was waiting
for him and his family. One of the pilots seized the bag from him and

stowed it in the cargo hold. Every new pilot who flew with Buffett was surprised to find him carrying his own bags from a car he drove himself. As he climbed the boarding stairs, he said hello to the flight attendant—someone new—and took a seat close to a window, which he would not look out of at any point during the flight. He was in a good mood; he had been looking forward to this vacation for weeks.

His son Peter and daughter-in-law Jennifer, his daughter Susan and her partner, and two of his grandchildren all sat in their own café au lait leather club chairs arranged around the 45-foot-long cabin. They swiveled their chairs away from the curving wall panels to make more room as the flight attendant served refreshments from the galley, which was packed with the family's favorite snacks and beverages. A stack of magazines sat close on the sofa: Vanity Fair, the New Yorker, Fortune, Yachting, the Robb Report, the Atlantic Monthly, the Economist, Vogue, and the Yoga Journal. Instead, she handed Buffett an armload of newspapers, a basket of potato chips, and a Cherry Coke to match his red Nebraska shirt. He commended her, talked for a few minutes to calm her nerves about flying for the first time with her boss, and told her she may notify the copilot that they were ready to take off. Then he hid his head in a newspaper as the plane rumbled down the runway and climbed to 40,000 feet. For the next two hours, six people hummed around him, watching videos, talking, and making phone calls, while the flight attendant laid out linens and orchid-filled bud vases on the bird's-eye maple dining tables before returning to the galley to make lunch. Buffett never moved. He sat reading, hiding behind his newspapers, as if he were alone in his home study.

They were flying in a $30 million aerial palace known as a "fractional" plane. It could have up to eight owners, but because it was part of a fleet, all could fly at the same time if they so desired. The pilots in the cockpit, the crew who kept it running, the schedulers who got it to the gate on six hours' notice, and the flight attendant who served them lunch were all employed by NetJets, a subsidiary of Warren Buffett's Berkshire Hathaway.

Later, the G-IV traversed the Snake River Plain and reached the Sawtooth Mountains, a massive Cretaceous upheaval of black and ancient granite mounds frying in the summer heat. It flew into the bright, clear air into the Wood River Valley, descending to 8,000 feet before beginning to buck on the mountain wave of turbulence projected into the sky by the brown hillsides below. Buffett read on,

unconcerned, as the plane rocked and his family shifted in their seats. Brush studded the higher elevations of a second ridge of hills, and rows of pines began to march up the ridges between ravines on the leeward side. The family beamed with anticipation. As the plane descended through the decreasing slot between the rising mountain peaks ahead, the midday sun cast a longer shadow over the historic mining town of Hailey, Idaho.

Seconds later, the wheels landed on the Friedman Memorial Airport runway. By the time the Buffetts had rushed down the stairs onto the tarmac, squinting in the July glare, two SUVs had passed through the gate and parked alongside the plane, driven by Hertz employees. All wore the company's gold and black shirts. Instead of Hertz, the logo read "Allen & Co."

The grandchildren bounced on their heels as the pilots unloaded the luggage, tennis rackets, and Buffett's red-and-white Coca-Cola golf bag into the SUVs. Then he and the others shook hands with the pilots, said goodbye to the flight attendant, and boarded the SUVs. Bypassing Sun Valley Aviation, a small trailer at the southern end of the runway, they swung through the chain-link gate and onto the road that went to the peaks beyond. About two minutes had passed since the plane's wheels initially touched the runway.

Eight minutes later, another jet arrived on time and took its own runway parking position.

Throughout the sunny afternoon, jet after jet flew into Idaho from the south and east, or swung around the peaks from the west and descended into Hailey: workhorse Cessna Citations, elegant, close-quarters Learjets, quick Hawkers, opulent Falcons, but especially the awe-inspiring G-IVs. As the afternoon progressed, dozens of massive, sparkling white planes lined the runway like a store window filled with tycoons' toys.

The Buffetts followed the road established by earlier SUVs a few miles from the airport to Ketchum, a tiny village on the border of the Sawtooth National Forest near the Elkhorn Pass turnoff. A few kilometers later, they rounded Dollar Mountain and saw a verdant paradise nestled among the brown slopes. Sun Valley, the Rockies' most fabled resort, is nestled among the lacy pines and dazzling aspens, where Ernest Hemingway began writing For Whom the Bell Tolls and where Olympic skiers and skaters have long called home.

The families they were joining on Tuesday afternoon all had some link to Allen & Co., a boutique investment bank specializing in the media and communications industries. Allen & Co. had orchestrated some of Hollywood's largest mergers and, for more than a decade, had hosted an annual series of debates and seminars for its clients and friends in Sun Valley, interspersed with outdoor activity. Herbert Allen, the firm's CEO, only invited persons he liked or with whom he was eager to conduct business.

As a result, the conference was always packed with famous and wealthy attendees, including Hollywood producers and stars Candice Bergen, Tom Hanks, Ron Howard, and Sydney Pollack, entertainment moguls Barry Diller, Rupert Murdoch, Robert Iger, and Michael Eisner, socially renowned journalists Tom Brokaw, Diane Sawyer, and Charlie Rose, and technology titans Bill Gates, Steve Jobs, and Andy Grove. Every year, a mob of reporters awaits them outside the Sun Valley Lodge.

The reporters had traveled to the Newark, New Jersey, airport or a similar embarkation point the day before to board a commercial flight to Salt Lake City, then raced to Concourse E's bullpen to sit among a crush of people waiting for flights to places like Casper, Wyoming, and Sioux City, Iowa, until it was time to cram themselves into a prop plane for the one-hour bronco ride to Sun Valley. When they arrived, their plane was directed to the opposite end of the airport, next to the tennis-court-sized terminal, where they saw a crew of tanned young Allen & Co. employees dressed in pastel "SV99" polo shirts and white shorts greeting the handful of Allen & Co. guests who had arrived early on commercial flights. These were easily identifiable among the other passengers: guys in Western boots and Paul Stuart shirts with jeans, and women in goatskin-suede jackets and marble-sized turquoise beads. The Allen staff had memorized the arrivals' faces from photos sent in advance. They hugged folks they'd known for years like old friends, swept away all the guests' bags, and took their charges to the SUVs parked steps away.

The reporters headed to the rental car desk and drove to the Lodge, now acutely aware of their low position. For the following few days, numerous portions of Sun Valley would be marked as "private," with closed doors, constant guards, hanging flower baskets, and enormous potted plants to keep prying eyes at bay. The reporters would hover about the edges, noses pressed against the bushes, oblivious to the exciting things going on inside. Since Disney's Michael Eisner and Capital Cities/ABC's Tom Murphy devised a plan to merge their companies at Sun Valley '95 (as if the conference had engulfed the entire resort, which, in a way, it had), the press coverage had grown to the point where it had the artificially giddy atmosphere of a business version of Cannes. However, the Sun Valley mergers were merely the tip of the iceberg. Sun Valley was about more than just making deals, although the agreements received the most of the attention. Every year, rumors circulated that one corporation or another was working on a deal at the mystery conclave in the Idaho mountains. As the SUVs arrived one by one at the porte cochere, the reporters looked through the front windows to see who was inside. When someone newsworthy arrived, they pursued their victim into the lodge, brandishing cameras and microphones.

When Warren Buffett came out of his SUV, the reporters noticed him right away. "The DNA of the conference had him built into it," remarked his buddy and Allen & Co. chairman Don Keough. The majority of the press liked Buffett, who went out of his way to avoid being despised by anyone. He also sparked their interest. His public image was one of a humble man, and he appeared sincere. However, he led a complex existence. He had five houses but only occupied two. He had ended himself with, effectively, two wives. He spoke in homely aphorisms with a benevolent twinkle in his eye and had a very close set of friends, but along the road he had gained a reputation as a difficult, even frigid dealmaker. He appeared to avoid publicity while attracting more of it than probably any other businessman on the planet.3 He flew throughout the country in a G-IV, frequently attended celebrity events, and had many famous friends, yet he claimed to enjoy Omaha, hamburgers, and thrift. He claimed that his success was built on a few simple investing ideas and tap-dancing to work with joy every day, but if that was true, why hadn't anyone else been able to imitate it?

Buffett, as usual, offered the photographers a willing wave and a grandfatherly smile as he passed. They photographed him before moving on to the next car.

The Buffetts drove around to their French-country-style condominium, one of the Wildflower group's desirable properties near to the pool and tennis courts, where Herbert Allen kept his VIPs. Inside, the typical bounty awaited them: a stack of Allen & Co. SV99 branded coats, baseball caps, zip fleeces, polo shirts (new colors each year), and a zipped notepad. Despite his fortune of more than $30 billion—enough to purchase a thousand of those G-IVs parked at the airport—Buffett enjoyed few things more than receiving a complimentary golf shirt from a buddy. He looked carefully over this year's stuff. What piqued his curiosity even more was Herbert Allen's handwritten note to each attendee, as well as the meticulously arranged conference notebook that detailed what Sun Valley had planned for him this year.

Buffett's itinerary was timed to the second, meticulously structured, and as crisp as Herbert Allen's French cuffs. It was put out hour by hour, day by day. The notebook listed the conference speakers and themes, which had previously been kept a secret, as well as the luncheons and dinners he planned to attend. Buffett, unlike the other visitors, was aware of most of this ahead of time, but he was nevertheless curious about what the notebook contained.

Herbert Allen, the so-called "Lord of Sun Valley" and the conference's quiet choreographer, established the casual luxury that dominated the gathering. People constantly praised him for his strong convictions, intellect, sound guidance, and generosity. "You'd like to die with the respect of somebody like Herbert Allen," according to a guest. Afraid of being barred from the meeting, those who expressed disapproval rarely went beyond vague hints that Herbert was "unusual," restless, impatient, and possessed of an enormous ego. Standing in the shadow of his tall, wiry form, it was difficult to keep up with the words, which came out like machine gun fire. He screamed questions and cut off responses in mid-sentence, lest they waste any of his time. He excelled in uttering the unsayable. "Ultimately, Wall Street will be eliminated," he once assured a reporter, despite the fact that he controlled a Wall Street bank. He called his competition "hot-dog vendors."

Allen kept his firm small, and his bankers invested their own money in their transactions. This unorthodox strategy transformed the firm into a partner rather than a mere servant to its clients, who were the Hollywood and media elites. Thus, when he hosted, his guests felt fortunate rather than like hostages being marketed by salesman at every turn. Every year, Allen & Co. planned a thorough social itinerary based on each guest's personal network of relationships—which the firm was aware of—and the new persons Allen's majordomos believed each should meet. Unspoken hierarchies determined the distances between the guests' condominiums and the Inn (where meetings were held), which meals the guests were invited to attend, and who they would be seated alongside.

Buffett's friend Tom Murphy referred to this type of event as "elephant-bumping." "Anytime a bunch of big shots get together," says Buffett, "you can get people to come, because it reassures them if they're at an elephant-bumping that they're an elephant too."

Sun Valley was always reassuring since, unlike most elephant bumps, you couldn't pay to get in. As a result, the elites established a kind of phony democracy. Part of the excitement of arriving was seeing who was not invited, and even more excitingly, who was denied an invitation. People did, however, form meaningful bonds within their social group. Allen & Co. promoted conviviality with expensive entertainment, beginning on the first evening, when visitors dressed in Western attire, hopped into old-fashioned horse-drawn carts, and accompanied cowboys up a winding road past a natural stone spire into road Creek Cabin meadow. Herbert Allen or one of his two sons met the visitors as the sun began to set. Cowboys performed rope stunts outside a large white tent adorned with urns of crimson petunias and blue sage, while the Sun Valley old guard reunited and welcomed newcomers as they stood in line, plate in hand, for a steak and salmon buffet. The Buffetts frequently closed the evening by gathering with friends around a bonfire beneath the starry western sky.

The fun continued on Wednesday afternoon with an optional, very moderate white-water kayak down the Salmon River. On this excursion, relationships flourished because Allen & Co. coordinated who sat where on the van to the embarkation point and on the rafts. The river guides kept quiet as they navigated through the mountain valley, not wanting to disrupt conversations or disrupt emerging partnerships. Spotters hired from the local community and ambulances flanked the route in case someone fell into the frigid water. When the guests put down their paddles and walked off the rafts, they were given warm towels and fed platters of BBQ.

Those not rafting could be found fly-fishing, horseback riding, shooting trap and skeet, mountain biking, playing bridge, learning to knit, studying nature photography, playing Frisbee with the ubiquitous canine conference guests, ice-skating on the outdoor rink, playing tennis on perfect clay courts, lounging at the pool, or golfing on immaculate greens, where they rode in carts stuffed full of Allen & Co. sunscreen, snacks, and bug spray.6 All the entertainment flowed. The babysitters, a hundred or so good-looking, predominantly blond, highly tanned youths dressed in the identical polo shirts and matching Allen & Co. backpacks, were Herbert Allen's secret weapon. As the parents and grandparents played, the sitters ensured that Joshua and Brittany were accompanied by their own playmate to whatever activity they chose—a tennis clinic, soccer, bicycling, kickball, a wagon ride, a horse show, ice skating, relay races, rafting, fishing, an art project, or pizza and ice cream. Each babysitter was personally chosen to ensure that every child had such a great time that they would beg to return year after year—while also delighting their parents with occasional glimpses of the very, very attractive young person who was allowing them to spend days of guilt-free time with other adults.

Buffett had always been one of the most grateful of Allen's recipients. He adored Sun Valley as a family holiday, since if left to his own devices at a ski resort with his grandchildren, he would have been completely at a loss for what to do. He had little interest in any outside hobbies other than golf. He never went skeet shooting or mountain biking, considered water "a prison of sorts," and would rather be handcuffed than ride on a raft. Instead, he settled into the heart of the elephant herd. He played a little golf and bridge, including a dollar bet standing golf game with Jack Valenti, president of the Motion Picture Association of America, and a bridge game with Meredith Brokaw, and spent the rest of his time socializing with people like Playboy CEO Christie Hefner and computer hardware CEO Michael Dell.

Often, however, he disappeared for long periods into his condo overlooking the golf course, where he read and watched business news in the living room seated next to an enormous stone fireplace.7 He barely noticed the view of pine-covered Baldy, the mountain outside his window, or the bank of blossoms like a Persian palace rug: pastel lupines and sapphire delphiniums towering over poppies and Indian paintbrush, crisp blue salvia and veronica nestled among the stonecrop a "The scenery is there, I guess," he remarked. He came for the friendly atmosphere Herbert Allen had created.8 He enjoyed spending time with his closest friends, including Kay Graham and her son Don, Bill and Melinda Gates, Mickie and Don Keough, Barry Diller and Diane von Furstenberg, and Andy Grove and his wife, Eva.

Above all, for Buffett, Sun Valley was about reuniting with his entire family during one of the few occasions the family was all together. "He likes us all being in the same house," his daughter, Susie Buffett Jr., adds. She lived in Omaha; her younger brother, Howie, and his wife, Devon, who are missing this year, lived in Decatur, Illinois; and their younger sibling, Peter, and his wife, Jennifer, lived in Milwaukee.

Susan, Buffett's separated wife of 47 years, had traveled in from her San Francisco home to meet them. Astrid Menks, his companion for over twenty years, remained in their Omaha home.

Warren dressed in a Hawaiian shirt and brought his wife to the annual Pool Party on the tennis courts near their condo on Friday night. The majority of the guests knew and liked Susie. She was always the star of the Pool Party, singing old-fashioned standards under the light of tiki torches in front of the lit Olympic pool.

This year, as the drinks and friendliness flowed, the chatter of a scarcely discernible new language—B2B, B2C, banner advertisements, bandwidth, broadband—competed with the sounds of Al Oehrle's band. A strange sense of dread had persisted throughout the week's lunches, dinners, and cocktails, like a silent cloud among the handshakes, kisses, and hugs. A new group of recently minted technology executives, filled with an unusual swagger, introduced themselves to people who had never heard of them a year before.9 Some displayed a hubris that was at odds with Sun Valley's usual atmosphere, where a determined informality reigned and Herbert Allen enforced an unwritten rule against pomposity, on penalty of expulsion.

The veil of arrogance hovered heaviest over the conference's keynote presentations. Company executives, high-ranking government officials, and other notable figures delivered speeches unlike any other, because rarely a word of what was said was ever whispered beyond the flower boxes hanging by the Sun Valley Inn's doors. Reporters were barred, and famous journalists and media barons who controlled television networks and newspapers sat in the audience but maintained a code of silence. Thus allowed to perform only for their peers, the speakers expressed essential and frequently accurate things that could never be articulated in front of the press because they were too direct, too nuanced, too terrifying, too readily satirized, or too easy to misunderstand. The workaday journalists waited outside, waiting for crumbs that were rarely thrown.

This year, the new Internet moguls had been strutting, boasting about their soaring expectations, trumpeting their newest mergers, and attempting to raise funds from the money managers in the crowd. The money people, who managed other people's pensions and savings, held so much wealth that it was difficult to comprehend: more than a trillion dollars. In 1999, a trillion dollars could cover everyone's income tax in the United States. You could provide a brand-new Bentley automobile to each household in more than nine states. You could purchase every piece of real estate in Chicago, New York City, and Los Angeles combined. Some of the companies giving presentations required that money, and they wanted this audience to provide it to them.

Early in the week, Tom Brokaw's panel, titled "The Internet and Our Lives," led a series of talks on how the Internet would transform the communications industry. Priceline's Jay Walker led the audience on a whirlwind tour of the Internet, comparing the information superhighway to the arrival of the railroad in 1869. One after the other, executives laid out the gleaming prospects for their companies, filling the room with the intoxicating vapor of a future unlimited by storage space and geography, so slick and visionary that while some were convinced that a whole new world was unfolding, others were reminded of snake-oil sellers. The people who headed technological corporations saw themselves as Promethean geniuses bringing fire to the mortals. Other enterprises that had worked in the ashes to produce the mundane basics of life—auto parts, lawn furniture—were now primarily interested in how much technology they could purchase. Some Internet stocks traded at infinite multiples of their nonexistent earnings, while "real companies" that manufactured real items fell in value. As technology stocks surpassed the "old economy," the Dow Jones Industrial Average broke beyond the previously distant 10,000-point mark only four months earlier, doubling in less than three and a half years.

Many of the newly wealthy gathered between speeches on a cordoned-off dining patio near the Duck Pond, where a pair of captive swans floated around a pool. Any guest—but not a reporter—could make their way past the crowds dressed in khaki slacks and cashmere cable sweaters to ask Bill Gates or Andy Grove questions. Meanwhile, the journalists pursued the Internet moguls as they traveled between the Inn and their condos, exacerbating the sense of inflated self-importance that pervaded Sun Valley this year.

Some of the new Internet czars spent Friday afternoon persuading Herbert Allen to include them in celebrity photographer Annie Leibovitz's Saturday afternoon shoot of the Media All-Star Team for Vanity Fair. They believed they had been invited to Sun Valley because they were the people of the moment, and they had difficulty believing Leibovitz made her own decisions about who to photograph. Why, for example, does she include Buffett? His involvement in media has come mostly through board memberships, a broad network of personal influence, and a track record of large and minor media investments. Furthermore, he was old media. They couldn't believe his portrait could still sell publications.

These would-be all-stars felt slighted since they were fully aware that the media balance had changed to the Internet. That was true even if Herbert Allen thought the "new paradigm" for valuing technology and media equities, which was focused on clicks and eyes and estimates of long-term development rather than a company's ability to earn cold hard cash, was crap. "New paradigm," he remarked. "It's like new sex." There's just no such thing.

The next morning, Buffett, a symbol of the old paradigm, got up early because he would be the year's final speaker. He consistently declined calls to speak at conferences sponsored by other firms, but when Herbert Allen asked him to speak at Sun Valley, he always agreed. The Saturday morning closing talk was the conference's main event, so instead of going straight to the golf course or grabbing a fishing rod, practically everyone walked to the Sun Valley Inn's breakfast buffet and took a seat. Today Buffett would be discussing the stock market.

In private, he had been scathing of the gunslinging, promoter-driven market that had sent technology stocks skyrocketing this year. Berkshire Hathaway's stock sat in the dust, and his strict rule of not investing in technology businesses appeared out of date. However, the criticism had no effect on his investment strategy, as he had just said in public that he never made market predictions. So his choice to get on stage at Sun Valley and do just that was unusual. Maybe it was the time. Buffett had a clear conviction and a strong desire to preach.

He had spent several weeks preparing for this speech. He recognized that the market was more than just people trading stocks like they were chips in a casino. The chips symbolized businesses. Buffett considered all the chips worth. How much were they worth? He next went over his history, drawing on an extensive mental file. This was hardly the first time that revolutionary new technologies had disrupted the stock market. Business history was littered with new technologies—railroads, telegraphs, telephones, automobiles, aircraft, and television: all revolutionary ways to connect things faster—but how many made investors wealthy? He was going to explain.

Clarke Keough approached the podium after finishing his morning buffet. Buffett had known the Keoughs for many years, as they had been neighbors in Omaha. Buffett's connections to Sun Valley came through Clarke's father, Don. Don Keough, the current chairman of Allen & Co. and former president of Coca-Cola, met Herbert Allen when he purchased Columbia Pictures from Allen & Co. for Coca-Cola in 1982. Keough and his employer, Coca-Cola CEO Roberto Goizueta, were so impressed with Herbert Allen's unsportsmanlike approach to selling that they persuaded him to join their board.

Keough, a Sioux City cattleman's son and former altar boy, had officially retired from Coca-Cola, but he still lived and breathed the brand, and he was frequently referred to as the company's shadow CEO.

When the Keoughs were his neighbors in Omaha in the 1950s, Warren asked Don how he planned to pay for his children's college and suggested that he invest $10,000 in Buffett's business. But Don was sending six kids to parochial school on $200 per week as a Butter-Nut coffee salesman. "We didn't have the money," his son Clarke informed the gathering. "This is part of my family's past that we will never forget."

Buffett joined Clarke on the podium, sporting his beloved Nebraska red sweater over a checkered shirt. He completed the story.

"The Keoughs were wonderful neighbors," he told me. "It's true that Don would occasionally comment that, unlike me, he had a job, but our relationship was great. My wife, Susie, once walked over and asked Don's wife, Mickie, for a cup of sugar, and she was given an entire sack. When I heard about it, I decided to see the Keoughs that night. I asked Don, 'Why don't you give me $25,000 for the partnership

to invest?' And the Keough family hardened slightly at that point, and I was turned down.

"I returned later and requested for the $10,000 Clarke mentioned, and received a similar response. But I was not proud. So I returned later and begged for $5,000. And at that point, I was rejected again.

"So one night in the summer of 1962, I started going to the Keough house. I'm not sure if I would have reduced it to $2500, but by the time I arrived at the Keough residence, everything was dark and silent. There was nothing to see. But I understood what was going on. "I stayed because I knew Don and Mickie were hiding upstairs."I rang the doorbell. I knocked. Nothing occurred. But Don and Mickie were upstairs, and it was pitch black.Too dark to read and too early to sleep. And I remember that day like it was yesterday. Clarke was born June 21, 1962.

"March twenty-first, 1963."

"It's small details like this that turn history on. So you should be delighted they didn't pay me the $10,000."

After charming the crowd with this little gift, Buffett returned to the topic at hand. "Now I am going to try to multitask today. Herb instructed me to include a couple slides. 'Show you've got it,' he said. When Herb says something, it's almost like an order in the Buffett home. Speeding past the specifics of "the Buffett household"—for Buffett considered his household to be no different than any other— he jumped into a joke about Allen. The secretary to the President of the United States raced into the Oval Office, apologizing for unintentionally scheduling two meetings at once. The President had to decide between seeing the Pope and Herbert Allen. Buffett paused for effect. *"'Send in the Pope,' said the President. 'At least I only have to kiss his ring.'*

"To all you fellow ring-kissers, I would like to talk today about the stock market," stated the man. "I will discuss stock pricing, but not their future course of action in the following month or year. Valuing is not synonymous with forecasting.In the short run, the market functions as a voting machine. Long term, it is a weighing machine.

"In the end, weight is important. However, votes have a short-term impact. And it's an extremely undemocratic method of voting. Unfortunately, there are no literacy exams for voting qualifications, as you've all discovered."

Buffett pressed a button, illuminating a PowerPoint slide on a large screen to his right. Bill Gates, sitting in the audience, had a moment to catch his breath before the notoriously clumsy Buffett managed to bring up the first slide.

DOW JONES
INDUSTRIAL AVERAGE
December 31, 1964 874.12
December 31, 1981 875.00

He came to the TV and began explaining.

"During these seventeen years, the economy expanded fivefold. The sales of the Fortune 500 businesses increased more than fivefold. Nonetheless, during these seventeen years, the stock market went nowhere.

He took one or two steps back. "When you invest, you are delaying spending and putting money aside now to receive more money later. And there are actually only two questions. There are two aspects to consider: the amount and timing of the return. Aesop was not a finance major, as he once observed, 'A bird in the hand is worth two in the bush.' But he doesn't specify when. Buffett noted that interest rates, or the cost of borrowing, are the price of "when." They are to finance what gravity is to physics. As interest rates fluctuate, the value of all financial assets—houses, stocks, bonds—changes, just as the price of birds does. And that's why sometimes a bird in the hand is better than two birds in the bush, and sometimes two in the bush is better than one in the hand."

Buffett compared Aesop to the huge 1990s bull market, which he dismissed as nonsense. Profits had grown significantly less than in the preceding period, but birds in the bush were pricey due to low interest rates. Fewer people wanted cash-- bird in hand—at such low rates. Investors were paying unprecedented sums for those birds in the woods. Buffett casually referred to this as the "greed factor."

The audience, which included IT experts who were transforming the world while profiting from the big bull market, remained mute. They were sat atop portfolios crammed with stocks trading at exorbitant prices. This made them very happy. This was a new paradigm, the dawning of the Internet age. They felt Buffett had no right to call them greedy. Warren—who had hoarded his money for years and given very little away, who was so cheap his license plate said "Thrifty," who spent most of his time thinking about how to get money, who had blown the technology boom and missed the boat—was spitting on their champagne.

Buffett continued. There were only three ways the stock market could keep rising 10 percent or more per year. One scenario was for interest rates to fall and remain below historical levels. The second was if the share of the economy that went to investors, rather than employees, the government, and other entities, increased over its already historically high level. Alternatively, he suggested that the economy may begin to grow quicker than usual. Using optimistic assumptions like this, he labeled "wishful thinking".

Some people, he claimed, did not believe that the entire market would prosper. They just assumed they could pick winners from the rest. Swinging his arms like an orchestra conductor, he was able to present another slide while stressing that, while invention has the potential to bring the globe out of poverty, those who invest in innovation have traditionally not been pleased.

"This is half of a page which comes from a list seventy pages long of all the auto companies in the United States." He waved the entire list in the air. *"There were two thousand vehicle companies: the most significant invention of the first half of the twentieth century. It had a huge impact on people's lives. If you had seen how this country would develop in relation to automobiles when the first cars were introduced, you would have exclaimed, 'This is the place I must be.' However, only three vehicle firms remained from the two thousand that existed a few years before. And, at one point or another, all three were selling for less than book value, which is the amount of money invested in the businesses and left there. So automobiles had a huge impact on America, but had the reverse effect on investors.*

He dropped the list to put his hand in his pocket. "Now, it's a lot easier to determine who lost. There was, I believe, an obvious choice then. "And, of course, you should have been shorting horses." Click. A slide on horses flashed up.

U.S. HORSE POPULATION
1900—17 million
1998—5 million

"To be honest, I'm upset that the Buffett family did not short horses over this era. "There are always losers."

Members of the audience chuckled softly. Their enterprises may be losing money, but they are convinced that they are winners, like supernovas on the verge of a seismic shift in the heavens. Undoubtedly, their names would eventually be on the pages of history books.

Click. Another slide appeared.

"The other significant invention of the first half of the century was the airplane. Between 1919 and 1939, there were around 200 firms. Imagine if you could have seen the future of the airline business in Kitty Hawk. You would have witnessed a world beyond your wildest dreams. "Assume you had the insight to see all of these people wishing to fly and do whatever you want in an airplane, and you decided this was the place to be."As of a few years ago, there has been no profit from the sum of all equity investments in the aviation sector throughout history.

"So I suggest to you: If I had been down there at Kitty Hawk, I believe I would have been farsighted and public-spirited enough to shoot Orville down. "I owed it to the future capitalists."

Another slight chuckle. Some people were growing tired of these musty old instances. But, out of respect, they let Buffett go forward with it.

Now he was discussing their businesses. "It's great to support new industries since they're extremely marketable. It is quite difficult to encourage investment in a banal product. There is no numerical guideline, making it much easier to pitch an esoteric product, especially one with losses." This was directly aimed at the audience, causing pain. "But people will keep returning to invest, you know. It reminds me of the story about the oil prospector who died and went to paradise. And St. Peter responded, "Well, I checked you out, and you meet all of the requirements." But there is one problem. He stated, "We have some tough zoning laws up here, and we keep all of the oil prospectors over in that pen." And, as you can see, it is incredibly jam-packed. "There is no room for you."And the prospector asked, "Do you mind if I just say four words?"

"St. Peter responded, 'No harm in that.'"The prospector cupped his hands and yelled, 'Oil discovered in hell!'.'""Once the lock is removed from the cage, the oil prospectors begin their descent."St. Peter commented, 'That's a pretty smart technique. So, he says, 'come in and make yourself at home. "There's plenty of room."The prospector pondered for a moment before saying, 'No, I guess I'll join the rest of the boys. There could be some truth to that rumor after all.

"Well, that is how people feel about equities. After all, it's pretty easy to believe the rumor is true.

This elicited a small giggle for a half second, which faded as soon as the audience realized Buffett's point, which was that, like the prospectors, they might be stupid enough to believe rumors and drill for oil in hell. He concluded by referring to the proverbial bird in the bush. There was no new paradigm, he stated. Finally, the stock market's valuation can only represent the economy's output. He showed a graphic demonstrating how, for several years, the market's value had outpaced the economy's growth by a large margin. This means, Buffett argued, that the next seventeen years might not look much better than the protracted period from 1964 to 1981 when the Dow went nowhere—unless the market plummets. "If I had to pick the most probable return over that period," he said, "it would probably be six percent." However, a recent PaineWebber-Gallup poll revealed that investors expected stocks to return 13 to 22%.

He walked over to the screen. Waggling his bushy brows, he motioned at a cartoon of a naked man and woman, borrowed from a classic stock market book, Where Are the Customers' Yachts? "The man said to the woman, 'There are certain things that cannot be adequately explained to a virgin either by words or pictures.'" The audience understood his argument, which was that individuals who bought Internet stocks were destined to get screwed. They sat in stone stillness. Nobody laughed. Nobody laughed, snickered, or guffawed.

Buffett appeared unconcerned when he returned to the podium and informed the audience about the goody bag he had brought from Berkshire Hathaway. "I just bought a company that sells fractional jets, NetJets," according to him. "I considered giving each of you a quarter share of a Gulfstream IV. But when I got to the airport, I understood it would be a step down for the majority of you." They laughed. So, he said, he gave each of them a jeweler's loupe, which he instructed them to use to examine one another's wives' rings—particularly the third wives'. That nailed the mark. The audience laughed and clapped. Then they paused. A hostile undertone flowed through the room. Sermonizing on the excesses of the stock market in Sun Valley in 1999 was akin to preaching chastity in a bad house. The speech might have glued the audience to their seats, but that didn't imply they'd go out and abstain.

21

Nonetheless, some believed they were hearing something crucial. "This is great; it's the basic tutorial on the stock market, all in one lesson," Gates jokes. The money managers, many of whom were looking for bargain stocks, found it reassuring and even cathartic.

Buffett waved his book in the air. "This book formed the conceptual foundation of the 1929 stock market frenzy. Edgar Lawrence Smith's Common Stocks as Long-Term Investments demonstrated that stocks consistently outperformed bonds. Smith listed five reasons, the most unique of which was that businesses kept some of their earnings and could reinvest them at the same rate of return. That was the plowback, a revolutionary concept in 1924! But, as my mentor, Ben Graham, used to say, 'You can get in a lot more trouble with a good idea than a poor idea,' because you forget that the excellent concept has limitations. In his preface to this book, Lord Keynes stated, "There is a danger in expecting the results of the future to be predicted from the past."

He had returned to the same subject: that one could not draw conclusions from the past few years of rising stock prices. "Now, is there anyone I haven't insulted?" He paused. The question was rhetorical; no one raised their hand.

"Thank you," he said, concluding.

"Praise by name, criticize by category" was Buffett's rule. The speech was intended to be provocative, not off-putting—because he cared deeply about what others thought of him. He had not named any offenders, and he assumed they would get over his jokes. His argument was so forceful, virtually impregnable, that he believed even those who disagreed with it had to admit its strength. And the audience's uneasiness was not spoken loudly. He addressed questions till the session concluded. People began to stand and give him an ovation. The speech, whether viewed as a masterful explanation on how to think about investing or the final roar of an old lion, was a tour de force by any standard.

Buffett has remained on top for forty-four years in a business where five years of strong performance was considered a significant accomplishment. Still, as the record progressed, the concern remained: when will he falter? Would he declare the end of his rule, or would a seismic upheaval depose him? Some believed that the time had come. It may have taken an invention as significant as the personal computer, along with a technology as prevalent as the Internet, to bring him down, but he appears to have ignored freely available information and denied the realities of the approaching millennium. As they whispered a courteous "wonderful speech, Warren," the young lions prowled restlessly. As a result, even in the ladies' room during recess, Silicon Valley women made scathing remarks.

It wasn't just that Buffett was wrong, as some believed, but that even if he were eventually proven correct—as others suspected—his bleak forecast of the investing future contrasted so strongly with Buffett's own fabled history. For in his early glory days, stocks were cheap, and Buffett snatched them up by the handful, nearly alone in seeing the golden apples laying untouched on the path. Barriers rose over time, making it more difficult to invest, gain an advantage, and discover what others did not know. So, now that it was their turn, who was Buffett to preach? Who was he to say they shouldn't profit from this amazing market?

Herbert Allen's visitors spent the rest of the quiet afternoon playing one last round of tennis or golf, or they went to the Duck Pond Lawn for a relaxing talk. Buffett spent the afternoon with old acquaintances, who praised him on his successful speech. He believed he had successfully swayed the audience. He hadn't given a speech full of such compelling information just to be on the record.

Buffett, who wanted to be liked, registered a standing ovation rather than mutterings. However, the less flattering interpretation is that many people were not convinced. They assumed Buffett was explaining his failure to capitalize on the technology boom, and they were surprised to see him offer such specific predictions, prophecies that would almost certainly prove incorrect. Beyond his earshot, the rumble continued: "Good ol' Warren. He missed the ferry. How could he have missed the tech boat? He is a friend of Bill Gates."

Later that evening, a few miles away at the River Run Lodge, with the closing dinner guests chosen according to some invisible plan, Herbert Allen finally spoke, thanking various people and reflecting on the week. Then Susie Buffett entered the stage beside the windows overlooking the pebbly Big Wood River and performed the old songs. Later, the guests returned to the Sun Valley Lodge terrace, where Olympic skaters performed axel and arabesque in the Saturday night ice show.

Sun Valley '99 was deemed another wonderful five-day extravaganza when fireworks blazed over the sky at the end of the evening. Most people will remember Buffett's talk about the stock market, which was his first forecast in exactly thirty years, rather than the rafting or the skating.

WARREN, WHAT'S WRONG?

Omaha and Atlanta • August–December 1999

Buffett invested nearly all of his $30 billion plus in Berkshire Hathaway stock, or 99 percent. He had discussed at Sun Valley how the market's weighing machine was more essential than its voting machine. But it was the voting machine's assessment of his stock price that provided the platform from which he preached. People paid attention to him because he was wealthy. So when he forecast that the market would disappoint investors for seventeen years, he was aware that he was standing on the verge of a precipice. If he was wrong, he would not only be the laughingstock of Sun Valley, but his own ranking in the record books of the world's wealthiest men would likely fall. Buffett paid great attention to that ranking.

Through the late 1990s, BRK (Berkshire Hathaway's stock ticker) increased his profile by outperforming the market, peaking at $80,900 a share in June 1998. A single share of Berkshire stock cost enough to buy a small condo, which was unusual among American corporations. To Buffett, the stock price was an easy indicator of his performance. It had risen steadily since he purchased BRK for $7.50 a share. Even though the market was volatile in the late 1990s, an investor who purchased BRK and held it until 1999 would have been better off.

Annual Stock Price Appreciation						
	1993	**1994**	**1995**	**1996**	**1997**	**1998**
BRK	39%	25%	57%	6%	35%	52%
S&P2	10%	1%	38%	23%	33%	29%

But now, Buffett found himself standing on the sinking platform of an unloved stock, watching the "T&T" (technology and telecommunications) stocks rise. By August 1999, BRK had dropped to $65,000. How much should someone pay for a huge, established corporation that generates $400 million in earnings each year? What was the price for a small, new business that's losing money?

• Toys "R" Us made $400 million per year and had sales of $11 billion.
• eToys lost $123 million per year on sales of $100 million.

The market's voting machine determined that eToys was worth $4.9 billion, whereas Toys "R" Us was valued nearly a billion less. The assumption was that eToys will crush Toys "R" Us on the Internet.

The calendar was the only source of uncertainty for the market. Experts predicted that tragedy would strike at midnight on December 31, 1999, because the world's computers were not set to handle dates beginning with a "2." Fearing panic, the Federal Reserve began rapidly increasing the supply of money to avoid cash shortages in the event that all of the country's ATMs stopped at the same time. Shortly after Sun Valley, the market skyrocketed like a Fourth of July firework. If you had put a dollar in the NASDAQ, a technology-heavy index, your gamble was now worth $25. The equivalent bet in BRK was only worth 80 cents. By December, the Dow Jones Industrial Average had gained 25% that year. The NASDAQ surged beyond the 4,000-point mark, up an astonishing 86 percent. BRK dropped to $56,100. BRK's five-year lead was wiped out within months. For over a year, financial experts mocked Buffett as a relic of the past. Now, on the eve of the millennium, Barron's, a weekly Wall Street must-read, has Buffett on its cover with the title "Warren, What's Wrong?" The accompanying piece said Berkshire had "stumbled" heavily. He was running a Pamplona of bad news unlike anything he had ever seen. "I know it's going to change," he said repeatedly. "I just don't know when." His screaming nerves urged him to fight. Rather, he did nothing. He didn't answer. Near the end of 1999, many veteran "value investors" who followed Buffett's style had either closed their firms or gave up and purchased technology stocks. Buffett didn't. What he dubbed his Inner Scorecard—a toughness about financial decisions that had been with him for as long as anyone could remember—kept him grounded.

"I feel like I'm on my back, painting in the Sistine Chapel. I appreciate it when people comment, 'Gee, that's a very nice painting.' But it's my painting, so when someone says, 'Why don't you use more red instead

of blue?' Good-bye. This is my painting. I don't care what they sell it for. The painting itself will never be completed. "That's one of its highlights. "The main question concerning how people behave is if they have an Inner or Outer Scorecard. It helps if you can be content with an Inner Scorecard. I always pose it this way. I say, 'Look at it. Would you rather be the world's greatest lover than have everyone think you're the worst lover? Or would you rather be the world's worst lover while having everyone believe you're the greatest lover? Now that's an intriguing question. "Here is another one. If the world couldn't see your results, would you rather be regarded as the world's greatest investor while actually having the world's worst track record? Imagine being labeled as the world's worst investor yet being the best.When it comes to teaching your children, I believe that the lesson they acquire at a young age is the one that their parents emphasize. If you focus solely on what the world will think of you, rather than how you actually behave, you will end up with an Outer Scorecard. My father was a firm believer in the Inner Scorecard methodology. He was truly a maverick. However, he was not a maverick simply for the purpose of being one. He simply didn't care what others thought. My father taught me to live life properly. "I've never seen anyone quite like him."

PART TWO

The Inner Scorecard

THE URGE TO PREACH

Nebraska, 1869–1928

John Buffett, the first known Buffett in the New World, was a serge weaver thought to be of French Huguenot origin. In the seventeenth century, he came to America to avoid religious persecution, settling as a farmer in Huntington, Long Island.

Little is known about the first Buffets in the United States other than that they were farmers.1 It is evident, however, that Warren Buffett's desire to preach is part of a family tradition. One of John Buffett's sons was known for sailing north across Long Island Sound to a coastal village in Connecticut, where he climbed a hill and began preaching religion to the heathens. However, it is unlikely that the outcasts, scofflaws, and unbelievers of Greenwich repented after hearing his speech, given history tells that lightning struck him down immediately.

Several generations later, Zebulon Buffett, a farmer in Dix Hills, Long Island, left his mark on the family tree as the first documented example of another Buffett trait—treating one's own relatives with extreme tightfistedness—when his grandson, Sidney Homan Buffett, quit his job working on Zebulon's farm in disgust over the insultingly low pay. Sidney, a gangly youngster, traveled west to Omaha, Nebraska, to work for his maternal grandfather, George Homan, who owned a livery stable. The year was 1867, and Omaha was a hamlet made up mostly of wooden shacks. Omaha has served as a trail-outfitting center for westbound prospectors during the Gold Rush, providing pioneers with necessities such as gaming, women, and alcohol. However, with the conclusion of the Civil War, it was about to be revolutionized. For the first time, the newly reunited states' coasts would be linked by a vast transcontinental railroad, and Abraham Lincoln himself decided that Omaha would serve as its headquarters. The arrival of the Union Pacific infused the town with a thriving business spirit and a feeling of purpose. Nonetheless, the town maintained its notoriety as a "rogue's rookery" and the Sodom of a religious state.

Sidney abandoned his job at the livery stable to build the first grocery store in a town without paved streets. In this respectable but modest business, he sold fruit, vegetables, and game until eleven p.m. every night: prairie chickens for a quarter, jackrabbits for a dime.6 His grandfather Zebulon was concerned about Sidney's prospects and bombarded him with letters containing advice, all of which his descendants still follow—with one significant exception.

"Try to be on time in all your dealings. Avoid interacting with certain males as they may be tough to cope with. Save your credit as it is more valuable than money. If you continue in business, be satisfied with moderate gains. Don't rush to get rich... I want you to be fit for both life and death."

Sidney, content with minor gains in an upward-scrambling, freewheeling environment, eventually grew the business into a success.8 He married Evelyn Ketchum and they had six children, several of whom died early. Ernest and Frank, two boys, were among those who survived.

It has been remarked that "no man was ever better named than Ernest Buffett." Born in 1877, he completed his formal education in the eighth grade and joined his father behind the counter during the Panic of 1893. Far more eccentric than his businesslike brother, Frank Buffett grew into a huge, stove-bellied guy, the heathen among the family's Puritans, who even drank on occasion.

One day, a lovely young woman arrived at the business looking for work. Her name was Henrietta Duvall, and she'd come to Omaha to escape an unkind stepmother. Both Frank and Ernest were instantly smitten, but Ernest, who was more attractive, married Henrietta in 1898. Ernest and Henrietta's first child, Clarence, was born within a year of their marriage, and they went on to have three more sons and a daughter. Shortly after the argument, Ernest formed a partnership with his father, Sidney. He later departed to open another grocery company. Frank was single for most of his life, and he and Ernest did not appear to speak for the following twenty-five years, as long as Henrietta was alive.

Ernest set out to establish himself as a community leader. At his new store, the "hours were long, pay low, opinions cast in iron, and foolishness zero." Always dressed in a dapper suit, he scowled from his desk on the mezzanine to stop his employees from idling, and penned letters demanding that suppliers "kindly speed up the celery." He charmed his lady customers, but never hesitated to judge. He carried a little black notebook to write down the names of people who irritated him—Democrats and people who didn't pay their groceries. "He always uses exclamation points and expected you to admit that he knew best," Buffett adds. In a letter to his son and daughter-in-law, instructing them to always have some ready cash, he branded the Buffetts as "bourgeois incarnate":

"I'd like to point out that no Buffett has ever left a substantial estate, but no Buffett has ever left nothing. They never spent all of their earnings, but always saved a portion of it, and it has all worked out fairly well.

"Spend less than you make" could have been the Buffett family slogan, if it was backed with the corollary, "Don't go into debt."

Henrietta, a French Huguenot, was as frugal, determined, and teetotal as her husband. She, a committed Campbellite, felt called to preach too. While Ernest was at the shop, she would tie the horses to the family's fringed surrey and assemble her children to go out into the countryside, knocking on farmhouse doors to distribute tracts. Her attitude did nothing to alleviate the Buffett family's inclinations. According to some accounts, Henrietta was the most preachy of all the Buffets that ever lived. The Buffetts were craftsmen, not merchants or professionals, but as pioneer settlers in Omaha, they were acutely aware of their place. Henrietta hoped her four sons and daughter would be the first in their family to graduate college. To pay for their education, she reduced her household budget—more than was technically necessary, even by Buffett's standards. When the boys were younger, they all worked in their family's store. Clarence then pursued a career in the oil industry, earning a doctorate degree in geology. George, her second child, earned a PhD in chemistry and eventually moved to the East Coast. Her three youngest children, Howard, Fred, and Alice, all graduated from the University of Nebraska. Fred began working in the family store, while Alice became a home-economics teacher.

Howard, the third son and Warren's father, was born in 1903. He had bad memories of feeling like an outcast when attending Central High School in the early 1920s. Omaha was run by a small group of families that owned the stockyards, banks, and department stores, and fortunes from the breweries that had closed due to Prohibition. "My clothes were pretty much hand-me-downs from my two older brothers," he added, "and I was a paperboy and the son of a grocery store owner." So the high school fraternities didn't look my way, and I was just one of the boys from what approximated outside of the rails." He felt these snubs intensely, and they instilled in him a deep resentment of rank and privilege obtained via birth. Howard studied journalism at the

University of Nebraska and worked for the student newspaper, the Daily Nebraska, where he was able to combine an outsider's passion of reporting on the activities of the powerful with his family's interest in politics. It wasn't long before he met Leila Stahl, a girl whose upbringing combined a shared interest in newspapers with self-consciousness about social position.

Leila's father, John Stahl, a sweet little dumpling of a man of good German-American descent, had traveled Cuming County, Nebraska, in a horse and buggy with a buffalo robe on his lap as superintendent of schools.19 According to family history, he adored his wife, Stella, who bore him three daughters—Edith, Leila, and Bernice—and one son, Marion. Stella, who was of English origin, was dissatisfied with her life at West Point, Nebraska, a community of German-American hausfraus where she felt out of place. She is supposed to have consoled herself by playing the pipe organ. Stella's mental collapse occurred in 1909. This must have appeared like an alarming recurrence of family history, as her mother, Susan Barber, who was characterized as "maniacal," had been a prisoner at the Nebraska State Insane Asylum, where she died in 1899. After an incident in which, according to family legend, Stella attacked Edie with the fireplace poker, John Stahl quit his traveling profession to care for their children. Stella withdrew to her gloomy room, where she sat, twirling her hair, clearly upset. This solitude was punctuated by intermittent moments of vicious behavior toward her husband and the girls.20 Stahl, realizing that he couldn't leave the children alone with their mother, purchased a newspaper, the Cuming County Democrat, to earn a living from home. From the time Leila was five, she and her sisters handled the household and assisted their father in distributing the newspaper. She learned to spell by typing. "When I was in the fourth grade," she recounted, "we had to come home from school and set type before we could go out and play." By the age of eleven, she could run a jackhammer of a Linotype press, and every Friday she missed school due to headaches from having to get out the paper on Thursday night. Living above the business in a mouse-infested house, the family banked all of their hopes for the future on Marion, the clever brother studying to be a lawyer.

During World War I, the Stahls' hardships increased. When the Cuming County Democrat came out against Germany in a German-American town, half of its subscribers deserted the publication and transferred to the West Point Republican, resulting in a financial catastrophe. John Stahl was a staunch follower of Democratic political titan William Jennings Bryan. Bryan was one of the most influential politicians of his time, coming close to becoming President of the United States. In his prime, he advocated for a type of "populism" that he outlined in his most famous speech:

"There are two ideas about government. Some argue that if you just legislation to make the wealthy rich, their wealth will trickle down to those who are less fortunate. The Democratic concept has been that if you legislation to make the masses prosperous, then prosperity would trickle up and through every class that depends on it. The Stahls saw themselves as members of the masses, the class the rest relied on. Their ability to carry that load was not improving. By 1918, Leila's sixteen-year-old sister Bernice—considered the dullard of the sisters with a measured IQ of 139—appeared to be giving up on life. She was certain that she, like her grandmother and mother, would become mentally ill and die at the Nebraska State Insane Asylum. During this period, Leila's educational schedule suggests a tumultuous home life. She put off going to college for two years to support her father. After one semester at the University of Nebraska in Lincoln, she came home for another year to help. Leila, the most energetic and brightest of the girls, later described this story in a different perspective, describing her family as perfect and stating that she stayed out of college for three years to pay her tuition.

When she arrived in Lincoln in 1923, she had one obvious and stated goal: to find a husband. She went straight to the college newspaper and asked for a job. Leila, a small-boned girl with a soft brown bob who bustled like the spring robin, smiled charmingly, softening the expression in her arrowhead-sharp eyes. Howard Buffett, who had started as a sportswriter for the Daily Nebraskan before becoming editor, hired her right away. Howard, who had black hair and a professorial appearance, was one of only thirteen students who had been "tackled" for the Innocents, a college club of excellent men fashioned after Harvard and Yale's prestigious societies. The Innocents, named after the thirteen Popes Innocent of Rome, declared themselves to be champions against evil. They also sponsored the prom and homecoming. When presented with such a large man on campus, Leila grabbed him immediately.

"Well, I don't know whether she worked very much on the Daily Nebraska," Howard commented later, "but she sure worked on me. I've never regretted it—don't get me wrong—it's the best deal I've ever made." However, Leila was an excellent student with a head for mathematics, so when she announced plans to drop out of college and get married, her calculus professor allegedly slammed down the textbook in dismay.

Howard, who was about to graduate, approached his father to explore his job options. He had no genuine interest in money, but at Ernest's insistence, he abandoned the lofty, low-paying industry of journalism and the prospect of law school in favor of selling insurance. The newlyweds settled into a little white four-room cottage near Omaha, which Ernest packed with groceries as a wedding present. Leila outfitted it from top to bottom for $366—items purchased at "sort of wholesale prices." From that point forward, she channeled her energy, ambition, and math talent—which by all accounts exceeded her husband's—into advancing Howard's career.

Doris Eleanor, the Buffetts' first child, was born in early 1928. Later that year, Leila's sister Bernice had a mental breakdown and left her teaching position. But Leila seemed to be spared of the melancholy listlessness that plagued her mother and sister. She was a flurry of energy who could chat for hours on end (even if she told the same stories). Howard called her the "Cyclone."

As the Buffetts settled into life as a young married couple, Leila persuaded Howard to join her own First Christian Church. She proudly recorded in her "day book" when he was appointed a deacon. Howard, who was still very engaged in politics, began to exhibit signs of the family's desire to preach. However, when he and Ernest turned the dinner table into a forum for long conversations on the subject, Howard's brother Fred became so tired that he fell asleep on the floor. Leila, on the other hand, had embraced her new husband's political views and was now a staunch Republican. The Buffetts praised Calvin Coolidge, who declared, "The chief business of the American people is business," and shared his philosophy in limited government and minimum regulation. Coolidge had reduced taxes and awarded citizenship to American Indians, but he generally remained silent and out of the spotlight. Herbert Hoover, his Vice President, was chosen as his successor in 1928, promising to keep pro-business policies in place. The stock market had thrived under Coolidge, and the Buffett's believed Hoover was the man to keep it going. "When I was a kid," Warren later said, "I got a lot of good stuff. I was fortunate to grow up in a family where people discussed intriguing topics, to have bright parents, and to attend good schools. I don't think I could have been raised by a nicer set of parents. That was extremely significant. I didn't receive money from my parents, and I didn't want it. But I was born at the appropriate time and location. "I won the 'Ovarian Lottery.'" Buffett has always attributed most of his success to luck. When it came to his family memories, he was creating some of his own reality. Few would argue that he could not have been reared by a better pair of parents. When he discussed the importance of parents having an Inner Scorecard when parenting their children, he always cited his father's Inner Scorecard as an example. He never mentioned his mother.

A THOUSAND WAYS

Omaha, 1939–1942

Warren Buffett got his first few cents selling packs of gum. And from the moment he began selling—at the age of six—he had an unwavering attitude toward his customers that foreshadowed much of his later style.

"I had this small green tray with five different sections." I'm sure my aunt Edie gave me that. It included containers for five various gum brands, including Juicy Fruit, Spearmint, Doublemint, and so on. I used to get packs of gum from my grandfather and sell them door to door in the neighborhood. Previously, I mostly did this in the evening.I remember Virginia Macoubrie saying, 'I'll take one stick of Juicy Fruit.' I answered, 'We don't split apart packets of gum.' I mean, I have standards. Mrs. Macoubrie said she wanted one stick, and I vividly remember her saying that. No, they were only available in five-stick packets. They cost a nickel, and she wanted to spend a cent with me."

Making a sale was appealing, but not enough to sway his decision. If he sold one stick to Virginia Macoubrie, he'd still have four sticks to sell to someone else, which wasn't worth the effort or danger. He made two cents profit on each pack. He could hold the pennies, heavy and solid, in his palm. They were the first few snowflakes in a snowball of money to come.

Warren was willing to split up red Coca-Cola cartons that he sold door-to-door on summer nights. He continued to sell them during family holidays, approaching sunbathers along the shores of Lake Okoboji in Iowa. Soda pop was more profitable than chewing gum: he earned a cent for every six bottles and proudly tucked the coins into the ballpark-style nickel-plated money changer on his belt. He also wore it when he went door-to-door hawking Saturday Evening Post and Liberty publications.

The money changer made him feel like a professional. It represented the selling aspect Warren enjoyed most: collecting. Although he now collected bottle caps, coins, and stamps, he primarily gathered cash. He stored his pennies in a drawer at home, occasionally adding to the $20 his father had given him when he was six, all recorded in a small maroon passbook—his first bank account.

By the time he was nine or ten, he and Stu Erickson were selling used golf balls at Elmwood Park Golf Course—until someone reported them and the cops kicked them out. When police spoke to Warren's parents, Howard and Leila were unconcerned. They just thought their son was ambitious. Warren, the Buffetts' only—and precocious—son, had a "halo," according to his sisters, and got away with a lot.

At the age of ten, he acquired a job selling peanuts and popcorn at University of Omaha football games. He marched around the stands, shouting, "Peanuts, popcorn, five cents, a nickel, half dime, fifth of a quarter, get your peanuts and popcorn here!" The 1940 presidential election campaign was underway, and he had acquired dozens of various Willkie-McNary buttons to wear on his shirt. His favorite quote was "Washington Wouldn't, Cleveland Couldn't, Roosevelt Shouldn't," which referenced FDR's outrageous—to the Buffetts— decision to run for a third term. While the United States has no constitutional term limits, the country has so far rejected the concept of an "imperial President." Howard saw FDR as a dictator who had grandstanded his way to popularity. The prospect of four more years with FDR nearly choked him.

Though he found Wendell Willkie too liberal for his standards, Howard believed that anyone could get rid of Roosevelt. Warren, who shared his father's political views, relished showing off his Willkie-McNary buttons at the stadium. Then his manager summoned him to the office and told, "Take those off. "You will get a reaction from the Roosevelt people."

Warren placed the buttons in his apron, and some of the dimes and nickels became trapped within the pins' backs. When he returned from the game, his manager instructed him to empty the contents of his pocket, pins included. Then he scooped them from the counter and hauled them away. "That was my introduction to business 101," Buffett explains. "I was pretty sad." And when Roosevelt won an unprecedented third term, the Buffetts were even sadder.

However, while Howard's major focus was politics and money was a sideline, his son had the opposite interests. Warren hung out at his father's office at the grand old Omaha National Bank building whenever possible, reading Barron's "The Trader" column and the books on his father's bookcase. He took up residence in Harris Upham & Co.'s customer room. At this regional stockbroking firm, down two flights of stairs from Howard's office, he thought it was the height of glamour to be able to "mark the board," chalking stock prices on a sluggish Saturday morning during the Depression. On weekends, the market continued to trade for two hours. Root-bound guys with nothing better to do sat in a semi-circle of seats in the client area, listlessly watching figures scroll by on the Trans-Lux, an electronic display of key stock prices. Occasionally, someone would leap up and rip a handful of tape from the lazily clicking ticker machine. Warren was accompanied by his maternal great-uncle John Barber and his paternal great-uncle Frank Buffett, the family misanthrope who had been heartbroken over losing Henrietta to his brother Ernest, who is now deceased. His lifelong habit of thinking solely in one direction imprisoned each man.

"Uncle Frank was a total bear on the world, whereas Uncle John was a total bull. I would sit between the two of them, and they would compete for my attention and try to persuade me that they were correct. They didn't like each other, so they didn't talk to each other, but they did talk to me in the meantime. Frank, my great-uncle, believed that the entire world was about to collapse.

"And when someone would come up to the counter behind the chairs and say, 'I want to purchase a hundred shares of U.S. Steel for twenty-three,' my uncle Frank would always yell out, 'U.S. STEEL? "IT IS GOING TO ZERO!" This was not good for business. "They couldn't kick him out, but everyone loathed him around here. "It was not an office designed for short sellers."

Warren sat snugly between his two great-uncles, staring at the blurry figures. His difficulty reading the Trans-Lux led to his family discovering that he was nearsighted. Warren noticed that after being fitted for spectacles, the numbers seemed to shift in accordance with their own immutable law. Although his great-uncles were both trying to persuade him of their respective—and extreme—points of view, Warren saw that their opinions appeared to have no link with the numbers flying overhead on the Trans-Lux. He was determined to find the pattern, but he wasn't sure how.

"My uncles Frank and John would compete to see who would take me to lunch, because it was a way of beating the other. With my uncle Frank, we'd go down to the old Paxton Hotel and get day-old meals for a quarter.

Warren, who valued spending time with adults, relished his uncles' attention. Actually, he relished being pursued by everyone. He desired attention from his other relatives and his parents' friends, but most of all from his father.

Howard took each of his children on an East Coast trip when they were 10, which was a pivotal moment in their development. Warren knew precisely what he wanted to do: "I told my father I wanted to see three things. I wanted to see the Scott Stamp and Coin Company. I wanted to see the Lionel Train Company. I wanted to visit the New York Stock Exchange. Scott Stamp and Coin was around 47th Street, Lionel was around 27th Street, and the Stock Exchange was all the way downtown.

Wall Street had begun to recover from the catastrophe by 1940, but it remained a chastened environment. The guys of Wall Street were like a band of tenacious mercenaries battling on after the majority of their friends had been killed in combat. With the 1929 Crash still fresh in people's minds, the method they made a living appeared faintly unsavory. Even while they didn't brag about it outside the bunker walls, several of these mercenaries were doing exceptionally well. Howard Buffett took his son to lower Manhattan and met with the head of one of the leading brokerage businesses. Warren Buffett was taking a peek inside the bunker's gold-plated doors.

"That's how I met Sidney Weinberg, the most famous man on Wall Street. My father had never met him. He had a little firm in Omaha. But Mr. Weinberg let us in, possibly because he was accompanying a small child. We talked for almost thirty minutes."

Weinberg, the senior partner at the financial bank Goldman Sachs, had spent a decade methodically rebuilding the firm's reputation following its shame for defrauding investors with a renowned pyramid scheme during the 1929 market crash.6 Warren had no idea Weinberg was an immigrant's child who began off as a porter's helper at Goldman Sachs, emptying cuspidors and polishing the partners' silk caps.7 But he knew he was in the presence of a big shot the moment he walked into Sidney Weinberg's walnut-paneled office, which was adorned with authentic letters, documents, and Abraham Lincoln paintings. And what Weinberg did at the end of their visit had a significant impact on him. "As I walked out, he threw his arm around me and asked, 'What stock do you like, Warren?'

"He'd forgotten it all the next day, but I remembered it forever."

Buffett would never forget that Weinberg, a prominent Wall Street figure, had paid such close attention to him and appeared to value his viewpoint.8

Howard drove Warren from Goldman Sachs to Broad Street, where he entered the New York Stock Exchange via a series of massive Corinthian columns. In the temple of money, guys in brightly colored jackets screamed and scribbled as they stood around wrought-iron trading tables, while clerks rushed back and forth, scattering paper scraps on the floor. Warren, however, was captivated by a sight from the Stock Exchange dining room.

"We had lunch at the Exchange with a Dutchman named At Mol, who is a member of the Stock Exchange and has an attractive appearance. After lunch, a man approached with a tray containing various tobacco leaves. He built a cigar for Mr. Mol, who chose the leaves he desired. And I thought, "This is it." It does not get better than this. A custom-made cigar."

A cigar that has been custom manufactured. The cigar images conjured in Warren's mathematical head! He had absolutely no interest in smoking a cigar. But, reasoning backward, he realized what hiring a man for such a trivial purpose meant. To justify the expense, the cigar man's employer had to be generating a lot of money, even if the rest of the country was still in the grip of the Great Depression. He got it right away. The Stock Exchange must send forth streams of money: rivers, fountains, cascades, and torrents of money, enough to engage a guy for the pure frivolity of rolling cigars—handmade, custom-made cigars—for the Stock Exchange members' own personal enjoyment.

That day, when he looked at the cigar vendor, a glimpse of his destiny was born.

He retained that idea when he returned to Omaha, now old enough to organize and pursue his search more systematically. Even as he played basketball and Ping-Pong and collected coins and stamps like any other boy; even as his family mourned his small, sweet grandfather, John Stahl, who died that year at the age of seventy-three—his first loss—he worked with a passion for the future he saw ahead of him, right there in sight. He wanted money.

"It may provide me independence. Then I could do whatever I pleased with my life. The main thing I wanted to accomplish was work for myself. I didn't want anyone to direct me. I valued the idea of being able to do what I wanted every day.

He quickly found himself with a useful tool. One day, at Benson Library, a book beckoned from the shelf. Its dazzling silver cover glittered like a pile of money, indicating the value of its contents. Captivated by the title, he opened it and was immediately hooked. It was referred to as One Thousand Ways to Make $1,000. One million dollars, in other terms!

Inside the cover, an image depicted a little man looking up at a huge amount of coins.

"Opportunity Knocks," reads the first page of the text. "Never in the history of the United States has the time been so favorable for a man with small capital to start his own business as it is today."

What a Message! "We have heard a lot about the opportunities of bygone years. Why, the prospects of yesterday pale in comparison to those that await today's daring, resourceful man! There are riches to be earned that will make those of Astor and Rockefeller appear insignificant." These comments were like wonderful images of heaven in Warren Buffett's eyes. He sped up his page turning.

"But," the book warned, "you cannot succeed unless you start. Starting is the first step towards earning money. Hundreds of thousands of people in this country who want to make a lot of money are unable to do it because they are waiting for something to happen. Begin it! The book was scolded and explained. One Thousand Ways to Make $1,000 began with "the story of money" and was written in a clear, pleasant language, as if someone were sitting on the front porch talking to a friend. It was jam-packed with practical business advice and money-making ideas. Some of its concepts were restricted, such as goat dairying and running doll hospitals, but others were more feasible. Warren was fascinated by the idea of pennyweight scales. If he had a weighing machine, he would weigh himself fifty times daily. He was confident others would pay money to do the same.

"The weighing machine was simple to understand. I'd buy a weighing machine and use the proceeds to acquire more weighing machines. Pretty soon, I'd have twenty weighing machines, and everyone would weigh themselves fifty times per day. I assumed that's where the money is.9 "What could be better than compounding?"

The concept of compounding struck him as vital. The book claimed he could earn a thousand dollars. If he began with a thousand dollars and increased it by 10 percent each year:

In five years, $1,000 became over $1,600.

In ten years, it became almost $2,600.

In twenty-five years, it became over $10,800.

The way numbers erupted as they multiplied at a consistent rate over time demonstrated how a tiny sum could become a fortune. He could see the numbers piling as vividly as if he rolled a snowball across the yard. Warren began to think differently. Compounding combines the present and the future. If a dollar today was going to be worth ten years from now, he considered the two to be the same.

Sitting on the doorstep of his buddy Stu Erickson's, Warren proclaimed that he would be a millionaire by the time he turned thirty-five.10 That was a daring, almost ridiculous-sounding assertion for a child to make in the sad world of 1941. But his calculations and the book indicated that it was doable. He was 25 and needed more money. Nonetheless, he was confident he could accomplish it. The more money he saved early on, the longer it could compound and the better his prospects of meeting his objective.

A year later, he revealed the essence of his reality. By the spring of 1942, his hoard had grown to $120, much to the amazement and pleasure of his family. He enlisted his sister Doris as a partner and purchased three shares of stock for each of them, totaling $114.75 for three shares of Cities Service Preferred. "I didn't understand that stock very well when I bought it," he says; all he knew was that it was a popular stock that Howard had been selling to his customers for years. The market reached a low in June, and Cities Service Preferred fell from $38.25 to $27 per share. Doris, he claims, "reminded" him every day on the way to school that her stock was declining. Warren claims he felt tremendously responsible. So, when the stock finally recovered, he sold for $40, making a $5 profit for the two of them. "That's when

I realized he knew what he was doing," Doris says. However, Cities Service immediately rose to $202 per share. Warren acquired three lessons and considers this experience to be one of the most important in his life. One lesson he learned was not to become overly concerned with the price he paid for a stock. The second rule was to avoid rushing to make a modest profit. He learned these two lessons by reflecting on the $492 he could have made if he had been more patient. It had taken him five years to save the $120 needed to acquire this stock, beginning when he was six years old. Based on how much he was now making from selling golf balls or peddling popcorn and peanuts at the ballgame, he figured it may take years to recoup the amount he had "lost." He would never, ever forget his error. The third lesson was investing in other people's money. If he committed a mistake, someone might be furious with him. So he didn't want to be responsible for other people's money until he was confident he could succeed.

THE RULES OF THE RACETRACK

Omaha and Washington, D.C. - 1940s

Warren's Dale Carnegie tests of behavior were a handicap, a mathematical experiment on human nature. The information he gathered showed him the likelihood that Carnegie was correct.

This mode of thinking grew out of his childhood habit of calculating the odds on the lives of hymn composers. However, his interest in longevity was more than abstract. Ernest Buffett, to whom Warren was deeply connected, died in September 1946 at age 69 while the family was in Omaha campaigning for Howard's third term. Warren was sixteen. Only Stella, aged 73, remained alive among his four grandparents, and she was confined to the Norfolk State Hospital. Warren had been worried with his own lifespan long before Ernest's death, and the most recent family tragedies did nothing to alleviate his concerns about either longevity or insanity. Warren's interest in handicapping, on the other hand, extended to many other things and had begun much earlier—long before he even realized the phrase existed—when he was a tiny child with marbles, registration plates, bottle caps, and a fingerprint kit for nuns. The art of handicapping is dependent on information. The trick was having more information than the other guy, then interpreting it correctly and applying it rationally. Warren first used this as a child at the Ak-Sar-Ben racetrack, where his friend Bob Russell's mother introduced the boys to the world of parimutuel betting. Warren and Russ were too young to gamble, but they quickly learned how to generate money. Thousands of discarded tickets peered out from the mud and sawdust of the Ak-Sar-Ben flooring like mushrooms on the forest floor, among the cigarette butts, beer slops, old programs, and hot-dog scraps. The boys turned into truffle hunters.

"They call it stopping.' Early in the racing season, you have all these individuals who have only seen races in movies. And they'd believe that if your horse finished second or third, you didn't get paid since all the attention is on the winner, so they'd discard place and show tickets. The other time you'd hit it big was when there was a contested race. That small light would turn on that indicated 'contested' or 'protest.' By then, some had ditched their tickets. Meanwhile, we were simply gobbling them up. We wouldn't look at them as we worked. At night, we'd go through them. It was disgusting; people spit on the floor. But we had a terrific time. If I found any winning tickets, my aunt Alice, who had no interest in racing, would cash them in for us, because they wouldn't cash them for children."

Warren wanted to race all the time. When Mrs. Russell wasn't taking him, "my dad would never go to the races," Buffett adds. "He did not believe in the races." Instead, his parents let his great-uncle Frank, the eccentric in the family, have him. Frank had long ago reconciled with Ernest and finally married a lady the family dubbed "the gold-digger." He had no special interest in horses, but he drove Warren to Ak-Sar-Ben because his great-nephew wanted to go. Warren learned how to read the tip sheet at Ak-Sar-Ben, which opened up a whole new world for him. Handicapping horses allowed him to combine two of his strengths: data collection and math. It was similar to counting cards in blackjack, except that the winning hand had four legs and went around a track. Soon, he and Russ knew enough to publish their own advice sheet, cleverly titled Stable-Boy Selections.

"We got away with it for a while." They were not the most popular sellers in the globe. I mean, a couple of tiny kids selling something they typed out in my basement on an ancient Royal typewriter. Carbons were the limiting issue back then. You could probably only fit in about five carbons. But I got on the Royal, and Bob Russell and I drugged out the horses, and then we typed up this thing."We were on the track, saying, 'Get your stable-boy selections!' However, the Blue

Sheet was the most popular tip sheet, and the racecourse received a commission for it. The Blue Sheet sold for somewhat more. At 25 cents, we were a low-cost product. They quickly closed Stable-Boy Selections because they were getting a cut on everything sold in the store except for us."

When the Buffetts moved to Washington, D.C., Warren's only advantage was the opportunity to improve his handicapping talents.

"The only thing I understood about Congress was that Congressmen had access to the Library of Congress, which contained everything that had ever been written. So when we arrived in Washington, I said, 'Pop, there's one thing I want. I want you to ask the Library of Congress for every book on horse handicapping. And my father remarked, 'Well, don't you think they'll think it's strange if the first thing a new Congressman asks for is all the books on horse handicapping?' I asked, "Pop, who was out at the county fairs stumping for your election?" Who was down there at the packinghouses, ready to call the cops if anything happened? I added, 'And you're up for reelection in two years. You are going to need me. So it's payment time. He brought me hundreds of books on horse handicapping."Then I would read all of these novels. I mailed it to a business on North Clark Street in Chicago where you could buy old race forms, months of them, for a low price. They were ancient; who wanted them? I'd go through them, handicapping one day and then seeing how it worked the next. I tested my handicapping abilities on a daily basis using several mental systems.There are two categories of handicappers. There are two types of handicappers: speed and class. Speed handicappers determine which horse has run the best times in the past. The fastest horse will win. Class handicappers believe that the horse that has performed well against ten-thousand-dollar horses and is now competing against five-thousand-dollar horses will defeat them. Because, as they say, the horse is quick enough to win.

"In horse racing, it is important to understand both methods of handicapping. But back then, I was primarily a speedster. "I was a quantitative guy to begin with."

As he experimented, thought, and observed, Warren discovered the Racetrack Rules:

1. Nobody leaves after the first race.
2. You don't have to recover it the same way you lost it.

The racecourse expects individuals to keep betting until they lose. Couldn't a smart handicapper reverse these rules and win?

"The market is also a racetrack." But I wasn't creating complicated hypotheses then. I was only a young kid."

Betting was extremely common in Washington.

"I would frequently visit my father's workplace, and there was a bookie in what was then known as the Old House workplace Building. If you yell 'Sammy!' in the elevator shaft, a kid will approach and take bets.I used to conduct some bookmaking for folks who wanted to gamble on the Preakness, or something like that. That was the end of the game I enjoyed, the fifteen percent take with no risk. My father, you know, was battling to keep this under control. He found it amusing, but he could see how it could go badly."

During his summer vacation, Warren returned to Omaha and went down at the Ak-Sar-Ben track with his friend Stu Erickson.3 Back in Washington, he met a new acquaintance to go to the racetrack with, someone who could help him improve his handicapping skills. Bob Dwyer, his high school golf coach, a potbellied, entrepreneurial young man, earned far more than his teacher's stipend by selling life insurance, ice chests, and other items during the summer months while school was out. The rest of the golf team thought Dwyer was gruff and crusty, but he liked Warren, who had a way about him and played heartily despite his glasses constantly fogging up. Warren once begged Dwyer to take him to the races. His trainer said he required permission. "The next morning," Dwyer recalls; "bright and early, he came prancing in with a note from his mother, saying it was all right to go to the races." So Dwyer made up an excuse to get Warren out of class 5, and they rode the Chesapeake & Ohio from Silver Spring, Maryland, to the racecourse in Charleston, West Virginia. Going to the races with a teacher helped Warren improve his handicapping skills. Dwyer showed Warren additional techniques for reading the Daily Racing Form, the most essential tip sheet.

"I would receive the Daily Racing Form ahead of time and calculate the odds of each horse winning the race. Then I'd compare the percentages to the odds. However, to avoid bias, I would not consider the odds first. Sometimes you'd come across a horse whose odds were drastically different from the actual probability. You figure the horse has a 10% chance of winning, yet it's going off at fifteen to one.

"The less complex the track, the better. People bet on the jockeys' colors, their birthdays and the names of the horses. The challenge, of course, is to be in a group where almost no one is analytical and you have a lot of information. So when I was a kid, I would spend a lot of time studying forms." Bill Gray, who was one grade behind Warren at Woodrow Wilson but slightly older, accompanied him to several horse races. "He was really good with numbers. Extremely chatty. Very outgoing. We would talk about baseball, batting averages, and sports."He knew the horses he was going to choose the moment he stepped off the train. He'd walk out to the track and say, "Well, this horse is too heavy, or this horse's performance in the last few races hasn't been good enough, or his times aren't fast enough." "He knew how to judge the horses." Warren placed six- to ten-dollar wagers, often on the nose. He only gambled big when the odds were excellent, but he had a method of putting part of his hard-earned paper-route money on the proper horse. "He might change his mind as the different races came forward," Gray said. "But for a sixteen-year-old, that's not so common, you know?"

Warren once went to Charleston by himself. And he lost the first race. But he did not go home. He kept betting and losing until he'd lost almost $175 and his pockets were practically empty. "I came back." I went to the Hot Shoppe and treated myself to the biggest thing they had—a gigantic fudge sundae or something—and there went the rest of my money. While I ate, I calculated how many newspapers I needed to deliver to offset what I had lost. I was going to have to work for over a week to make up the money. And I did it for idiotic reasons. "You shouldn't wager on every race. I had made the biggest sin: falling behind and believing you had to break even that day. The first rule is that no one goes home after the first race, and the second rule is that you don't have to return the same way you left it. That is so fundamental, you understand." Was he aware that he had taken an emotional decision? "Oh, yes. Oh, I was sick. It was the last time I had done something like that."

MISS NEBRASKA

New York City and Omaha, 1950 –1952

Warren had always been unpopular with girls. He wished to have a girlfriend, but his unique characteristics thwarted his efforts. "Nobody was more shy than I was with girls," he admits. "But my reaction to that was probably to turn into a talking machine." When he ran out of words to say about stocks or politics, he grunted instead. He was afraid to ask girls. He summoned the courage when a girl did something that made him believe he wouldn't be rejected, but his overall attitude was, "Why would they want to go out with me?"As a result, he did not go on many dates in high school or college. And whenever he did, something seemed to go wrong.

The highlight of a date to a baseball game with a girl named Jackie Gillian was hitting a cow with his car on the way home. He took another girl to a driving range to practice hitting golf balls. Driving a hearse to pick up Barbara Weigand, he claims, was "sort of desperate," not a stunt. It may have worked as an icebreaker, but what else could be said? On a date with a shy girl like Ann Beck, he went silent; he was so insecure that he didn't know what to do. Girls did not want to hear about Ben Graham or the margin of safety. What hope did he have if he couldn't get to first base with Bobbie Worley, whom he had dated for the entire summer? Very little, he reasoned, and perhaps the girls could sense it.

Finally, in the summer of 1950, before he went to Columbia, his sister Bertie set him up on a date with her roommate from Northwestern. Susan Thompson, a round-cheeked brunette, had quickly impressed Bertie, who was a year and a half younger, as a special girl with a knack for understanding people. When Warren met Susie, he was fascinated, but suspected she was too good to be true: "I bet she was a fake at first. She fascinated me and pursued her, but I was determined to find the hole in the dike. I couldn't believe anyone could be like her." Susie, on the other hand, had no interest in him. She was in love with someone.

After leaving for Columbia, Warren read in Earl Wilson's gossip column4 in the New York Post that Miss Nebraska 1949, Vanita Mae Brown, was living at the Webster women's residence5 and performing on a television show with singer and teen idol Eddie Fisher.

Vanita had attended the University of Nebraska at the same time as Warren, but she had escaped his attention and ambition until now. Something about the situation made him less shy. Since the glamorous Miss Nebraska lived in New York, he called her at the Webster.

Vanita took the bait. She and Mr. Omaha soon found themselves on a date. He discovered that her upbringing was very different from his own. She grew up in South Omaha, near the stockyards, and after school she cleaned chickens at Omaha Cold Storage. Her pinup physique and girl-next-door demeanor had been her ticket out. She worked as an usherette at the Paramount Theater in Omaha before winning a local beauty pageant thanks to her love of putting herself on display. "I think her talent was bedazzling the judges," Buffett says. After winning Miss Nebraska, she went on to represent her state as Princess Nebraska at the Cherry Blossom Festival in Washington, D.C. She then relocated to New York City, where she was desperately trying to break into the entertainment industry.

Warren was not the type of guy who would take a girl to dinner at the Stork Club or a show at the Copacabana, but she must have appreciated seeing a familiar face. Soon they were exploring New York's streets together. They went to Marble Collegiate Church to listen to Dr. Norman Vincent Peale, a well-known self-help author and speaker. On the Hudson River bank, Warren serenaded her with "Sweet Georgia Brown" on his ukulele while carrying cheese sandwiches for a riverside picnic.

Despite her dislike for cheese sandwiches6, Vanita appeared to want to continue seeing him. He found her so entertaining and quick-witted that talking to her was like playing verbal Ping-Pong.7 Her Technicolor aura drew him in. Vanita's interest, however, did not distract him from his woefully lacking social skills. With each passing year, he became more determined to improve them. He saw an advertisement for a Dale Carnegie-style public speaking course. Warren trusted Dale Carnegie, who had previously helped him improve his interpersonal skills. He attended a Carnegie course in New York with a $100 check in his pocket.

"I went to Dale Carnegie because I was painfully aware of my social maladjustment." And I went and gave them a check, but I stopped paying for it because I lost my nerve."

Warren's social deficiencies did not bode well for his chances with Susan Thompson, to whom he had been writing all fall. She wasn't encouraging, but she didn't explicitly tell him to stop bothering her. Warren quickly devised the plan to become friends with Susie's parents to gain access to their daughter. He joined them for a Northwestern football game in Evanston over Thanksgiving. Later, the three had dinner with Susie, but she left early to go on a date.

Warren returned to New York after the holiday, discouraged but still intrigued. He continued to see Vanita. "She had one of the most imaginative minds I've ever run into," he jokes.

In fact, dating her became more unpredictable and risky. She threatened to go down to Washington when Howard was speaking in Congress and throw herself at his feet, shrieking, "Your son is the father of my unborn child!"Warren believed she might actually do it. Another time, as they were leaving a movie theater, she caused such a scene that he hoisted her up and stuffed her, jackknifed, into a wire-mesh trash basket on the street corner. She hung there, suspended and screaming, as he stalked away.

Vanita was beautiful, smart, and entertaining. She was also dangerous, and Warren knew it was risky to become more involved with her. But there must have been some thrill. Dating Vanita was like taking a leopard on a leash to see if it would make a good pet. However, "Vanita could handle herself well. She had no trouble carrying it. The only question was whether she would want to pull it off. You didn't have to worry about her embarrassing you unless she chose to."

Warren once invited her to a dinner at the New York Athletic Club for Frank Matthews, a renowned lawyer and Secretary of the Navy. Having the lovely Miss Nebraska on his arm would be a bonus. Matthews was from Nebraska, the audience was full of people worth knowing, and Warren wanted to be recognized. During the cocktail hour, Vanita ensured that he was mentioned. He introduced her as his date, but she corrected him and insisted she was his wife. "I don't know why he does this," she explained. Is he ashamed of me? Would you be ashamed of me? Every time we go out, he acts like I'm just his date, and we've been married."

Warren finally realized that, while Vanita could handle herself well when she wanted to, "the truth was that she would always want to embarrass me." "She preferred acting that way with me," he says, and she did it frequently. Vanita was fascinated by her, and if he hadn't had an alternative, who knows what would have happened.10

Warren saw Susan Thompson as much as she allowed whenever he returned to Nebraska, which wasn't much. To him, she appeared extremely sophisticated, even authoritative, and generous with her emotions. "Susie was way, way, way more mature than I was," he notes. He began to fall hard for her and distanced himself from Vanita, although "it was obvious I wasn't Number One" with Susie11. "My intentions were clear," he claims; "they just weren't having any effect on her."

Susan Thompson's family was well known to the Buffetts—her father, "Doc Thompson," had managed Howard's only failed reelection campaign—but in most ways, they were diametrically opposed to Warren's. Dorothy Thompson, Susie's mother, was a sweet, tiny woman, warm, genuine, and wise to the world. She was known in the family as the "wife who went along." She made sure dinner was on the table at six p.m. Sharp and supportive of the many lives her husband, Dr. William Thompson, led. A smallish, silver-haired peacock of a man who wore bow ties and three-piece wool suits in lavender, cotton-candy pink, or chartreuse, he cut a striking figure and carried himself with the confidence of someone who knew he was being admired. He came, he said, "from a long line of teachers and preachers," and seemed to want to duplicate all of their labors at once.

As dean of the University of Omaha's College of Arts and Sciences, he oversaw operations while teaching psychology. As assistant athletic director, he oversaw the university's athletic programs and directed them with the enthusiasm of a former football player and sports fanatic. This role made him so prominent that "every cop in town knew him," says Buffett, "which was a good thing, because of the way he drove." He also designed IQ tests and psychology tests, and supervised the testing of all the city's schoolchildren.13 Not content to enjoy a day of rest from bossing people around and testing their children, he donned the vestments of an ordained minister and preached v-e-r-y s-l-o-w-l-y in a deep, booming voice at the tiny Irvington

Doc Thompson smiled as he expressed his wishes, insisting on immediate obedience. He emphasized the importance of women while expecting them to wait on him. His work focused on the inner self, but he was clearly vain. He clung to those he loved, becoming nervous when they were out of sight. He was a chronically anxious hypochondriac who frequently predicted disaster for those he cared about. He lavished affection on those who met his demanding standards.

Dorothy, or Dottie, the Thompsons' older daughter, was not one of those. According to family legend, during the first few years of Dottie's life, when her father was particularly dissatisfied with her, he locked her in a closet. A charitable interpretation would be that the pressure of completing his PhD with a toddler underfoot unbalanced him.

Susie, their second daughter, was born seven years after Dottie had arrived. Dorothy Thompson, seeing how badly Dottie was reacting to her husband's harsh child-rearing methods, allegedly asserted herself and told him, "That one was yours, I'm raising the next."

Susie was sick from birth. During her first eighteen months, she suffered from allergies and chronic ear infections, requiring a dozen ear lancings. From kindergarten to second grade, she had long bouts of rheumatic fever, which kept her at home for four to five months at a time. She later recalled watching her friends play outside her window during these periods and wishing she could join them.16

Throughout her many illnesses, the Thompsons were constantly comforting, cuddling, and rocking their daughter. Her father lavished her with affection. "There was nothing in his life remotely approaching her," according to Warren. "Susie could do no wrong, but everything Dottie did was incorrect. They were constantly critical of her."

A family home video shows Susie, about four years old, screaming, "No!" and ordering around 11-year-old Dottie as they played with a tea set.

When Susie was finally well and no longer confined to her bedroom, she never chose to play sports or games outside, but was always eager to make new friends.18 It was people she had missed during her long days of illness.

"When you've had pain," Susie later reflected, "the release from it can be completely liberating. It's magnificent. Being pain free is a wonderful state of being. I learned this at a young age. Knowing this allows you to approach life with a very simple mindset. And then you meet people and think, "Wow, people are really fascinating."19

Susie's girlish round cheeks and breathy, deceptively childlike voice remained intact as she grew older. During her adolescence, she attended Omaha's Central High, an integrated school with students of various faiths and races, which was unusual for the 1940s. Even though she was part of a crowd that some considered snobbish, her classmates recall her as having friends from all these groups.20 Her exuberant warmth and ethereal way of speaking could come across as "a little phony," even "a little loopy,"21 but her friends said there was nothing phony about her. Her interests were in speech and performing arts rather than academics. She argued passionately and persuasively on the Central High debate team, and people noticed that her politics had diverged from her father's. She performed charmingly in school plays and sang in smooth contralto in school operettas and as a member of the choir. Her performance as the sweetly harebrained lead in Our Hearts Were Young and Gay sparkled so much that her teachers remembered it for years after.22 Indeed, her charm and strength of personality made her "Most Popular," a "lady in waiting" to the school sweetheart, Miss Central, and led her classmates to elect her senior class president.

Susie's first boyfriend was John Gillmore, a quiet, unassuming boy who she openly adored. By the time he became her steady at Central High, Gillmore towered over her by nearly a foot, but despite her "kittenish" demeanor, she dominated him.

During those years, she also started dating a nice, smart guy she met at a freshman debate competition. Milton Brown, a tall, dark-haired young man with a warm, wide smile, attended Thomas Jefferson High School in Council Bluffs, Iowa, just across the Missouri River from Omaha. They saw each other several times a week throughout high school. While her close friends knew about Milt, it was Gillmore who remained her consistent date for parties and school events.

Susie's father disapproved of Brown, the son of an unschooled Russian-Jewish immigrant worker on the Union Pacific Railroad. Doc Thompson made him feel unwelcome on the three or four occasions she dared to bring him to the house, lecturing him on FDR and Truman. Susie's father made no secret of his desire to prevent his daughter from dating a Jew. Doc Thompson, like the Buffets, had all of Omaha's prejudices, where different ethnic and religious groups kept to themselves, and life for a mixed-religion couple would be difficult at best. Susie, however, dared to cross these social lines while maintaining a separate life as a conventional, popular high school girl. Susie navigated these turbulent waters until she entered college, where she and Milt embarked on a journey to freedom—together—at Northwestern University in Evanston, Illinois. There, she shared a room with Bertie Buffett and pledged sororities. Bertie breezed through her classes and was promptly crowned the Phi Delt "Pajama Queen." Susie, a journalism major, had her schedule planned so she could see Milt almost every day.

Susie's unconventional choice to openly date a Jewish boy clashed with her life as a typical coed, and members of her sorority forbade her from bringing Brown to a dance because he had pledged a Jewish fraternity. Susie, though hurt, did not abandon her faith. Instead, she and Milt began to study Zen Buddhism in search of a faith that reflected their shared spiritual beliefs.

Warren made his futile Thanksgiving trip to Evanston, unaware of this, and then spent the winter holidays with Susie in Omaha. By then, he had decided to pursue her seriously. She possessed the qualities he'd always sought in a woman. She described herself as "one of the few fortunate people who grew up feeling unconditionally loved." That's the best gift you can give anyone."30 But she wanted to give her unconditional love to Milt Brown.

Milt was elected president of the sophomore class in the spring of 1951, with Bertie serving as vice president. Susie cried whenever she opened a letter from home demanding that she end her relationship with Brown. Bertie was aware of what was going on, but Susie never confided in her, despite the fact that they had become friends.31 She seemed to have a way of never allowing anyone into her head. Then, as the semester ended, the two were sitting in their dorm room when the phone rang. It was Doc Thompson. "Come home now," he ordered. He wanted her away from Milt, and he informed her that she would not be returning to Northwestern in the fall. Susie collapsed, sobbing, but she could never appeal her father's decisions.

Warren, who graduated from Columbia that spring, also returned to Omaha. He would be living in his parents' home while they were away in Washington, but he would have to spend part of the first summer after returning to fulfill his National Guard obligations. Though he wasn't particularly well suited to the Guard, it was preferable to fighting in Korea. However, the Guard required him to attend a several-week training camp in La Crosse, Wisconsin, each year. Training camp didn't help him mature.

"The guys in the National Guard were initially suspicious of me because my father served in Congress. They assumed I was going to be a prima donna or something. But it didn't last long.It's a highly democratic organization. What you do outside doesn't matter much. To fit in, you simply had to be willing to read comic books. About an hour after I arrived, I was reading comics. Everyone else was reading

comic books; why shouldn't I? My vocabulary was reduced to about four words, and you can guess what they were.

"I discovered that it pays to associate with people who are better than you, because you will rise a little bit. And if you hang out with people who behave worse than you, you'll eventually start sliding down the pole. "It just works that way."

The experience inspired Warren to fulfill another promise once he returned from National Guard camp. "I was scared of public speaking. You wouldn't believe what I was if I had to give a speech. I was terrified and couldn't do it. I'd throw up. In fact, I planned my life so I never had to face anyone. When I returned to Omaha after graduation, I noticed another advertisement. And I knew I'd have to give public speeches from time to time. The agony was so intense that I enrolled in the course again just to relieve the pain." That wasn't his only goal: he knew he needed to be able to communicate with Susan Thompson to win her heart. The odds were stacked against him with Susie, but he would do anything to improve them, and this summer might be his last chance.

The Dale Carnegie class met at the Rome Hotel, a favorite among cattlemen. *"I took a hundred bucks in cash and gave it to Wally Keenan, the instructor, and said, 'Take it before I change my mind.'"There were about 25 to 30 of us in there. We were all absolutely terrified. We couldn't pronounce our names. We all stood there silently, refusing to speak to one another. Meanwhile, Wally's ability to remember all of our names after only meeting once impressed me. He was a good teacher, and he attempted to teach us the memory association trick, but I never learned it.*

"They gave us this book of speeches—keynote speech, election speech, lieutenant governor's speech—and told us to deliver them every week. The way it works is that you learn to get outside yourself. Why should you be able to talk to someone alone for five minutes and then freeze in front of a group? So they teach you psychological techniques to overcome this. Some of it is simply practice—just doing and practicing. We really helped each other out. And it worked. That's the most important degree I possess."

Warren, on the other hand, was unable to test his new skills on Susie, who avoided him. Warren, aware of Doc Thompson's influence on his daughter, showed up every night, ukulele in hand, to romance her father in her stead. "She would go out with other guys," says Buffett, "and I had nothing to do when I went over there. So I would flirt with him instead, and we would talk about it." Doc Thompson, who enjoyed the summer heat, sat outside on the screened porch on hot July nights, dressed in a three-piece pastel wool suit, while Susie secretly went out with Milt. Doc Thompson played the mandolin as Warren sweated and sang, accompanied by the ukulele.

Warren felt at ease with Doc Thompson, whose style reminded him of his father's insistence that the world was going to hell because of the Democrats. Witness, Whittaker Chambers' autobiography about his conversion from Communist spy to Cold War anti-Communist, had just been released. Warren was particularly intrigued by this book, which described the Alger Hiss case. Chambers had accused Hiss of being a Communist spy, but the Buffetts' political enemies, the Truman crowd, dismissed the charge. Only Richard Nixon, a young senator on the House Un-American Activities Committee, pursued Hiss, leading to his conviction for perjury in January 1950. Doc Thompson could eat this stuff. Unlike Howard, he also discussed sports. He didn't have any sons and thought Warren was the best thing since bubble gum. Warren was smart, Protestant, Republican, and, most importantly, he was not Milt Brown.

Bill Thompson's support was not as beneficial as it appeared. Warren faced stiff odds in winning Susie's heart. She could look past his baggy socks and cheap suits; it was the rest that worked against him. He came across to her as a Congressman's son, someone considered "special," a boy with every advantage—a graduate degree and a lot of money—and who was clearly on his way to success. He constantly brought up stocks, which she had no interest in. He entertained his date by telling rehearsed jokes, riddles, and brainteasers. Her father's fondness for Warren led her to view Warren as an extension of her father's control. Doc Thompson "practically threw Susie at Warren." "It was two against one," Buffett explains.

Milt, who needed her, faced the injustice of being a Jew from the wrong side of the tracks. He was especially appealing because he was the guy her father couldn't stand.

That summer, Brown worked in Council Bluffs. When he received a letter from Northwestern informing him of a tuition increase, he realized he couldn't afford to return to Evanston, so he went over to the Buffett home and handed Bertie, his class vice president, a letter stating that he was transferring to the University of Iowa.34 Susie was enrolled at the University of Omaha that fall, and by then, she and Milt had to admit that their relationship was "off and on" due to her father. She spent the summer in tears.

Meanwhile, despite her initial lack of interest in Warren, Susie could never spend time with someone without wanting to know everything about them. She soon realised her first impression had been incorrect. He wasn't the privileged, cocky, self-assured guy she imagined. "I was a wreck," he says, jittering on the verge of a nervous breakdown. "I felt odd, I was socially inept, but beyond that, I hadn't found a cruising speed in life." Even her friends noticed the vulnerability beneath his outward confidence. Susie gradually realized how worthless he felt internally. All of the confident chatter about stocks, the aura of a prodigy, and the tinny twang of the ukulele were wrapped around a fragile, needy core: a boy stumbling through his days in a shroud of despair. "I was a mess," he admits. "It was incredible the way Susie saw through some of that." Susie loved it when someone felt like a wreck and a mess. Warren later explained that she needed to turn him into a cause because he "was Jewish enough for Susie, but not too Jewish" for her father. So she started to come around.

Warren, who was nearly blind to how others dressed—even women— had grown so in love with Susie that he noticed her clothes. He'd never forget the blue dress she wore on their dates, or the black-and-white print ensemble he dubbed the "newspaper dress." They stumbled around the dance floor to the sounds of a Glenn Miller song in the Peony Park pavilion, surrounded by summer fireflies. Warren had yet to learn to dance despite his best efforts. He was as comfortable on the dance floor as a sixth-grader at a sorority social. "I would have done anything she asked," he admits. "I would have let her put worms down the back of my shirt."

By Labor Day, when Warren took her to the state fair, they were a couple. Susie enrolled at the university as a sophomore studying journalism, joined the debate team, and joined the Association for the Study of Group Dynamics, a psychology organization.

In October 1951, Warren jokingly wrote to his aunt Dorothy Stahl, "Things in the girl department are at an all-time peak...".One of the local gals has sunk the hooks pretty deep into me. As soon as I get permission from [my uncle] Fred and you, I'll move forward. This girl has only one disadvantage: she knows nothing about stocks.

Otherwise, she is unbeatable, and I suppose I can overlook her weakness."

"Proceeding further" with caution was the correct wording. Warren built up his nerve. Instead of proposing marriage, he "just sort of assumed it, and kept talking." Susie, for her part, "realized she had been chosen," though "she wasn't sure how."

Warren, triumphant, arrived on time for his Dale Carnegie class. "That was the week I won the pencil." They gave a pencil award for completing a difficult task and contributing the most to the training. Susie proposed the same week she won the pencil. She then wrote a long, sad letter to Milton Brown. He was shocked. He knew she had gone on some dates with Warren, but he had no idea it was serious.

Warren spoke with Susie's father for his approval. He was well aware that this would be easy to obtain. But Doc Thompson took a long time to get to the point. He began by stating that Harry Truman and the Democrats were leading the country straight to hell. Pouring money into Europe after the war through the Marshall Plan and the Berlin Airlift42 proved that Roosevelt's policies remained in place, and Truman was driving the country into bankruptcy. Consider how the Soviets obtained the atomic bomb shortly after Truman dismantled portions of the military. Senator Joe McCarthy's House Un-American Activities Committee was proving what Doc Thompson had suspected all along: the government was riddled with communists. HUAC was finding Communists everywhere. When it came to dealing with Communism, the government was completely ineffective, if not worse. Truman had lost China to democracy. He would never be forgiven for firing the heroic General Douglas MacArthur for insubordination after he repeatedly attempted to circumvent Truman and obtain permission to attack the Chinese communists in Manchuria. However, it was likely that even MacArthur could not save the country at this point. The Communists were taking over the world, and stocks would be nothing more than worthless paper. So Warren's plan to work in the stock market would fail. Doc Thompson would never blame Warren for his daughter's starvation. He was an intelligent young man. If the Democrats hadn't ruined the country, he'd probably be fine. Susie's miserable future would not be Warren's fault.

Warren, who had grown up hearing this kind of talk from both his father and Susie, waited patiently for the crucial word "yes." Three hours later, Doc Thompson came to a decision and gave his permission. Susie and Warren had already started planning their April wedding by Thanksgiving.

STAGE FRIGHT

Omaha, Summer 1951–Spring 1952

Warren understood Doc Thompson's concern about how he would support a family, despite having no doubts himself. Since he couldn't work for Graham-Newman, he decided to become a stockbroker and do so in Omaha, far from the canyons of Wall Street. According to conventional wisdom, the best place to make money in the stock market was New York, so his decision was unusual. But he felt liberated from the conventions of Wall Street; he wanted to work with his father; Susie was in Omaha; and he was never happy away from home.

Warren was almost twenty-one and extremely confident in his investment abilities. By the end of 1951, he'd increased his capital from $9,804 to $19,738. He had earned 75% in a single year.1 Naturally, he sought advice from his father and Ben Graham. To his surprise, both replied, "Maybe you should wait a few years." Graham, as always, believed the market was too high. Howard, a pessimist, preferred mining stocks, gold stocks, and other investments aimed at protecting against inflation. He didn't believe any other type of business would be a wise investment, and he was concerned about his son's future.

That did not make sense to Warren. Since 1929, the value of businesses has increased significantly.

"It was exactly the opposite effect of what you saw in other times, when the market was staggeringly overvalued. I had looked into companies. I couldn't understand why you wouldn't want to own them. It was on a micro level, not an economic growth assessment, and I was working with micro money. But it just seemed crazy not to own them. On the other hand, Ben, with his two hundred IQ and extensive experience, tells me to wait. And my father, who, if he had told me to walk out the window, I would have done so." Still, defying his father's and Ben Graham's advice was a huge step for him. It required him to consider the possibility that his judgment was superior to theirs, and that the two men he most admired were not thinking rationally. But he was certain he was correct. He might have walked out a window if his father had told him to, but not if it meant leaving behind a Moody's Manual filled with cheap stocks.

Indeed, the opportunities he saw were plentiful to justify his first loan. He was willing to take on debt equivalent to one-quarter of his net worth. "I was already running out of money to invest. If I was enthusiastic about a stock, I would have to sell something else to acquire it. I was averse to borrowing money, but the Omaha National Bank gave me a loan for about $5,000. I was under 21, and my father had to cosign the loan. Mr. Davis, the banker, treated it like a rite of passage. He said something like, 'You're going into manhood now,' and referred to the $5,000, saying, 'It's a solemn obligation, and we know you've got the character to repay it.' This lasted for half an hour while I was sitting next to this large desk."

Howard probably felt both proud and silly cosigning a loan for his son, who had been a successful businessman for at least a dozen years. Since Warren had made his decision, Howard was willing to hire him at his own firm, Buffett-Falk—but only after suggesting that he interview at a prominent local firm, Kirkpatrick Pettis Co., to see what the best of Omaha stockbroking had to offer.

"I went to see Stewart Kirkpatrick and mentioned in the interview that I wanted intelligent customers. I intended to look for people who could understand things. And Kirkpatrick said, in effect, don't worry about their intelligence; worry about their wealth. Which is fine; you can't blame him for it. But I wouldn't have wanted to work anywhere but at my father's firm."

Warren was assigned to one of Buffett-Falk's four private unair-conditioned offices, adjacent to the "cage," a glassed-in area where a clerk handled money and securities. He began by selling his favorite stock to the safest people he knew: his aunt and his college friends, including his first roommate at Wharton, Chuck Peterson, who was now a real estate agent in Omaha and with whom he had reconnected. "My aunt Alice was the first person I called, and I sold her 100 shares of GEICO. She made me feel better about myself. She was interested in me. After that, Fred Stanback, Chuck Peterson, and anyone else I could convince to buy it. But mostly, I convinced myself to buy it, because if others didn't, I'd figure out how to buy five more shares myself. I had a big ambition: I was going to own one-tenth of one percent of the company. It had 175,000 outstanding shares, and I figured that if the company became worth a billion dollars someday and I owned that many, I'd be worth a million. So, I needed 175 shares.2

In the meantime, Warren's job required him to sell on commission, which he found nearly impossible outside of this narrow circle. When the grand old families of Omaha—the owners of the banks, stockyards, breweries, and big department stores—peered down their noses at the grandson of a grocer, he got a sense of the challenges his father had faced in building his brokerage business. Warren, now alone in Omaha with his parents in Washington, felt disrespected.

Previously, full-service stockbrokers sold all stocks, and most people purchased individual stocks rather than mutual funds. Everybody paid a fixed commission of six cents per share. Transactions were completed in person or by phone as part of a relationship. Every trade was preceded by a brief conversation with "your broker," who served as a combination salesman, adviser, and friend. Your broker may live in your neighborhood; you've seen him at parties, golfed with him at your country club, and he attended your daughter's wedding. General Motors introduced new car models every year. A businessman may trade his car more frequently than his stocks. That is, if he held any stocks.

Important accounts did not take Warren seriously. Nebraska Consolidated Mills, a client of his father's, once scheduled him to come out at 5:30 a.m.3. "I was twenty-one. And I'd go around to all these people and sell them stocks, and when I was done, they'd say, 'What does your dad think?' "I get that all the time." Warren, who resembled a "dork," struggled to generate sales.4 He couldn't read people, make small talk, and was definitely not a good listener. His mode of communication was broadcast rather than received. When he was nervous, he sprayed information about his favorite stocks like a fire hose. Some potential clients listened to his pitch, checked with other sources, and implemented his ideas, but they purchased the stocks through other brokers, so he did not receive the commission. He was taken aback by the dishonesty of people he'd met in person and would encounter again around town. He felt cheated. Sometimes he was simply perplexed. He once walked in on a man in his seventies sitting at his desk with a pile of dollar bills and a secretary in his lap. Every time she kissed him, the man handed her a dollar bill.

"My father had not taught me what to do in this situation." In general, I wasn't receiving reinforcement. When I first started selling GEICO,

Buffett-Falk had a small office downtown, and the stock certificates came in with Jerome Newman's name on them. He was the seller I was purchasing from. And the guys at Buffett-Falk said, "What the hell." "If you believe you are smarter than Jerry Newman..."

In fact, Graham-Newman was forming a new partnership, and some of the investors had given the firm GEICO shares to help fund the venture. So, in effect, they were selling, not Graham-Newman. Warren was unaware of that.5 But when it came to GEICO, he didn't care who sold. It never occurred to him to ask anyone at the firm why they were selling. He was unwaveringly certain of his own opinion. He did not hide this fact.

"I was kind of a wise guy, with this graduate degree, among people who hadn't attended college. Ralph Campbell, an insurance agent, once came in to see Mr. Falk and asked, 'What's this kid doing promoting this company?' GEICO was a company that did not employ insurance agents. And I said, as a wise man, 'Mr. Campbell, you better buy this stock for unemployment insurance.'"

The full significance of Dale Carnegie's first rule, don't criticize, had yet to sink in. Warren used what would later become Buffett's trademark wit to demonstrate that he knew more than everyone else, but why would anyone believe that from a twenty-one-year-old? And yet, he did. It must have stunned Buffett-Falk employees to see him ripping through manuals from morning to night, adding to his knowledge file cabinets.

"I read the Moody's Manuals page by page. The Moody's Industrial, Transportation, Banks, and Finance Manuals contain ten thousand pages—twice. I looked at every business, though I didn't look too closely at some."

Despite his insatiable interest in the game of stock picking, Warren aspired to be more than just an investor and a salesman. He wanted to be a teacher, like Ben Graham. He enrolled in night classes at the University of Omaha.

At first, he collaborated with his stockbroker friend Bob Soener to teach the first four weeks of "Profitable Investing in Stocks." While Soener taught the class the fundamentals of reading the Wall Street Journal, Warren stood in the hallway, listening for any good investment ideas. Then he took over for the following six weeks.6 Eventually, he taught the entire course and gave it the more cautious title of "Sound Investing in Stocks." He lit up in front of his classroom, pacing the floor as if he couldn't get the words out fast enough, although the students were struggling not to drown in the flood of information he threw their way. But, despite his extensive knowledge, he never promised the class that they would become wealthy or that taking his class would cause any specific outcome. He also didn't brag about his own investment success.

His students included stock-market professionals and housewives, doctors, and retirees with no business background. They symbolized a subtle shift: long-absent investors were returning for the first time since the 1920s, which contributed to Graham's belief that the market was overvalued. Warren tailored his instruction to the scope of their knowledge and abilities. He modeled his teaching style after Graham's, employing the "Company A, Company B" method and some of his mentor's other teaching techniques. He assigned grades with the strictest fairness. His aunt Alice took the course and sat in the classroom, staring at him with adoration.7 He graded her a C.

People were constantly throwing out stock names and asking him to buy or sell. He could speak from memory for five or ten minutes about any stock they mentioned: its financial data, price/earnings ratio, trading volume—and it appeared that he could do this for hundreds of stocks, as if he were quoting baseball statistics.8 A woman in the front row would occasionally say, "My late mother gave me ABC stock, and it has since risen slightly. "What should I do?" Then he would say, "Well, I think I would sell that, and maybe buy...," giving three or four options such as GEICO or one of the stocks he was completely confident about (and already owned).9 When asked how to invest, the students remarked on his unusual conservatism.

Meanwhile, in April, Warren was working like a woodpecker to support himself. He was about to start a family, so his income would be divided into two streams. Part of what he produced—his stream— would return to the mill and continue to grow. And part of it would be spent on him and Susie's survival, which was a significant change in his situation. Until now, he had been able to cut costs by living in the maid's room at Columbia, eating cheese sandwiches, and accompanying his dates to lectures or playing the ukulele for them rather than escorting them to the posh "21" Club. Now that he was back in Nebraska, he was able to save even more money by living in his parents' house, although it meant only seeing Leila on occasion when they returned from Washington.

He had never needed motivation to work his capital as hard as he could, and now he sat in the Buffett-Falk office with his feet on his desk, systematically searching the Graham and Dodd book for more ideas.10 He discovered a stock, Philadelphia and Reading Coal & Iron Company, which mined anthracite coal. It appeared cheap because it was selling for $19 and a fraction, but it actually had about $8 worth of culm banks per share. Warren would happily spend hours calculating the value of coal mines and culm banks to make an informed stock investment decision. He purchased Philadelphia and Reading Coal & Iron shares for himself and sold them to his aunt Alice and Chuck Peterson. When the stock immediately fell to $9 per share, he saw it as an opportunity to buy even more.

He purchased Cleveland Worsted Mills, a textile company. It had current assets of $146 per share, but the stock was trading for less than that. He believed the price did not accurately reflect the value of "several well-equipped mills."

Warren wrote a brief report about the stock. He liked how the company paid out a large portion of its profits to shareholders, giving them an advantage. "The $8 dividend provides a well-protected 7% yield on the current price of approximately $115," the report stated.11 He wrote "well-protected" because he believed Cleveland Worsted Mills' earnings were sufficient to cover its dividend. That proved to be less than prescient.

"I called it Cleveland's Worst Mill after they stopped paying the dividend." Warren was so upset that he decided to spend some money to figure out what was wrong. "I flew all the way to Cleveland to attend the annual meeting of Cleveland's Worst Mill. I arrived about five minutes late, and the meeting had ended. And here I was, a twenty-two-year-old kid from Omaha, investing my own money in stocks. The chairman said, 'Sorry, it's too late.' But then their sales agent, who was on the board of directors, took pity on me and got me off to the side, talked to me, and answered some questions." The answers, however, made no difference. Warren felt terrible; he had convinced others to buy Cleveland's Worst Mill as well.

Nothing irritated him more than selling people investments that resulted in losses. He couldn't stand disappointing others. This was what it was like in sixth grade, when the Cities Service Preferred stock he'd convinced Doris to invest in was wiped out. She had not hesitated to "remind" him of it, and he felt responsible. Now, he'd do anything to avoid the feeling of disappointing someone.

Warren began looking for any way to reduce his reliance on the job he was growing to despise. He had always enjoyed owning businesses and decided to purchase a gas station with a National Guard friend, Jim Schaeffer. They purchased a Sinclair station adjacent to a Texaco station "that consistently out-sold us, which drove us crazy." Warren and his brother-in-law Truman Wood, who had married Doris, even worked at the station on weekends. They washed windshields "with a smile"—despite Warren's dislike for manual labor—and did everything they could to attract new customers, but drivers continued to pull into the Texaco station across the street. Its owner "was well-known and well-liked. He outperformed us every month. That's when I realized the value of customer loyalty. The guy had been in business a long time and had a clientele. Nothing we could do would change that.

"My service station was the dumbest thing; I lost $2,000, which was a lot of money for me at the time. I'd never suffered serious damage in a loss. "It was painful."

Warren felt that almost everything he did in Omaha reinforced his youth and inexperience. He was no longer a precocious boy acting like a man, but a young man about to marry who still looked and acted like a boy. Kaiser-Frazer, the stock he had shorted in Bob Soener's office two years before, remained stubbornly priced at five dollars per share rather than falling to zero as he had anticipated. Carl Falk was constantly giving him funny looks and questioning his judgment. Warren became increasingly concerned about the nature of his job. He began to see himself as "a prescriptionist." "I had to explain to people who didn't know enough about whether they should take aspirin or Anacin," and people would do whatever the "guy in the white coat"—the stockbroker—told them. The stockbroker was paid based on turnover rather than advice. In other words, "he's paid based on the number of pills he sells." He gets paid more for certain pills than others. You wouldn't go to a doctor whose pay was entirely dependent on how many pills you took." However, this was how the stockbroking business worked at the time.

Warren saw a conflict of interest inherent in the business. He'd recommend stocks like GEICO to his friends and family, telling them that the best thing to do was to hold onto them for twenty years. That meant he wouldn't receive any more commissions from them. "You cannot make a living that way. "The system pits your interests against your clients."

Nonetheless, he had started to build a small clientele through his network of graduate school friends. In spring 1952, he traveled to Salisbury, North Carolina, to celebrate Easter with Fred Stanback. He charmed and amused Fred's parents, as well as the family, by discussing stocks, quoting Ben Graham, and ordering a Pepsi-Cola and a ham sandwich for breakfast.12 Soon after, back in Omaha, Fred Stanback's father gave him an order to sell some stock in Thor Corporation, a washing-machine company. Warren found a buyer through another broker, Harris Upham. Then he received another call from Stanback's bank regarding the sale and assumed he had two orders. He sold Thor Corporation stock twice, the second time accidentally selling stock he did not own. Now he had to find more shares, which he ended up buying at a loss to cover the second sale.

Despite his mistake, Mr. Stanback treated him graciously. He accepted the entire loss, even though Warren was at fault. Warren was thankful and never forgot it. He was more concerned about the second buyer, a man known as "Mad Dog" Baxter, who was a relic of Omaha's past as a major gambling layoff center and an associate in some of the city's numerous illegal betting parlors. Baxter had arrived at Buffett-Falk in person, walked up to the cashier's cage, and pulled out a wad of $100 bills, waving them around ostentatiously. Again, "Carl Falk looked at me questioningly." Was Buffett-Falk being used to launder illegal gambling funds? Situations like this fueled Warren's disdain for his job. Even when he wasn't selling stocks, he was conflicted. He had transformed Buffett-Falk into a "market maker," a company that acted as a middleman, buying and selling stocks as a dealer.13 The company profited by selling a stock to clients at a slightly higher price than it paid, and buying stock from clients at a lower price than it sold the stock for. The difference, or "spread," was the profit. Customers were unable to detect the spread. Acting as a market maker elevated a brokerage firm from a mere order taker to a player on Wall Street. Warren was proud of his ability to set Buffett-Falk up as a market maker, but the conflict bothered him.

"I do not want to be on the opposite side of the table from the customer. I never sold anything because I didn't believe in myself or own it. However, there was an undisclosed markup. If anyone asked, I told them. But I don't like things like that. I want to be on the same side as my partners, so everyone knows what's going on. And a promoter, by nature, does not do that.

No matter how Warren viewed his job as a stockbroker, there was always the possibility of a conflict of interest, and the risk of losing money for his clients and disappointing them. He would much rather manage people's money than sell them stocks, as his interests are aligned with those of the customers. Unfortunately, there were no such opportunities in Omaha. But in the spring of 1952, he wrote an article about GEICO that piqued the interest of a powerful man, and his fortunes appeared to change. The article "The Security I Like Best," published in the Commercial and Financial Chronicle, was more than just an advertisement for Warren's favorite stock; it also explained his investment philosophy. It piqued the interest of Bill Rosenwald, the son of Julius Rosenwald, a philanthropist and longtime chairman of Sears, Roebuck and Company. The younger Rosenwald ran American Securities, a money management firm founded with family stock in Sears14 that aimed for high returns while minimizing risk and preserving capital. Rosenwald approached Ben Graham, who gave Warren a glowing recommendation, and offered Warren a job. Few jobs in money management were more prestigious, and Warren was eager to accept it, even if it meant returning to New York City. To do so, he needed permission from the National Guard to leave Omaha.

"I asked my commanding officer if it was possible to transfer to New York to take this position. He said, 'You'll have to go down and see the commanding general.' So I went down to Lincoln, sat in the state capitol, waited a while, went in to see General Henninger, and said, 'Corporal Buffett reporting.' I'd written to him ahead of time explaining and requesting permission.

"And immediately he said, 'Permission denied.'"

"That was the last of it. That meant I was in Omaha while he wanted to keep me captive.

So Warren was stuck at Buffett-Falk, writing prescriptions for a living. His fiancée was his main source of comfort during the difficult first year in Omaha. He had started to lean on Susie. All the while, she was trying to figure out Warren. She began to realize the harm Leila Buffett's rages had done to her son's self-esteem, and she began attempting to repair it. She knew that the most important thing he needed was to feel loved and not criticized. He also needed to believe he could succeed socially. "People accepted me more when I was with her," he jokes. Even though she was still at the University of Omaha while he was working, he was like a toddler looking up at a parent about his relationship with his future wife. Both were still living at their parents' homes. Warren had developed a strategy for dealing with his mother that involved avoiding being alone with her and taking advantage of her dutiful nature when she was present by bombarding her with demands and requests. However, the long stretches of time he had spent away from her while in college had reduced rather than increased his tolerance for Leila's company. When she and Howard returned from Washington for Warren and Susie's wedding, Susie noticed that her fiancé tried to avoid his mother as much as possible. When forced to be in her presence, he would turn away from her and clench his teeth.

Warren's lease was up. He called Chuck Peterson and said, "Chas-o, I haven't got a place for us to live," and Chas-o rented him a small apartment a few miles from downtown. When Warren gave Susie, who had a strong sense of self-expression, a $1,500 allowance to furnish their first apartment, she and her future sister-in-law Doris set out for Chicago to shop for furniture in the colorful modern style she preferred.15

As the wedding date, April 19, 1952, approached, it became unclear whether the ceremony would take place at all. The Missouri River had flooded upstream Omaha last week. With the waters flowing south, officials predicted it would crest above the riverbank and flood the city over the weekend. This increased the likelihood that the National Guard would be called out.

"The entire town came out with sandbags. I had all these buddies coming in for the wedding, including Fred Stanback as best man, and various ushers and guests. They were all mocking me because I was in the National Guard. They joke, 'Well, don't worry about it, because we'll substitute for you on the honeymoon. "This was going on all week."

Days before, Howard drove Warren and Fred to the river. Thousands of volunteers were constructing double sandbag walls that were six feet high and four feet deep. The earth sank beneath the wheels of the massive trucks hauling sand and dirt, as if they were driving over rubber.16 Warren held his breath, hoping that he would not be called upon to sandbag and that the temporary levee would hold.

"Saturday arrived, and we were getting married around three in the afternoon. Around noon, the phone rang. My mother said, 'It's for you.' I answered the phone. The guy on the other end said, "C-C-C-Corporal Buffett?"' I had a commander with a very distinctive stutter. 'This is C-C-C, Captain Murphy,' he announced.

"If he hadn't stuttered, I would have said something that would have gotten me court-martialed, because I would have assumed the guys were playing a trick on me. But as it was, he said, 'We've been activated. What time can you arrive at the Armory? Warren nearly had a heart attack. "And I said, 'Well, I'm getting married at three o'clock,' and 'I could probably be there by five.' He said, 'Report for duty. We're going to be p-p-p-patrolling East Omaha d-d-down by the river." I replied, "Yes, sir."

"I got off the phone feeling extremely depressed. I then receive a call an hour later. And this guy had a completely normal voice. He asks, "Corporal Buffett?"' I said, 'Yes, sir.' He said, 'This is General Wood.' General Wood was the commanding general of the Thirty-fourth Division, and he lived way out in west Nebraska. General Wood stated, 'I'm opposing Captain Murphy's order. Have a good time!"

He had two hours until the biggest event of his life. Warren arrived at the soaring Gothic sanctuary of Dundee Presbyterian Church well before three o'clock. The wedding of a Congressman's son and Doc Thompson's daughter was a huge deal in Omaha. Several hundred guests, including many of Omaha's most prominent figures, were expected.

"Doc Thompson was so proud that he was pushing buttons all over the place. I was so nervous that I just figured—well, I didn't wear my glasses so I wouldn't be able to see all those people out there." Warren also asked the normally reserved Stanback to distract him by talking so he wouldn't have to pay attention to what was going on.

As maid of honor, Bertie supported Susie, while Dottie, Susie's sister, served as matron of honor. After the photos, the guests drank nonalcoholic punch and kate wedding cake in the church basement, which had linoleum floors. That was normal; the Thompsons and Buffets were not club members. Susie smiled as wide as an ivory fan. Warren glowed brightly and wrapped his arm around her waist, as if to keep them from flying away. After more photos, they changed into their departure attire and dashed through the crowd of cheering guests to get into Alice Buffett's car, which she had lent them for the honeymoon. Warren had already packed the backseat with Moody's manuals and ledgers. Susie suddenly saw the writing on the wall. And from Omaha, the newlyweds embarked on their honeymoon, a cross-country road trip.

"On my wedding night, I had chicken fried steak at the Wigwam Café in Wahoo, Nebraska," Buffett tells me. The Wigwam was a small hole-in-the-wall less than an hour from Omaha, with a few booths and cowboy decorations. Warren and Susie then drove thirty miles to the Cornhusker Hotel in Lincoln, where they spent the night, "and that's all I'll say on that subject," Buffet says.

"The next day, I bought a copy of the Omaha World-Herald, and it had run an article that said, 'Only love can stop the Guard.'" The 1952 flood was Omaha's worst in modern times, and the effort to avert it was Herculean. "The other guys spent days sandbagging, patrolling the flood with the snakes and rats. "I was the only guy who wasn't called out."

The newlyweds traveled throughout the western and southwestern United States. Warren had never been to the West Coast, but Susie was very familiar with it. They visited her family, saw the sights, went to the Grand Canyon, and had a great time. "We did not stop to visit companies and look at investments, as has been reported," Buffett explains. On the way back, they stopped in Las Vegas, which was crowded with ex-Omaha residents. Eddie Barrick and Sam Ziegman, the "layoff bookies," had recently moved to the area and purchased the Flamingo Hotel. Another associate, Jackie Gaughan, who had invested in casinos from the Flamingo to the Barbary Coast joined them soon. All of these characters had shopped at the Buffett grocery store, and Fred Buffett, despite not being a gambler, got along well with them. For Warren, Vegas felt almost like home, with echoes of the racetrack and a crowd of people who knew his family. So he wasn't afraid of the house. "Susie won a jackpot at the slot machine. She was only 19. They refused to pay her because she was underage. I told them, 'Lookit, you took her nickels.' They paid her.

After Vegas, the Buffetts returned to Omaha. Warren couldn't stop laughing at his Guard colleagues' bad luck. "Oh, the honeymoon was wonderful. It was great. Three weeks. And all the time, these Guardsmen were sloshing it up."

PART THREE

THE
RACETRACK

GRAHAM-NEWMAN

Omaha and New York City, 1952–1955

Susie traveled to Chicago with her parents and new in-laws for the Republican convention in July 1952, just months after their wedding. The Thompsons and Buffets arrived in Chicago, not as delegates, but as members of an army. Politically speaking, they were now one united family, and this election year they were on a crusade to reclaim the White House for the Republicans after twenty agonizing years under Democratic rule. Doris would be working behind the scenes with her father, while the much younger Bertie and Susie, innocent spectators, would spend their time gawking at celebrities such as John Wayne, who had come to the Grand Old Party.

Warren, of course, remained in Omaha, grinding. Politics captivated him, but not like money. He still despised his job as a "prescriptionist," but he persisted in his efforts to find an alternative. His former teacher, David Dodd, tried to assist him by referring him to the Value Line Investment Survey, an investment adviser and research publisher looking for "new men." The job would have paid well—"at least $7,000 per year." However, Warren did not intend to be an anonymous researcher. So he kept trying to sell GEICO to uninterested customers while reading the convention news, which was being reported under inch-high headlines in newspapers. For the first time in history, a convention was broadcast on television, and Warren was fascinated by the medium's ability to magnify and influence events.

Senator Robert Taft of Ohio was the front-runner heading into the convention. Taft, known as "Mr. Integrity," led a minority wing of the Republican Party centered on isolationist Midwesterners who wanted the government to be small, stay out of everyone's business, and, most importantly, go after Communism more aggressively than Truman had. Taft appointed his friend Howard Buffett as the head of both his Nebraska presidential campaign and his speakers bureau. To oppose Taft, Howard's despised Eastern Liberal Establishment6 drafted retired General Dwight D. Eisenhower, a moderate who had served as Supreme Commander of Allied Forces in Europe during WWII and was the first Supreme Commander of NATO forces. Eisenhower, a politically astute diplomat with exceptional leadership abilities, was a popular figure and widely regarded as a war hero. As the convention approached, "Ike" began to gain traction in the polls.

What would become the most contentious Republican convention in history took place in Chicago, as Eisenhower supporters pushed through an amendment to the convention rules that, after a contentious vote, gave him the delegates needed to win the nomination on the first ballot. Taft's outraged supporters felt robbed. However, Eisenhower quickly made peace with them by promising to combat "creeping socialism," and Taft insisted that his supporters swallow their outrage and vote for Eisenhower to reclaim the White House. The Republicans rallied behind him and his running mate, Richard Nixon, and "I Like Ike" buttons appeared everywhere. Everywhere except Howard Buffett's chest. He broke with the party by refusing to support Eisenhower.

This was a case of political suicide. His popularity within the party dwindled overnight. He was left to stand on principle—alone. Warren realized that his father had "painted himself into a corner." Warren had been trying to avoid broken promises, burned bridges, and confrontation since he was a child. Howard's struggles instilled three principles in his son: allies are essential, commitments are so sacred that they should be rare, and grandstanding rarely gets anything done. Eisenhower defeated Adlai Stevenson in the November election, and Warren's parents returned to Washington in January to serve out the remainder of Howard's lame duck term. Warren, who had long recognized obsessive qualities in Howard and Leila that harmed them in various ways, had begun to adopt some of his in-laws' style. Dorothy Thompson was laid-back, and her husband, while autocratic, was more personable and astute in human relations than the rigidly idealistic Howard Buffett. The longer he spent with Susie and her family, the more they influenced him.

"Warren," said Doc Thompson, delivering advice with the authority of the Sermon on the Mount, "always surround yourself with women." They are more loyal and work harder." His son-in-law didn't really need to be told that. Warren had always wanted to be taken care of by women, as long as they didn't try to boss him around. Susie could tell he was eager for her to take on a maternal role. So she wrapped herself around her husband and worked on "fixing" him, the wreck, the mess. "Oh, my God," she exclaimed. "He was a case." When they met, she said, "I had never seen anyone in so much pain."

Warren may not have been aware of the depths or dimensions of his pain, but he does describe the significant role she played in his life.

"Susie had an equal or greater influence on me than my father, albeit differently." I had all these defense mechanisms that she could describe, but I can't. She probably noticed things about me that others didn't. But she knew it would take time and plenty of nourishment to bring it out. She made me believe that I had someone with a small sprinkling can who would ensure that the flowers grew."

Susie recognized Warren's vulnerability and his need to be soothed, comforted, and reassured. She became increasingly aware of the impact his mother had on her children. Doris was more severely damaged, but Leila had persuaded both Warren and Doris that they were worthless. Susie discovered that her husband was plagued by self-doubt in all aspects of his life except business. He had never felt loved, and she could tell he didn't feel lovable.

"I needed her like crazy," he says. "I was happy at work, but not with myself. She actually saved my life. She resurrected me. She put me together. It was the same kind of unconditional love you'd expect from a parent."

Warren expected many things from his wife that a parent would normally provide. Furthermore, he grew up with a mother who did everything for him. Susie took over. Although their basic model of married life was typical of the time—he made the money, she looked after him and handled the domestic duties—their arrangement was extreme. Everything in the Buffett household revolved around Warren and his business. Susie recognized that her husband was special, and she willingly became the cocoon for his embryonic ambitions. He worked during the day and studied Moody's Manual at night. He also planned his schedule to allow for leisure time to play golf and Ping-Pong, even enrolling as a junior member of the Omaha Country Club. Susie, barely twenty years old, was no Betty Crocker, but she had taken up rudimentary cooking and basic housekeeping like any 1950s wife—at a time when Omaha women auditioned for the local television show Typical Housewife on KTMV. She devoted herself to meeting her husband's few but specific needs: Pepsi in the fridge, a lightbulb in his reading lamp, some indifferently cooked meat and potatoes for dinner, a salt shaker, popcorn in the pantry, and ice cream in the freezer. He also required assistance getting dressed, dealing with people, tenderness, head rubs, cuddling, and hugs. She even cut his hair because he said he was afraid to go to the barbershop.

Warren was "nuts about Susie, and she felt things" within him, he claims. He describes her as the giver and himself as the receiver. "She was absorbing more about me and sensing much more about me than I was sensing about her." They were always kissing and cuddling, with Susie frequently sitting on Warren's lap, which she said reminded her of her father.

Susie became pregnant six months after the wedding and dropped out of the University of Omaha. Her sister, Dottie, was pregnant with her second child. She and Susie had stayed particularly close. Dottie, a dark-haired beauty, shared her father's intelligence and, according to family lore, had the highest IQ in the school when she attended Central High. But in appearance and domesticity, she was more like her mother. She had married Homer Rogers, a pilot and war hero with a deep baritone voice who everyone referred to as Buck Rogers, despite his modesty about his military exploits. Homer was a boisterous, energetic cattleman, as muscular as the oversize steers he purchased and sold. The Rogerses always had a party at their house, with Dottie playing piano and Homer singing something like "Katie, Katie, get off the table, the money's for the beer." Susie and Warren did not participate in the Rogerses' active social life because they were more serious and did not consume alcohol, but the sisters spent a lot of time together on their own. Dottie had always struggled to make decisions, and after having her first son, Billy, she appeared dazed by the demands of motherhood. Susie, naturally, took charge and assisted her.

Susie had also become close to her sister-in-law Doris, who had recently married and was working as a schoolteacher in Omaha. Her husband, Truman Wood, was a handsome man with a pleasant personality who came from a prominent Omaha family, but Doris began to wonder if she was a racing filly married to a Clydesdale. Doris, an action-oriented girl, told Truman to get his act together. He ambled a little faster, but not significantly.

Susie's protectiveness of Warren and his sister increased in January 1953, after Eisenhower was sworn in, when Howard's final congressional term expired and he and Leila returned to Nebraska permanently. Doris and Warren felt the strain of Leila's return to town. Warren couldn't bear being in the same room as his mother, who continued to turn on Doris on occasion.

Howard was lost in Omaha. Warren formed Buffett & Buffett, a partnership that formalized their occasional stock purchases together. Howard contributed some capital, and Warren contributed a small sum of money, but mostly ideas and labor. However, Howard was dissatisfied with the prospect of returning to the stockbroking business for the third time. Warren had been tending his old accounts while in Congress, but Howard knew Warren despised it, had never stopped trying to persuade Ben Graham to hire him, and would leave in an instant if he could move to New York. Howard, for his part, missed his true love: politics. He had a desire to join the Senate, especially now that a Republican was in the White House. However, his ambitions clashed with his extreme political beliefs.

Susie and Warren had their first child, a daughter, on July 30, 1953, Alice Buffett's birthday. Her name was Susan Alice, and she was also known as Little Susie, or Little Sooz. Susie went on to become a passionate, playful, and devoted mother.

Little Susie was Howard and Leila's first grandchild. A week later, Susie's sister, Dottie, gave birth to her second son, Tommy. Doris became pregnant with her first child, a daughter named Robin Wood, within months. By spring 1954, Susie was expecting her second child. The Buffetts and Thompsons had a new focus: grandchildren.

A few months later, it appeared that Howard's time had arrived. Hugh Butler, Nebraska's senior senator, was rushed to the hospital with a stroke and was not expected to live, according to news reports from Washington. The deadline to enter the primary to fill his Senate seat was that same night. Howard's sense of propriety prevented him from filing the papers to run until Butler had died, so the Buffetts waited anxiously all day for news. They knew that Howard's name recognition in Douglas County meant that if he ran in a special election without going through the party nominating process, even if the party leaders were dissatisfied with him, he would have a good chance of winning.

Butler's death was announced in the early evening, after Secretary of State Frank Marsh's office closed at five p.m. as usual. Howard threw his candidacy paperwork into the car, and he and Leila drove to Lincoln, assuming they had plenty of time because the deadline was midnight. They attempted to file the papers at Marsh's home, but he refused, despite Howard having paid the filing fee earlier in the day. Infuriated, they returned to Omaha.

The state Republican convention was in session at the time, and when Butler died, delegates on the floor elected a temporary successor to finish his term. Anyone currently serving would almost certainly be elected to Butler's position in November. Howard, the state's top Republican, was an obvious choice. However, he was viewed as a zealot, a guy who tilted at windmills, unyielding on minor ethical issues, and disloyal to his own party for not supporting Eisenhower. Instead, the convention elected Roman Hruska, a popular Congressman who had taken Howard's seat when he retired. Howard and Leila returned to Lincoln and promptly filed a lawsuit in the State Supreme Court to force the party to accept his nomination. But twenty-four hours later, they abandoned the futile fight and dropped the lawsuit.

Warren was furious when he learned about Hruska. "They slit Daddy's throat from ear to ear," he told me. How dare the party reward Howard's decades of loyalty this way?

Howard, at age fifty-one, had just seen his future disappear. As his rage subsided, his depression worsened. Until now, a retired senior party politician like him would have had a role to play, but he had been barred from the arena that had been the focal point of his life and made him feel useful in the world. He applied for a teaching position at the University of Omaha, which the family thought was reasonable given his business experience and tenure as a Congressman. However, Howard was considered such an oddball locally that the school refused to hire him, although his own son taught there and Doc Thompson was the dean of the College of Arts and Sciences. He ended up returning to work at Buffett-Falk. He eventually found a part-time teaching position as a lecturer at Midland Lutheran College, located 30 miles from Omaha. The family harbored resentment toward the local establishment, which they felt had effectively driven Howard out of town.

Leila dissolved into a pool of misery. Howard's position in the world may have meant more to her than to him because of the reflected glory it bestowed upon her. Her sister Edie was now living in Brazil, Bertie was in Chicago, and her relationships with Doris and Warren were strained at best, leaving her with only twenty-two-year-old Susie to rely on. However, Susie was a busy, pregnant young mother who was also responsible for Warren.

Susie would soon leave Omaha. Warren had been corresponding with Ben Graham for two years. He suggested stock ideas like Greif Bros. Cooperage, a company he and his father had purchased as a partnership. He visited Graham-Newman on occasion during his trips to New York.

"I would always try to see Mr. Graham."

It wasn't common for former students to hang out at Graham-Newman.

"No, well, I was persistent."

Warren was already on his way to New York when the local Republican Party slammed the door on his father's Senate nomination. "Ben wrote to say, 'Come on back.' Jerry Newman, his partner, explained, 'You know, we just checked you out a little further.' "I felt like I had hit the jackpot." Whether he would accept the position was never a question. This time, the National Guard said yes.

Warren was so excited to be hired that he arrived in New York on August 1, 1954, and arrived at Graham-Newman on August 2, a month before his scheduled start date. He discovered Ben Graham had been tragically killed a week earlier. Warren wrote his father four weeks before his own twenty-fourth birthday, saying, "Ben Graham's son Newton (26) committed suicide last week while serving in the Army in France. He had always been a little off. Graham didn't realize it was a suicide until he read it in the New York Times about an Army release, which is obviously extremely difficult."18 When Ben traveled to France to collect his son's remains, he met Newton's girlfriend, Marie Louise Amingues, aka Malou, who was several years older than Newton. He returned weeks later but was never the same. He also began to correspond with Malou and made regular trips back to France. But Warren had no idea about his idol's personal life then.

Instead, he had to focus on his own, as one of his first tasks was to find a place for his family to live. Susie and Little Susie had stayed in Omaha throughout his first month in New York City. "I attempted to live at Peter Cooper Village first, one of two large projects built by Metropolitan Life immediately following World War II. Fred Kuhlken, a friend from Columbia, lived with Peter Cooper. Walter Schloss lived with Peter Cooper. Everyone wanted to get into Peter Cooper. It was very reasonable, about $70 or $80 per month, under some kind of special section of the law. I applied before going and received a postcard about two years later stating that I had been accepted. "If I had been accepted earlier, I would have lived in the city.

Instead, Warren looked far and wide for a low-cost apartment. Despite the impersonal location and lengthy commute, he eventually settled on a three-bedroom apartment in a white-brick building in the middle-class suburb of White Plains, about thirty miles away in Westchester County, New York. When Susie and Little Susie arrived weeks later, the apartment was still not ready. The family moved into a room in a Westchester house that was so small they had to make a makeshift crib out of a dresser drawer. The Buffetts stayed only a day or two.

But such were the stories later told about Warren's frugal habits that this story grew legs and scuttled into the legend that he was too cheap to buy Little Susie a crib, so she slept in a drawer for much of her White Plains infancy.

Warren took the New York Central train to Grand Central every morning while Susie, who was pregnant, unpacked and organized her new home while caring for their baby and getting to know the neighbors. In that first month, he parked himself in Graham-Newman's file room and, eager to learn everything about the company, began reading through every single piece of paper in every single drawer in an entire room filled with large wooden files.

There were only eight people working there: Ben Graham, Jerry Newman, his son Mickey Newman, Bernie Warner, the treasurer; Walter Schloss, two female secretaries; and Warren. Warren finally had the thin gray laboratory-style jacket he had coveted. "It was a big deal when they handed me my jacket. We all wore them. Ben wore it. Jerry Newman wore it. "We were all equal in our jackets."

Well, not exactly. Warren and Walter sat at desks in a windowless room that housed the ticker machine, direct lines to brokerage houses, and some reference books and documents. Walter sat near the direct lines, making most calls to brokers. Ben, Mickey Newman, or, more commonly, Jerry Newman appeared from their private offices to check the ticker machine. "We'd look up information and read. We would look through Standard & Poor's or Moody's Manual for companies that are selling below their working capital. Schloss recalls, "There were a lot back then."

These companies were what Graham referred to as "cigar butts": cheap and unloved stocks that had been discarded like a sticky, mashed stub of a stogie found on the sidewalk. Graham specialized in spotting these unappealing remnants that everyone else ignored. He coaxed them to light and sucked out one final free puff.

Graham knew that a certain number of cigar butts would be bad, so he thought it was pointless to spend time examining the quality of each cigar butt. The law of averages stated that the majority of them were fit for puff. He was always thinking about how much companies would be worth if they died, or what their assets would be worth if liquidated. Buying at a discount to that value was his "margin of safety"—his insurance against the percentage that was likely to go bankrupt. As a backup, he purchased small positions in a large number of stocks—the principle of diversification. Graham's concept of diversification was extreme, with some of his positions as small as $1,000.

Warren, who was so confident in his own judgment, saw no reason to hedge his bets in this manner and internally rolled his eyes at diversification. He and Walter gathered data from the Moody's Manuals and completed hundreds of the simple forms that Graham-Newman used to make decisions. Warren wanted to know all the basic facts about each company. After reviewing the field, he narrowed it down to a few stocks that warranted further investigation, and he focused his money on what he thought were the best bets. He was willing to put most of his eggs in one basket, as he had with GEICO. By that point, he had sold his GEICO stock because he never seemed to have enough money to invest. Every decision had an opportunity cost, and he had to weigh each investment opportunity against the next best option. As much as he admired GEICO, he had made the difficult decision to sell it after discovering another stock that he coveted even more, Western Insurance. This company earned $29 per share and its stock sold for as little as $3.

It was like finding a slot machine that would always pay cherries. If you put in 25 cents and pulled the handle, the Western Insurance machine was almost guaranteed to pay at least two dollars. Anyone sane would play that slot for as long as she could remain awake. It was the cheapest stock with the best margin of safety he'd ever seen. He bought as much as he could and let his friends in on the deal.

Warren was always looking for something free or inexpensive. With his remarkable ability to absorb and analyze numbers, he quickly became Graham-Newman's fair-haired boy. Ben Graham's cigar butts resembled his old hobby of stooping at the racetrack for discarded winning tickets.

He paid close attention to what was going on in the back, where the partners—Ben, Jerry, and Mickey—were working. Ben Graham served on the board of Philadelphia and Reading Coal & Iron Company, and Graham-Newman controlled the company. Warren discovered this stock on his own, and by the end of 1954, he had invested $35,000. His boss would have been horrified, but Warren was unconcerned—and eavesdropped with interest. Philadelphia and Reading, which sold anthracite coal and owned the supposedly valuable culm banks, were not particularly profitable businesses. It was eventually going nowhere. However, it was generating excess cash that it could use to improve its business by acquiring another.

"I was just a peon sitting in the outer office. A man named Jack Goldfarb came into the office to see Graham-Newman. He negotiated with them, and they acquired the Union Underwear Company in exchange for Philadelphia and Reading Coal and Iron, forming the Philadelphia and Reading Corporation. That marked the start of the company's transformation into something more diverse. I wasn't in the inner circle, but I was very interested because I knew something was going on."

By keeping his ears open, Warren was learning the art of capital allocation—placing money where it would yield the highest return. In this case, Graham-Newman used funds from one business to acquire a more profitable one. Over time, it may mean the difference between bankruptcy and success.

Transactions like this made Warren feel as if he was sitting on the windowsill, watching high finance take place. However, as he quickly discovered, Graham did not behave like anyone else on Wall Street. He was constantly mentally reciting poetry or quoting Virgil and was prone to losing packages on the subway. Like Warren, he didn't care how he looked. When someone said, "That's an interesting pair of shoes," Graham looked down at the brown oxford on one foot and the black one on the other and said, "Yes, as a matter of fact, I've got another pair just like them at home." Unlike Warren, he had no interest in money for its own sake or trading as a competitive game. He saw stock picking as an intellectual exercise.

"Once, we were waiting for an elevator. We planned to eat in the cafeteria at the bottom of the Chanin Building at Forty-second and Lex. And Ben told me, "Remember one thing, Warren: money doesn't make a big difference in how you and I live." We're both going to the cafeteria for lunch, working every day, and having a good time. So don't be too concerned about money; it won't make much difference in how you live."

Warren admired Ben Graham, but he was primarily concerned with money. He wanted to collect a large amount of it and saw it as a competitive game. When asked to give up some of his money, Warren reacted like a dog fiercely guarding its bones, or as if he had been attacked. His inability to let go of even the smallest sums of money was so obvious that it was as if the money owed him rather than the other way around.

Susie had learned this too well. Warren quickly established a reputation for tightfistedness and eccentricity within their apartment building. It wasn't until he was embarrassed by the state of his shirts at work—Susie never ironed more than the collar, front placket, and cuffs—that he let her send them to the laundry. He made an agreement with a local newsstand to buy week-old magazines at a discount because they were about to be thrown away. He didn't have a car, and when he borrowed one from a neighbor, he never filled the tank. (When he finally got a car, he washed it only when it was raining, allowing the rain to perform the manual labor of rinsing.)

Holding on to every penny in this manner since selling that first pack of chewing gum was one of the two things that had made Warren relatively wealthy at the age of twenty-five. The other was collecting more money. Since Columbia, he has been making money at an increasing rate. Warren now spent a lot of time in a reverie, with statistics about businesses and stock prices racing through his mind. When he wasn't studying, he was teaching it. To keep his Dale Carnegie skills in shape so he wouldn't freeze in front of an audience, he got a job teaching investing at Scarsdale Adult School, a high school in a nearby suburb. Meanwhile, the Buffetts' social circles included couples whose breadwinners were primarily interested in stocks.

He and Susie were occasionally invited to country clubs or dinner parties with other young Wall Street couples. Bill Ruane had introduced him to several new acquaintances, including Henry Brandt, a stockbroker who resembled a disheveled Jerry Lewis and graduated at the top of his class from Harvard Business School, and his wife, Roxanne. Warren was regarded as the "luckiest person you ever saw" by some on Wall Street. However, when he began talking about stocks, the others sat transfixed at his feet, like "Jesus and the apostles," according to Roxanne Brandt.

The wives sat alone and had their own conversations. Susie stood out among the men as much as her husband. Warren cast financial spells, and Susie enchanted the wives with her appealing simplicity. She wanted to know everything about their children and their plans to have children. She knew how to get others to open up to her. She would inquire about a significant life decision and then, with a soulful expression, ask, "Any regrets?" Out would come the other person's most intimate emotions. Someone she had met half an hour before felt like she had a new best friend, even though Susie never confided in her. People adored her for being so invested in them.

Susie was mostly on her own as she awaited the birth of their second child, spending her days doing laundry, shopping, cleaning, and cooking, and feeding, changing, and playing with Little Susie. Everything felt right and normal for both. Three years ago, Ricky Ricardo stated in the first season of I Love Lucy, "I want a wife who's just a wife." Lucy's ambitions and her futile attempts to realize them made the show comedic. So, as Susie fed Warren dinner, she supported him at work as if it were a daily sacrament, and she recognized his admiration for Mr. Graham. However, she also watched from afar. Warren did not discuss the specifics of his job, which, in any case, did not interest her. She kept up the patient work of boosting his confidence and "putting him together" by showering him with love and teaching him about people. One thing she insisted on at home was that he bonds with their daughter. Warren was not the type to play peekaboo or take over diaper changing, but he did sing to Little Susie each night.

"I sang 'Over the Rainbow' all the time. It became hypnotic, much like Pavlov's dogs. I'm not sure if it was too boring or what, but she fell asleep as soon as I started. I would put her on my shoulder, and she would just melt in my arms."

Warren never changed his system after he discovered it was reliable. While singing, he could easily be lost in his thoughts. So it was "Over the Rainbow" night after night.

Susie, who was housekeeping, raising a baby, and caring for Warren in a sterile suburb of New York, could have welcomed anyone who came to the door. One day in late 1954, a Parents magazine salesman stopped by the apartment. Whatever the salesman told Susie, when

Warren got home, he realized that the paperwork she signed committed them to less favorable terms than she had anticipated. He was outraged that his wife had been misled. He called several times and spoke with magazine representatives, but they reportedly said "nothing doing" when he asked for his money back.

Warren organized a crusade. He wanted more than just his $17 back; he wanted to right a wrong, to bring the despicable Parents magazine to its knees. He went around the apartment building and found several others who were willing to join the cause. He filed a small-claims lawsuit against the magazine in Manhattan and planned to testify on behalf of all allegedly defrauded Parents magazine subscribers. He clicked his heels with delight at the prospect of the magazine's lawyers running their meters. There was a hint of his father in this episode, but with a financial bent and better chances of winning, so his mother would have approved.

To his chagrin, he received a check in the mail before the trial. Parents magazine had settled. The crusade was foiled.

Warren had returned home from work on December 15, 1954, as Susie's labor was about to begin, when he heard a knock at the door. Susie answered it and discovered a door-to-door missionary who had come to visit. She politely invited him to the salon. And she listened. Warren thought to himself that only Susie would have let the man in. Warren began to encourage the conversation to conclude. He had been an agnostic for several years and had no desire to be converted, and his wife was in labor. They had to go to the hospital.

Susie kept listening. "Tell me more," she asked. She pulsed and moaned occasionally as the missionary spoke. She ignored Warren's signals, clearly believing it was more important to be polite to the visitor and make him feel understood than to get to the hospital. The caller seemed unaware she was at work. Warren sat there, helpless and agitated, until the preacher ran out of steam. "I wanted to kill the guy," he says. They reached the hospital on time, and Howard Graham Buffett arrived early the next morning.

THE LOCOMOTIVE

New York City and Omaha, 1958–1962

Warren and Susie seemed ordinary people. They maintained a low profile. Their house was large, but not ostentatious. It had a log cabin in the backyard for the children. The back door was never locked, allowing neighborhood children to wander in and out. Inside the house, the Buffett's clickety-clack on their various tracks with increasing speed. As Susie added stop after stop to her local itinerary, Warren set out on a nonstop journey to Dollar Mountain.

Until 1958, his straightforward approach was to purchase a stock and wait for the cigar butt to light. Then he usually sold the stock, sometimes with regret, to buy another he wanted more, his ambitions being limited by the capital of his partnerships.

Now, he was managing more than $1 million in seven partnerships, and Buffett & Buffett and his personal funds, allowing him to operate on a different scale. His network of business associates, including Stanback, Knapp, Brandt, Cowin, Schloss, and Ruane, had expanded with the addition of Munger; the two of them ran up outrageous—by their standards—phone bills every month. Munger had introduced him to his friend Roy Tolles, a lanky former Marine fighter pilot who wore a constant placid smile and kept his thoughts to himself—except for the occasional barbed zinger he threw out, which made people "want to keep a few Band-Aids around," as one friend put it. Buffett, like Munger, could parry and riposte like a pro, and he added Tolles to his collection. This ability to recruit volunteers for his cause had resulted in a large, albeit loosely organized, support structure. Warren more or less automatically Tom-Sawyered these supporters, who were divided into several cells, into assisting his interests, which had grown so quickly that he could no longer carry out every detail on his own.

Warren's days of simply sitting in his home study and picking stocks from Security Analysis or Moody's Manuals were over. He began to work on larger, more lucrative projects that required time and planning to complete—even more so than purchasing National American insurance shares. These projects would sometimes turn into complicated, even dramatic episodes that would occupy his attention for months, or even years at a time. Several of these investment projects were occasionally active at the same time. He was already preoccupied to the point where he was rarely present to his family, and this increase in scale would exacerbate that tendency while binding him more tightly to his friends.

The first of these complicated episodes involved a company called Sanborn Maps. It published minutely detailed maps of power lines, water mains, driveways, building engineering, roof composition, and emergency stairwells for all cities in the United States, which were primarily purchased by insurance companies. The company was no winner, with its customer base gradually shrinking as insurers merged. However, its stock was cheap at $45 per share, considering Sanborn's investment portfolio alone was worth $65 per share. To acquire that investment portfolio, Warren required not only money from his partnerships, but also assistance from others.

From November 1958, he invested more than a third of the partnership's assets in Sanborn. He purchased the stock for himself and Susie. He had his aunt Alice, father, mother, and sisters buy it. He passed the Sanborn idea on to Cowin, Stanback, Knapp, and Schloss. Some people got in on it as a favor for him. He leveraged his capital by taking an override (a percentage of profits) from others. To increase his shareholding, he added Don Danly, his high school pinball and pilferage buddy; his father's best friend, Vic Spittler; Dottie's husband, Homer Rogers; and Howard Browne, the head of Tweedy, Browne, and Reilly, the brokerage firm where Tom Knapp worked. He also included Catherine Elberfeld and Anne Gottschaldt, the aunt and mother of his friend Fred Kuhlken, in the stock. Since he had not yet brought Gottschaldt and Elberfeld into a partnership, this strongly implied that he thought Sanborn was a sure thing. He eventually gained enough control over Sanborn's shares to be elected to the board. Warren made one of his regular trips to New York in March 1959, staying on Long Island at Anne Gottschaldt's small white colonial house. By now, she and her sister had adopted him as a surrogate son to replace the long-deceased Fred. Warren kept spare sets of underwear and pajamas at her house, and Gottschaldt served him hamburgers for breakfast. On those trips, he always left with a list of ten to thirty goals. He would visit the Standard & Poor's library to find information. He would visit companies and brokers, but he would always spend time with his New York City network, which included Brandt, Cowin, Schloss, Knapp, and Ruane.

This particular trip lasted approximately ten days. He met potential partners and attended his first board meeting at Sanborn Map.

Sanborn's board was almost entirely made up of representatives from insurance companies, its largest customers, so it operated more like a club than a business, except that the board meeting was not followed by a round of golf. None of the board members held more than a token amount of stock.3 At the meeting, Warren proposed that the company distribute the investments to its shareholders. However, since the Great Depression and World War II, American businesses have treated money as a scarce commodity that must be hoarded and managed carefully. This way of thinking had become automatic, its underlying premise unquestioned, although the economic justification for it had long since vanished. The board dismissed the idea of separating the investment portfolio from the map business as absurd. The board then pulled out the humidor near the end of the meeting and passed out cigars. While they smoked, Warren sat fuming. "That's my money, paying for those cigars," he reasoned. On the way back to the airport, he took photos of his children from his wallet and looked at them to lower his blood pressure.

Frustrated, Warren resolved to take the company away from Sanborn's undeserving board on behalf of the other shareholders. They deserved more. As a result, Buffett's group of investors, including Fred Stanback, Walter Schloss, Alice Buffett, Dan Cowin, Henry Brandt, Catherine Elberfeld, Anne Gottschaldt, and others, kept buying. Warren also used new money coming into partnerships. He had Howard transfer a number of his brokerage clients to Sanborn. Warren was probably doing his father a financial favor while tightening his grip on the company.

Before long, Warren supporters, including famous money manager Phil Carret, who had purchased Greif Bros. and Cleveland's Worst Mill after hearing about them through Warren, had amassed approximately 24,000 shares. When they had effective control, Warren decided it was time to act. The stock market was high, and he wanted Sanborn to sell its investments at the right time. Booz Allen Hamilton, the company's strategic consultants, had already submitted a plan to accomplish this,4 but taxes were the sticking point. If Sanborn sold the investments, it would face a tax bill of approximately $2 million. Warren proposed a solution similar to Rockwood & Co.'s tax strategy of exchanging tax-free investments for stock.

Another board meeting was held, but nothing happened except that more of the investors' money went up in cigar smoke. Buffett rode back to the airport again, this time looking at pictures of his children to calm himself down. Three days later, he threatened to hold a special meeting and seize control of the company unless the directors acted by October 31.5 His patience had run out.

Now the board had no choice. It agreed to separate the two businesses. Nonetheless, the question of how to handle the tax persisted. One insurance representative suggested, "Let's just swallow the tax."And I said, "Wait a minute." Let's—"Let's" is a contraction. It means, "Let us." Who are we? If everyone at the table wants to do it per capita, that's fine; but if you want to do it in terms of shares owned, and you get ten shares' worth of tax while I get twenty-four thousand, forget it. He was talking about paying two million dollars in taxes just to avoid having to do the share buyback.6 I remember the cigars being passed around. I was paying 30% of each of those cigars. I was the only guy not smoking a cigar. "They should have paid for one-third of my bubble gum."

In the end, however, the board caved. Thus, in early 1960, Warren won the fight through sheer willpower, organization, and energy. Sanborn made a Rockwood-style offer to shareholders, converting a portion of the investment portfolio into stock.

The Sanborn transaction set a new high-water mark: Buffett could use his brains and his partners' money to change the course of even the most stubborn and unwilling company.

During this episode, Buffett traveled back and forth to New York to work on the Sanborn project, figuring out where to get the stock he needed for control, how to get the board to agree, and how not to swallow the tax, all while looking for other investment ideas, his mind whirled with the thousands of numbers that clicked and spun inside his head. At home, he would go upstairs to read and think.

Susie saw his work as a sort of holy mission. Nonetheless, she attempted to bring him out of his study and into the family's world through planned outings, vacations, and dinners in restaurants. She used to say, "Anyone can be a father, but you have to be a daddy too." However, she was speaking to someone who had never had the type of father to whom she was referring. "Let's go to Broncos," she'd say, packing a group of neighborhood kids into the car for a burger run. Warren would laugh and appear interested at the table, but he rarely spoke. His mind could've been anywhere. On a vacation in California, he took a group of kids to Disneyland one night and sat on a bench reading while the kids ran around and had a great time.

Peter was almost two years old, Howie was five, and Little Sooz, who lived in her own pink checked-gingham kingdom with a canopy bed up a separate flight of stairs, was six and a half. Howie used destruction to see how much it would take to elicit a response from his parents. He targeted Peter, who was slow to begin speaking, prodding him as if he were a science experiment to see how he would react. Little Susie kept them both under control. She began devising ways to retaliate against Howie, including instructing him to poke holes in the bottom of a milk carton with a fork. While Howie was enjoying the sight of milk spurting all over the kitchen table, she dashed upstairs, crying, "Mommmmmm, Howie's being bad again!" Warren simply turned to Susie to deal with his son's explosive energy. Howie recalls that his mother "never got angry, and was always supportive."

Susie juggled all of this while portraying the standard upper-middle-class wife circa 1960: appearing every day in her signature look, a tailored dress or pantsuit, often in sunshine yellow, and a lacquered bouffant wig; taking perfect care of her husband and family; becoming a community leader; and gracefully entertaining her husband's business associates as if this required no more effort than tossing a Swanson TV Dinner into the oven. Warren allowed her to hire help, and soon a group of au pairs moved into an airy, light-filled room on the second floor with its own bath. Letha Clark, the new housekeeper, took on some of the burden. Susie usually began her day around noon by hosting a charity luncheon. After school, she took Little Susie to Blue Birds. She always described herself as simple, but she gradually added layers of complexity to her life. She was organizing a group called the Volunteer Bureau14 to do office work and teach swimming at the University of Omaha. "You, too, can be a Paul Revere" was its motto, evoking the image of a single person saving an entire nation through daring and self-sacrificing actions.

Susie, like Paul Revere, was impatient to mount and ride;15 she juggled family obligations and an increasing number of people vying for her attention. Many were marginalized or traumatized in some way.

Bella Eisenberg, her closest friend, was an Auschwitz survivor who had traveled to America and Omaha after the camp was liberated. She imagined Susie as someone you could call at four a.m. when the demons had taken hold of you.16 Eunice Denenberg was only a child when she discovered her father's suicide. The Buffetts, unlike most well-off white families, had black friends, including Bob Gibson, baseball's most intimidating pitcher, and his wife, Charlene. Being a star athlete meant little in 1960, especially if you were black. "Those were the days when white people wouldn't be seen with black people in Omaha," Buffett's childhood friend Byron Swanson recalls.

Susie reached out to everyone; in fact, the more troubled the person, the more eagerly she assisted. She developed a keen interest in the personal lives of people she barely knew. Warren recalls leaving her in line at a concession stand during a football game. When he returned from the men's room, the woman standing next to Susie said, "Now, I've never told anybody this before in my life..." Susie listened, fascinated. Almost everyone she met glowed under this kind of attention and was moved by the experience. Even with her closest friends, Susie almost always avoided discussing her own problems.

She played the same role of ministering angel to her own family, particularly her sister. Dottie, who was musical like Susie, founded the Opera Guild and remained the family's beauty, but she appeared vacant and, as one person put it, "valiantly unhappy." She maintained a pleasant demeanor while telling Susie that she never cried because if she did, she would never stop. Her husband, Homer, appeared frustrated because he was unable to penetrate his wife's cocoon. Nonetheless, the Rogerses maintained their active social life, and at night, amid the drinks and merriment, their two young sons roamed underfoot. Homer sometimes punished them harshly, and Dottie teased Billy cruelly, so Susie raised her nephews alongside her own children.

She also assisted the senior Buffets, who were dealing with both Howard's health issues and his ideology. Just as the rest of America had caught up to his level of paranoia about Communism, Howard jumped ahead. By the late Eisenhower years, Americans believed their country, which had grown soft and fat from prosperity, was losing the arms race, and they were haunted by the terrifying image of Premier Nikita Khrushchev banging his shoe on a table at the United Nations and thundering, "We will bury you." All 180 million Americans ducked and covered during air-raid drills, with the youngest crouched under their elementary school desks. Over a billion people lived under communism in nearly twenty countries around the world. Communism's rapid spread took aback much of the country across so much of the globe. Howard joined the John Birch Society, a newly formed group that combined fear of Communism with concern for the "moral and spiritual problem of America, which would be with us even if Communism were stopped tomorrow." He covered the walls of his office with maps depicting Communism's menacing red advance. He and Doris were instrumental in bringing the Christian Anti-Communist Crusade to Omaha, and they supported an ideological conservative movement centered on Arizona Senator Barry Goldwater. Howard was regarded as a philosophical purist by the libertarian wing of the Republican Party, but anyone associated with the Birchers sparked alarm and ridicule. After he went to the local press to defend his Birch membership, people began to dismiss him as eccentric. Warren found it upsetting that Omaha mocked his revered father.

His concern for Howard, however, stemmed from eighteen months of mysterious symptoms that doctors were unable to diagnose despite a trip to the Mayo Clinic in Rochester, Minnesota. Finally, in May 1958, Howard was told he had colon cancer and needed immediate surgery.21 Warren was upset by the diagnosis, but even more so by the inexcusable delay. Susie had kept him in the dark about his father's illness ever since.22 She gave him head rubs and maintained the household schedule. She also devoted herself to supporting Leila during Howard's surgery and prolonged recovery. She did all of this cheerfully, and she appeared to thrive as the calm, soothing presence on which everyone could rely in this crisis. She helped her older children understand the illness and ensured that everyone, including little Peter, paid regular visits to their grandfather. Howie spent his afternoons watching college football with Howard, who would sit in his recliner and switch sides during games, cheering for the losing team. When Howie asked why, he replied, "They're the underdogs now."

Throughout his father's ordeal, Warren used business to distract him. He kept his head buried in American Banker or the Oil & Gas Journal, except for brief interludes when he wandered into the kitchen for some popcorn or a Pepsi from the wooden crates that only he was permitted to touch.

Despite Howard's distress and illness, the quiet, withdrawn man who his family saw as Warren Buffett became a presence in public, regardless of what was happening at home. He exuded authority, an almost electric charge of energy, which radiated to the audience. "He just used to ooze that stuff wherever he went," Chuck Peterson says. The man who had so impressed Charlie Munger spoke constantly and convincingly about investing and partnerships. He raised funds as quickly as he could talk—but not as quickly as he could invest.

Munger listened to Buffett's investing and fundraising exploits on their almost daily phone calls, marveling at the natural salesmanship that allowed Buffett to promote himself so effectively. His trips to New York became more frequent as Henry Brandt prospected for him. Cash poured into the partnership's coffers, and 1960 was a watershed year. Warren's aunt Katie and uncle Fred invested nearly $8,000 in Buffett Associates earlier in the year. Chuck Peterson's connections helped bring in another $51,000 for Underwood. "Then Chuck told me, 'I'd like you and Susie to come to dinner and meet the Angles.'" Well, I didn't recognize them. He said they're both doctors and very smart people."

Carol and Bill Angle lived across the street from Peterson. Bill Angle, a cardiologist, was a whimsical man who would stay up all night in the winter, spraying water around his front yard and creating perfectly glazed snowmen, frosty replicas of his chubby self, standing next to frozen "ponds." His wife specialized in pediatric research.

"We picked them up, and there were six of us in the car. We headed to the Omaha Country Club. Carol Angle was a beautiful and intelligent woman. She kept her gaze fixed on me throughout dinner. I mean, she was simply fascinated. I was going crazy, talking about everything and desperately trying to impress her. And she was simply taking in every word."

Following the presentation, which Peterson describes as typically persuasive, "we left the country club and drove back." She could not take her gaze away from me the entire time we were driving. We dropped the Angels off. And I told Chuck, 'I made quite an impression tonight.' He replied, 'No, dummy. She is deaf. She is reading your lips. Because I couldn't stop talking, she couldn't stop looking at me."

But he had clearly made an impression, because the Angles later hosted a dinner at the Hilltop House for a dozen doctors they knew, at which Bill Angle proposed that they form a partnership and each contribute $10,000. One doctor asked, "What happens if we lose all of our money?"Bill Angle gave him a disgusting look. And he said, "Okay, then we form another partnership."

The Emdee partnership, Buffett's eighth, began August 15, 1960, with $110,000. The twelfth doctor, who was concerned about losing all his money, did not participate.

There were other skeptics. Not everyone in Omaha liked what they learned about Warren Buffett. His secrecy turned people off. Some thought the young hotshot would never amount to anything, and that the authority he exuded was unearned arrogance. Some opposed the notion of a nobody succeeding without kowtowing his way to the top. Buffett's name came up while one member of a prominent Omaha family was having lunch with a half-dozen others at the Blackstone Hotel. "He'll be broke in a year," the man stated. "Just give him a year and he's gone." A partner at Kirkpatrick Pettis, which Howard's firm merged with in 1957, repeatedly stated, "The jury's still out on him." That fall, the already frothy stock market went on a tear. The economy had been mired in a mild recession, and the country's mood was bleak because the Soviets appeared to be winning the arms and space races. But when John F. Kennedy won the presidency in a nail-biting race. The prospect of a new administration led by a man from a vibrant young generation raised the nation. In one of his early speeches, Kennedy set a goal of sending a man to the moon and back. The market soared, prompting comparisons to 1929. Warren had never been through a speculative market, but he remained calm. It was as if he had been anticipating this moment. Instead of retreating, as Graham might have done, he accomplished something remarkable. He went into overdrive raising funds for the partnerships.

He formed Buffett Associates, the original partnership, with Bertie and her husband, his uncle George from Albuquerque, and his cousin Bill. Wayne Eves, his friend John Cleary's partner, also got on board. And he finally included Fred Kulhken's mother and aunt, Anne Gottschaldt and Catherine Elberfeld, in the partnership. Their presence indicated that he believed the timing was not only advantageous but also safe.

Three more people entered Underwood. Warren met Frank Matthews Jr., son of the former Secretary of the Navy to whom Vanita Mae Brown had previously claimed to be married, while waiting for a cab in the rain after attending one of Ben Graham's lectures in New York. Matthews became a partner. Warren formed Ann Investments, his ninth partnership, for Elizabeth Storz, a member of another well-known Omaha family. He placed Mattie Topp, the owner of the fanciest dress shop in town, in the tenth, Buffett-TD, with her two daughters and sons-in-law and $250,000.

Legally, he could only take on 100 partners without having to register with the SEC as an investment adviser. As the partnerships grew, he began encouraging people to form informal groups and come in as individual partners. Eventually, he would put people in pools and combine their money. He later described the tactic as questionable— but effective. His desire to acquire more money, to earn more money, drove him forward. Warren was on fire, racing back and forth to New York at breakneck speed. He began to experience stress-related back pain. It often worsened when he was on an airplane, and he tried everything to alleviate it—except staying at home.

His name had become a secret by this point. Invest with Warren Buffett to become wealthy. However, the routine had changed. By 1960, admission cost at least $8,000. And he stopped asking people to invest with him. They needed to bring it up. It had to be their idea. People would not only have no idea what he was doing, but they would have to put themselves in this situation. It turned them into Buffett supporters and reduced the likelihood of them complaining about anything he did. Instead of requesting a favor, he was granting one. People felt obligated to him for accepting their money. Making people ask gave him psychological control. He would continue to use this technique in various contexts for the rest of his life. Along with getting him what he wanted, it seemed to allay his persistent fears about being responsible for other people's lives.

Though his insecurity remained as strong as ever, his success, combined with Susie's care and tutoring, had given him a bit of polish and flair. He was beginning to appear powerful, not vulnerable. Many people were eager to ask him to invest in them. Buffett formed his eleventh and final partnership, Buffett-Holland, on May 16, 1961, for Dick and Mary Holland, whom he met through his lawyer and partner Dan Monen. When Dick Holland decided to invest in the partnership, his family members urged him not to. Buffett's abilities were obvious to him, Holland claims, even though people in Omaha were still "laughing up their sleeves" about Warren's ambitions.30 However, in 1959, the partnerships outperformed the market by 6%. In 1960, they jumped to nearly $1.9 million in assets, outperforming the market by 29%. Even more impressive than any single year's profits was the compounding power of consistent growth. A $1,000 investment in the Buffett Fund, the second partnership, was worth $2,407 four years later. If invested in the Dow Jones Industrial Average, it would have only been worth $1,426.31 More importantly, he achieved this higher return by taking less risk than the market as a whole.

By the end of 1960, Buffett had earned $243,494 from his fees, which had been reinvested. Over thirteen percent of the partnership's assets now belonged to him alone. Even as his share of the partnerships grew, he had made the partners so wealthy that they were no longer simply pleased; many looked up to him with admiration.

Bill Angle, his Emdee partner, was foremost among them. He Tom-Sawyered himself into becoming Warren's "partner" in building a massive model train set with a HO gauge track on the third floor of the Buffetts' house, which had previously been a ballroom but was now the family attic. Warranty, the boy who had lingered at the Brandeis store every Christmas, yearning for the enormous, magical model train that he couldn't have, awoke within the grown man. He "supervised" as Angle completed all the work to create Warren's childhood fantasy. Warren also urged Tom-Sawyer Chuck Peterson to invest. "Warren, you must be out of your mind," Peterson said. "Why would I want to go fifty-fifty with you on a train that you possess?" But Warren didn't get it because he was so excited about the train and its accoutrements. "You can come over and use it," he said.

The train occupied most of the former ballroom's space. It was built on pilings and had passageways underneath to allow visitors to view the diorama from the inside. Three locomotives carrying long chains of cars raced down a massive spiraling track. They sped past villages and dove through forests, vanished into tunnels, climbed mountains and dipped through valleys, stopping and staring at signals and derailing just enough to add excitement when Buffett turned on the engines.

The train was Warren's totem, gleaming with the reflected glow of a delayed childhood and adorned with the patina of Omaha's railroad history. His children were not allowed to go near it. His relentless obsession with money and disregard for his family had become a running joke among his friends. "Warren, those are your children—you recognize them, don't you?" individuals responded. When he wasn't traveling, he could be found wandering around the house, nose deep in an annual report. The family gathered around him and his holy pursuit—the disengaged, silent figure, feet up in his stringy bathrobe, eyes fixed on the Wall Street Journal at breakfast.

The bookkeeping, banking, safety depositing, and post-officing requirements for his complex empire, which had grown to nearly four million dollars, eleven partnerships, and well over a hundred investors, had become almost overwhelming. Surprisingly, Warren was still handling all the money and doing all the clerical work himself: filing tax returns, typing letters, depositing dividend and capital checks, stopping for a meal at the Spare Time Café along the way, and stuffing stock certificates into the safety deposit box.

On January 1, 1962, Buffett merged all of the partnerships into a single entity, Buffett Partnership, Ltd.—or BPL. In 1961, the partnerships returned a whopping 46 percent, while the Dow returned only 22 percent. After the partners invested more money on January 1, the new Buffett Partnership, Ltd. began the year with net assets of $7.2 million. In just six years, his partnerships had outgrown Graham-Newman. However, when Peat, Marwick, Mitchell audited it, the auditor, Verne McKenzie, examined the BPL files not in a conference room on Wall Street, but in an alcove off Warren's bedroom upstairs, where the two worked side by side.

Even Buffett realized that his growing collection of files, phone bills, and stock trades had outpaced his ability to work from home. He disliked having overhead, but he could afford it.

Warren had become a millionaire at the age of thirty, with his outside investments totaling well over half a million dollars. So he rented office space in Kiewit Plaza, a new white granite building just down Farnam Street, about twenty blocks from his house and less than two miles from downtown. Warren's long-held ambition of sharing space with his father was now realized, as was the addition of a secretary. But Howard was clearly ill. He walked stiffly into the office, making an effort. Warren's face would darken when he heard some new ominous news about his father's health, but he mostly avoided knowing the specifics.

The new secretary tried telling Warren what to do. "She thought she was a little motherly," he said, "in the sense of trying to steer me."

Nobody steered Warren Buffett. He fired her on the spot.

But he needed help. Just before moving into Kiewit Plaza, he hired Bill Scott, a trust officer at U.S. National Bank who had read Warren's article in the Commercial & Financial Chronicle about an obscure insurance company. Scott enrolled in Buffett's investing course and then, he admits, "I set out to suck up to him until I got a job." Buffett began visiting the Scotts' home on Sunday mornings after dropping his children off at church to discuss stocks, eventually offering him a job. Scott began to assist Buffett as he moved money into the partnership as quickly as the two of them could open the mail. Buffett invited his mother to join for the first time, as well as Scott, Don Danly, and Marge Loring, the widow of Warren's bridge partner Russ Loring, and even Fred Stanback, who had a family business and had previously only worked with Warren on specific ideas. And for the first time, Warren invested his own money—nearly $450,000—in the partnership. After six years of work, his and Susie's share of the partnership increased to more than a million dollars; together, they owned 14% of BPL.

The timing was superb. In mid-March 1962, the market finally crashed. It continued to decline until the end of June. Stocks became cheaper than they had been in years. Buffett was now sitting on a single partnership with a large amount of cash to invest. Its portfolio fared relatively well during the downturn—"Compared to more conventional (often termed conservative, which is not synonymous) methods of common stock investing, it would appear that our method involved considerably less risk," he wrote in a letter to his partners. He raced through the stock tables. He frequently paraphrased Graham, saying, "Be afraid when others are greedy, and greedy when others are fearful." Now was the time to be greedy.

EASY, SAFE, PROFITABLE, AND PLEASANT

Omaha, 1968–1969

Buffett had issued a call to his fellow Grahamites in January 1968, summoning them for the first time as a meeting of the faithful in the midst of a raging stock market. "[T]here has been a tremendous change in attitude in the last few years, and I think the gang that is assembling in La Jolla is about all that is left of the old guard,"1 he wrote, inviting Graham's former students Bill Ruane, Walter Schloss, Marshall Weinberg, Jack Alexander, and Tom Knapp. He also invited Charlie Munger, whom he had introduced to Graham, Munger's partner, Roy Tolles, and Jack Alexander's partner, Buddy Fox. Ed Anderson, who had left Munger's partnership to join Tweedy, Browne, was also on the guest list, as was Sandy Gottesman, whom Buffett described as "a good friend of mine and a great admirer of you." At last, he commented, "I think you probably remember Henry [Brandt], who works very closely with us."

Fred Stanback, Buffett's business partner and best man at his wedding, was unable to attend. A few years after graduating from Columbia, Warren and Miss Nebraska 1949, Vanita Mae Brown, met for dinner in New York. They made it a double date by bringing Susie and Fred, who had previously met Vanita through Warren. She was then known as Vanita Mae Brown Nederlander, and she had a brief marriage to a member of the Nederlander family, which owned theaters and was part of an American entertainment dynasty. After the dinner, Fred, Warren's most introverted friend, became, as one friend put it, "putty in her hands," as if to demonstrate the old adage that opposites attract. Initially, their marriage probably appeared to be a charming end to Warren's career at Columbia: a couple brought into the Buffetts' circle from that era. He did have a tendency to organize his friends' lives, asking them to partner with him, putting them on his companies' boards, and generally incorporating them into his life through various ties. Two friends getting married may have seemed like a compliment to Fred, but it turned out to be the worst decision he ever made.

He and Vanita had been living in Salisbury, North Carolina, where Fred grew up and his family founded the "Snap Back with Stanback" headache-powder company. Fred needed boxcar loads of headache powder to get out of this pulse-pounding marriage. Vanita had completely established herself in tiny Salisbury and remained there to torment him with all of her considerable creativity while they fought in court. Thus, unlike the rest of the Grahamites, Fred's focus on the stock market had been temporarily diverted. It came at a time when the market was becoming increasingly unappealing: hundreds of millions of dollars had been poured into it by people who had no more than a few years of proven ability to profit. More than fifty new investment funds had entered the market, with nearly sixty-five more in the pipeline.3 For the first time in American history, it became fashionable for a diverse group of people to own stocks.4 Buffett described this phase as "an ever-widening circle of chain letters," even a "mania," populated primarily by "the hopeful, credulous, and greedy, grasping for an excuse to believe."

Trading volume had reached such a high point in a business that was still conducted using paper trade tickets and physical delivery of stock certificates that the market was nearly crushed by the weight of paperwork. Large numbers of orders were duplicated or never executed, tickets were misplaced or simply thrown away, and file rooms' worth of stock certificates vanished, presumed stolen, amid rumors that the Mafia had infiltrated the market. In a desperate attempt to catch up, a slew of reforms were enacted in 1967 and 1968, automating and computerizing trading systems. One of the most important would be to close the old "under-the-counter" market. The National Association of Securities Dealers announced that it was about to launch a new system called NASDAQ, which would quote prices for smaller stocks.6 Instead of appearing on stale Pink Sheets the moment they were printed, the prices of most non-stock exchange companies would now be posted and updated electronically as they changed. Market makers had to show their hands and back up the quotes they posted. Any trader with extensive knowledge, negotiating skills, and a strong backbone would dislike the new system. Amidst an already difficult market, it would make Buffett's job harder.

Warren issued instructions to each of the Grahamites who arrived in La Jolla. "Please do not bring anything more current than a 1934 edition of Security Analysis along with you," he wrote to me. Regardless of their age, wives would stay home.

In his letter, Buffett reminded them that they were there to listen to Graham, the Great Man, not each other. Several members of the group, including Munger, Anderson, and Ruane, were known for their talkativeness. When it came to investing, no one was more prone to this tendency than Buffett. At thirty-seven, he had finally attained peerage and was able to address his former teacher as "Ben," but he still occasionally slipped and said "Mr. Graham." So he was probably reminding himself not to try to take over as the best student in the class.

As instructed, the dozen Graham worshippers gathered at the Hotel del Coronado, located across the bay from San Diego. Warren had preferred to meet at a much lower-cost location, such as a Holiday Inn; he made it clear to the group that the extravagant pink-and-white Victorian confection of a resort was Graham's idea.

When the dozen arrived in San Diego, a massive storm had hit, bringing lashing rain and churning seas. But no one cared because they were there to talk about stocks. Buffett was ecstatic to have orchestrated a tribute to his teacher and an opportunity to demonstrate Ben Graham's wisdom to his new friends. Graham arrived at the

Coronado late. Even the teacher, once he arrived, administered an exam.

Graham was almost unbearable to listen to under any circumstances. Every sentence was complex and filled with classical allusions. The exam he gave them was very similar. "They weren't terribly complicated questions, though some were about French history or something. But you thought you knew some of the answers," Buffett explains.

They did not. Only Roy Tolles received over half. He scored eleven out of twenty by answering everything "true" except for a couple of questions he was certain were false. The "little exam" turned out to be one of Graham's teaching tricks, intended to demonstrate how even a seemingly simple game can be rigged. Buffett would later say that knowing a smart guy is stacking the deck does not guarantee protection.

Graham was amused by the discussions of stock promotion, manufactured performance, phony accounting, institutional speculation, and the "chain-letter acquisition syndrome" that took place throughout the meeting. However, he was no longer interested; instead, he wanted to tell riddles and participate enthusiastically in brainteasers, word and number games.

Buffett, on the other hand, remained as engaged as ever, despite the tone of his letter to his partners in October 1967, in which he stated that he would now limit himself to activities that were "easy, safe, profitable, and pleasant." When he returned to Omaha from San Diego, he focused intensely on the partnership's problems. He needed to inform the partners that things were not going well at some of the businesses they owned, and his next two letters dropped subtle hints. After eloquently describing the travails of textiles in 1967, he made no further mention of the business in 1968, although the prospects and results of the Berkshire mills remained unchanged. DRC's earnings were falling due to Hochschild-Kohn. However, Buffett did not take the logical next step of selling Berkshire Hathaway and Hochschild-Kohn.

Here, his commercial instincts clashed with some of his other characteristics: the desire to collect, the need to be liked, and the preoccupation with avoiding confrontation following the Dempster windmill war. In an intricate minuet of rationalization, he explained his thinking in his January 1968 letter to the partners: "When I am dealing with people I like in businesses I find stimulating (what business isn't?), and achieving worthwhile overall returns on capital employed (say, ten to twelve percent), it appears foolish to rush from situation to situation to earn a few more percentage points. It also does not appear prudent to me to trade known pleasant personal relationships with high-quality people at a reasonable rate of return for possible irritation, aggravation, or worse at potentially higher returns." Some of the growing crowd of Buffett watchers may have been surprised to read these words. Measuring by "overall" returns allowed some businesses to perform significantly worse than average. It was astonishing to see Buffett, who squeezed the last tenth of a percentage point from a buck like a miser gripping a toothpaste tube, dismissively waving away "a few more percentage points".

However, his performance silenced critics because, even as he lowered expectations, he continued to outperform himself. Despite the deadweights, the partnership had averaged more than a 31% return over its twelve-year history, while the Dow had produced 9%. Buffett's insistence on a margin of safety had significantly skewed the odds in his favor. Along with his investing ability, the cumulative impact on his batting average meant that $1,000 invested in the Dow was now worth $2,857, whereas he had made nearly ten times that, $27,106. Buffett's partners had come to rely on him to consistently deliver more than he promised. He demonstrated predictability and certainty in 1968, a turbulent year in which students took over and closed Columbia University, flower-child protests turned militant, and activists nominated a pig for President.

But by mid-1968, Buffett had decided to try to get rid of the intractable Berkshire Hathaway—a business that was neither easy, safe, profitable, nor enjoyable—and its unfortunate textile workers. He offered to sell the business to Munger and Gottesman. They traveled to Omaha to visit and talk. After three days of deliberation, however, neither man wanted to buy something Buffett believed he would be better off without. He was stuck with Berkshire Hathaway.

Buffett was forced to act because the Apparel and Box Loom divisions were not self-sustaining and would require a large sum of money to keep them operating. Deploying capital with no expectation of a return was a cardinal sin for him. He instructed Ken Chace what to do. Chace was irritated, but in typical stoic fashion, he followed orders and shut down the two divisions. Still, Buffett couldn't bring himself to bury the entire thing with a spike.

As a result, he was left with a partnership that owned two businesses, one thriving (National Indemnity) and one failing (Berkshire Hathaway), as well as eighty percent of DRC, the retail holding company, and, of course, stock in a variety of other companies. As 1968 came to a close, stocks on the market's periphery began to fall, and investors focused on the biggest, safest names. Indeed, Buffett began buying the blandest, most popular stocks that were still reasonably priced: $18 million in AT&T, $9.6 million in BF Goodrich, $8.4 million in AMK Corp. (later United Brands), and $8.7 million in Jones & Laughlin Steel. Above all, he continued to accumulate more Berkshire Hathaway stock, despite his prohibition on purchasing any more bad businesses and the textile industry's demise. He had only recently attempted to sell it to Munger and Gottesman, but now that he was unable to do so, he appeared to want as much of the stock as possible.

He and Munger had also discovered another promising company and were investing heavily in it. This was Blue Chip Stamps, a trading stamp company. They would buy it separately and together, and Blue Chip would eventually dramatically alter the course of both men's careers.

The trading stamp was given as a marketing incentive. Retailers gave their customers stamps with their change. Customers put them in a drawer and pasted them into small booklets. When enough booklets were redeemed, they could choose between a toaster oven, a fishing rod, and a tetherball set. The small thrill of saving stamps fit neatly into a disappearing world: a world of thrift, a world that feared debt, a world that saw these "free gifts" as the reward for going to the trouble of collecting and saving stamps, and a world where nothing was wasted.

But the stamps were not actually free. The stores paid for them and then marked up the merchandise accordingly. Sperry & Hutchinson was the national leader in trading stamps, except in California. A group of chains had shut out the S&H Green Stamp by creating their own trading stamp, Blue Chip, and selling it to themselves at a discounted rate. Blue Chip held a classic monopoly.

"When all of the major oil companies and grocers distributed a single stamp, it became like money. People would leave their change and

collect the stamps. Morticians handed out stamps. Prostitutes gave them. I always thought it would be hilarious if the madam called in one of the girls and said, 'From now on, I think you better double-stamp, honey.' It was ubiquitous. Everyone had them. People even created counterfeits."

In 1963, the Department of Justice sued Blue Chip for trade restraint and monopolization of the California trading stamp business. S&H also sued it. With the stock in a slump, Rick Guerin, who had formed his own partnership, Pacific Partners, noticed Blue Chip and brought it to Munger. Buffett had noticed it, too. "Blue Chip did not have an immaculate conception," Charlie Munger admits, but they all decided to take a calculated risk that Blue Chip could work its way out of its problems—the S&H lawsuit being the most serious.

They wanted it because Blue Chip offered something called "float." The stamps were paid in advance, while the prizes were redeemed later. Meanwhile, Blue Chip had access to the funds, which could last years. Buffett had first encountered this intriguing concept with GEICO, which was one of the reasons he wanted to own National Indemnity. Insurers, too, were paid premiums before the claims arrived. That meant they could invest in the steadily increasing stream of "float." Such a business appealed to Buffett, who was supremely confident in his investing abilities.

All types of businesses had floats. Deposits in banks were also floating. Customers often thought banks were doing them a favor by keeping their money safe. However, the bank invested the deposits in loans with the highest interest rates it could offer. They turned a profit. That was "float."

Buffett, Munger, and Guerin understood how to reverse any financial situation. If someone offered them trading stamps, they flipped the situation and thought, "Hmm, it's probably better to own the trading-stamp company," before figuring out why. They would not save time trading stamps for a hibachi or a croquet set any more than they would wear their great-aunt Betsy's petticoats to work. Even Buffett, a boyhood stamp collector who occasionally fantasized about counting stamps and kept a sentimental stash of Blue Eagle stamps in his basement, would rather own Blue Chip stock than collect Blue Chip stamps.

In 1968, Blue Chip began settling lawsuits brought against it by competitors.18 It entered into a "consent decree" with the Justice

Department, which required the grocery chains that owned it to sell 45 percent of the company to the retailers who distributed the stamps.19 To remove even more control from the grocers who had given Blue Chip its less-than-ideal conception, the Justice Department required the company to find another buyer for one-third of its stamp business. Still, it appeared that Blue Chip had survived this stage of the legal battle.

Munger's partnership bought 20,000 shares, and Guerin purchased a similar number. Munger developed the same proprietary attitude toward Blue Chip that Buffett had toward Berkshire Hathaway during this process. He warned others against it. "We don't want anyone buying Blue Chip," he informed them. "We don't want anyone buying this."

As the market rose, Buffett increased the partnership's temporary cash position to tens of millions of dollars, although he continued to buy stocks in large quantities. His partnership also purchased large blocks of Blue Chip stock from Lucky Stores, Market Basket, and Alexander's Markets, and would continue to do so for the next few months until it had more than 70,000 shares. For National Indemnity and Diversification, he also bought a 5% stake in Thriftimart Stores, one of Blue Chip's largest shareholders. Buffett believed he could eventually persuade Thriftimart to swap its Blue Chip for its own stock. Fortunately, they were betting primarily on the S&H lawsuit settling; otherwise, the timing would have been disastrous.

Just as he, Munger, and Guerin were making large investments in Blue Chip, its steadily growing sales peaked. Women had begun to lose interest in sitting at home and collecting trading stamps in a book. The burgeoning women's liberation movement meant that they had more time and money, as well as a sense of entitlement, which meant that if they wanted an electric blender or a fondue set, they went out and bought it rather than fussing over stamp books to trade in. Social roles and conventions had flipped upside down, and the Establishment culture was so despised that young people declared categorically, "Don't trust anyone over thirty." Buffett, at thirty-eight, did not feel old personally—he never would—but "I am in the geriatric ward, philosophically," he wrote to the partners. He was out of touch with current culture and finance.

In 1968, the prospect of Vietnam peace talks in Paris sparked another market rally. Though proud of having grown his partnership from seven investors and $105,000 to over 300 people and $105 million with little risk, Buffett had become an elder of the market, seemingly eclipsed by young barnstormers who could flash a couple of years' worth of showy numbers and joy-ride new investors into giving them $500 million almost overnight.

He appeared particularly—and comfortably—antiquated when it came to all of the new technology companies that were emerging. At Grinnell College, he arrived for a meeting to find his fellow trustee, Bob Noyce, eager to leave Fairchild Semiconductor. Noyce, Gordon Moore (its research director), and Andy Grove, its assistant director of research and development, decided to start a nameless new company in Mountain View, California, with the vague goal of extending circuit technology to "higher levels of integration." Joe Rosenfield and the college endowment fund each pledged $100,000, joining dozens of others in raising $2.5 million for the new company, which would soon be known as Intel (Integrated Electronics).

Buffett had a long history of being skeptical of technology investments, believing they lacked a safety margin. Years ago, in 1957, Katie Buffett, Warren's uncle Fred Buffett's wife, knocked on his back door with a question. Should she and Fred invest in her brother Bill's new business? Bill Norris was leaving Remington Rand's UNIVAC computer division to found Control Data Corporation, which would compete with IBM.

Warren was horrified. "Bill believed Remington Rand was behind IBM." I thought he had lost his mind. He left Remington Rand with six children and no money to speak of. I don't believe Bill left to get rich. I think he left because he was frustrated. Everything had to be sent to New York for approval and returned. Aunt Katie and Uncle Fred wanted to put some money into Control Data right away. Bill did not have any money. Nobody had any money, in a sense." Well, except Warren and Susie. "I could have funded half of it if I'd wanted. I was very negative about it. I told them, 'It doesn't seem like much to me. "Who needs another computer company?"

But because Bill was Katie's brother, she and Fred ignored Warren's advice and invested $400 anyway, purchasing the stock for sixteen cents per share.

Buffett's view of technology remained unchanged despite Control Data's ability to shower investors with cash. Many other technology companies that launched around the same time had failed. Buffett, however, approved a technology investment for Grinnell because he cared about Rosenfield more than anything. "We were betting on the jockey, not the horse," as he put it. More importantly, Rosenfield provided a margin of safety by guaranteeing the college's investment. And, as much as Buffett admired Noyce, he did not buy Intel for the partnership, missing one of his life's best investment opportunities. While he had lowered his investing standards in difficult environments and would do so again, he would never compromise on his margin of safety. This particular quality—passing up potential riches if he couldn't limit his risk—was what defined Warren Buffett. However, the entire market began to look like Intel to him. His 1968 year-end letter was sobering, stating that investment ideas had reached an all-time low. "Nostalgia just isn't what it used to be," he said. As he later explained: "It was a multi-trillion-dollar market, and I couldn't figure out how to invest $105 million wisely. I knew I didn't want to manage other people's money in an environment where I didn't believe I could do well but felt obligated to do so. That attitude was markedly different from 1962, when the market was also soaring. Both times, he lamented it. But he had raised funds with vigour that belied his inability to put them to use.

The partners were taken aback by the contrast between his somber words and the way he appeared to be making money for them. Some began to instill in him an almost supernatural sense of confidence. The more he defied his own pessimistic predictions, the more the legend appeared to grow. But he knew it wouldn't last.

THE UNWINDING

Omaha, 1969

Gladys Kaiser was stationed on the eighth floor of Kiewit Plaza, guarding Warren Buffett's doorway. Gladys, rail-thin and perfectly made up, chain-smoking through her platinum hair, dispatched paperwork, phone calls, bills, and nonsense with brisk efficiency.1 She kept Buffett away from everyone, including his family at times. Susie was furious, but she couldn't do anything because Gladys was guarding the door.

Susie blamed Gladys. And, of course, Warren would never give Gladys an order to keep Susie away. However, everyone in his office understood what he wanted from his subtle way of saying something without directly stating it. Nobody would cough if they thought he disapproved. People had to follow hints and signals as if they were written rules just to work at the Buffett Partnership. Beetled brows and "hmmmf" meant "don't even consider it." "Really?" asked. "I disagree but won't say so directly." An averted head, crinkled eyes, and backpedaling spelled "Help me, I can't." Gladys would not tolerate nonsense when it came to following these unspoken requests and orders, and sometimes people's feelings were hurt. But her job was to protect her boss, which required doing things he couldn't bring himself to do. She needed to be strong enough to take the blame. Framed newspaper clippings from the 1929 crash hung on the dingy walls above her head. The offices were furnished with dented metal furniture and an old ticker machine. Down the short linoleum hallway beyond. Gladys sat with others who understood Buffett's signals and signs. To the left was Bill Scott's small office, where he yelled "Hurry up, I'm busy!" at the brokers who were executing Buffett's trades. Part-time bookkeeper Donna Walters worked down the hallway to the right, in a workroom crammed with files and Gladys' small refrigerator filled with Pepsi bottles, meticulously keeping the partnership's records and preparing tax returns.2 Just past Walters sat John Harding, who oversaw the partners' and partnership's affairs. Buffett's personal space was directly behind Gladys, complete with a couple of reclining armchairs, a desk, and a plethora of newspapers and magazines. Its main feature was a large portrait of Howard Buffett on the wall across from his desk.

Every morning, Warren arrived, hung up his hat, and went into his sanctuary to read the newspapers. After a while, he came out and told Gladys, "Get me Charlie." Then he closed the door, picked up the phone, and spent the rest of the day alternating between the phone and his reading, spelunking for companies and stocks to buy. He would occasionally reappear and tell Bill Scott about a trade.

Scott was less busy these days, thanks to the strong stock market. Buffett, with his pockets full of money from National Indemnity, was looking for entire businesses whose prices were less susceptible to investor whims. He had discovered the Illinois National Bank & Trust, one of the most profitable banks he had ever seen, run by seventy-one-year-old Eugene Abegg of Rockford, Illinois. Buffett desired the crusty Abegg as part of the deal. Abegg looked like Ben Rosner, who had counted sheets of toilet paper. Buffett discussed with Abegg a few changes he wanted to make in the business before saying, "I've dropped all the shoes. I am not a centipede. If you want to go ahead, that's fine; if not, we're still friends.

"Gene had already agreed to sell the bank to somebody else. But the buyer began to criticize it, or they requested an audit. He had never been audited before, so he wanted out. "He was a dominant figure who acted conservatively in all aspects."He carried thousands of dollars in his pocket and cashed checks for others on weekends. He carried a list of unrented safe-deposit box numbers with him wherever he went, and he would try to rent you one at a cocktail party. Keep in mind that at the time, this was the largest bank in Illinois' second-largest city. He set every salary and paid every employee in cash, so the head of the trust department had no idea how much his own secretaries earned. So I went out there and named a number that turned out to be about a million dollars lower than the other guy. And Gene, who owned a quarter of the stock, called his largest shareholder, who owned more than half of the stock, and said, 'This young guy from Omaha's come here and offered this. I'm sick of those guys from XYZ Company. If you want to sell to them, you must run this bank, because I will not."

Sure enough, Abegg accepted his offer. And doing business with him reinforced Buffett's belief that strong-willed and ethical entrepreneurs were often more concerned with how the new owners treated them and the companies they had built than with grabbing the last nickel in a sale.

The Illinois National Bank, which Buffett soon came to refer to as Rockford Bank, was established before the United States Treasury assumed exclusive control over coining money. Buffett was fascinated to learn that it still issued its own currency. The ten-dollar bills featured Abegg's image. Buffett, who had a net worth of more than $26 million, could have bought almost anything, but not this. Gene Abegg had done him one better. He and the United States Treasury were able to issue their own currency, but not the Buffett Partnership or Berkshire Hathaway.3 The concept of legal tender bearing your own image piqued his interest. He began to carry a Rockford bill in his wallet.

Previously, Buffett did not want his picture on a bill or anywhere else. He had largely avoided the partnership spotlight. True, more stories and photographs of his family had made their way into the local paper than one might expect from someone who desired privacy.4

Nonetheless, aside from his letters to the partners, he had kept his lips sealed throughout the 1960s—he didn't want anyone to coattail him. He did not discuss how he invested or broadcast his results, in contrast to the flash and razzle-dazzle displayed by other money managers of the time, whose self-promotion propelled them to near-instant fame.

Even when an opportunity to promote himself presented itself, he did not take advantage of it. Years ago, a securities salesman named John Loomis visited Buffett at Kiewit Plaza. Carol, Loomis' wife, wrote Fortune magazine's investment column. She once interviewed a money manager named Bill Ruane, who told her Omaha was home to the smartest investor in the United States. Her husband arrived at Kiewit Plaza and made his way upstairs to the 227½-square-foot space, which looked nothing like the office of one of the richest men in town.

Buffett took him to the Blackstone Hotel restaurant across the street, where he drank a strawberry malt and told Loomis what he had done. Loomis discussed his wife's job as a journalist, which Buffett found interesting. He said had he not become a money manager, he would have chosen journalism as a career.

Warren and Susie met the Loomises shortly after arriving in New York. "They got us a special little room someplace where we had lunch," Buffett informs me. The well-connected young money manager from Omaha with a stellar track record and the ambitious Fortune reporter discovered they shared many characteristics: a zeal for exposing fat cats' shady dealings, a magpie obsession with minutiae, and a competitive streak as long as the interstate from New York to Omaha. Carol Loomis was a tall, athletic-looking, no-nonsense woman with short brown hair who tolerated poor journalism as much as Buffett tolerated losing money, and she was a meticulous editor. They began to correspond, and she introduced him to the world of big-league journalism. He started helping her with her story ideas. "Carol very quickly became my best friend other than Charlie," he admits.6 Initially, she did not publish anything about Buffett.

However, by the late 1960s, the rising market had made the partnership's stock investment less viable. The benefit of having a higher profile when attempting to acquire entire businesses began to outweigh the benefit of secrecy when purchasing stocks. Thus, in the late 1960s, Buffett's long-standing interest in newspapers and publishing converged with his newly recast investing goals and desire for personal attention in a way that fundamentally altered his world.

Buffett quickly plunged into the black-and-white world of journalism. Newspapers fell page by page, covering the litter of financial reports from newspaper and magazine publishers that lay scattered on his desk. When he fell asleep, more newspapers—pulled from a bundle and folded into neat packets—flew through his dreams. On his most restless nights, he fantasized about sleeping over his childhood paper route.

Buffett's fortune had grown large enough that he could afford to buy a newspaper, a magazine, or both. His ambition was to become a publisher rather than just an investor, to wield the power that comes with owning the means by which the general public learns about news. Around 1968, he and some friends attempted to purchase the entertainment newspaper Variety but were unsuccessful.[8] Then another acquaintance yielded fruit. Stanford Lipsey was Susie's friend who enjoyed going to clubs with her and listening to jazz. He showed up in Warren's office one day and expressed an interest in selling the Omaha Sun Newspapers. Buffett was immediately interested; he had already attempted to acquire it once.

Stan and Jeannie Blacker Lipsey inherited The Sun, a chain of weekly neighborhood newspapers, from her father. It published seven editions in the Omaha suburbs; its meat-and-potatoes stories included the police blotter, local society news, neighborhood business dealings, high school sports—and gossip about who was going steady with whom, making it a must-read for both parents and children. Although the Sun was the underdog in Omaha, its editor, Paul Williams, specialized in investigative journalism and competed by publishing stories that the leading paper, the Omaha World-Herald, overlooked, often stories that exposed the follies and misdeeds of city officials, stories that would offend major World-Herald advertisers. Usually, these advertisers avoided the Sun.

Despite his own rise to prominence in Omaha, Buffett was particularly drawn to the Sun's muckraking. He'd wanted to play cop ever since he started collecting license plate numbers to track down bank robbers. "He'd always had this huge admiration for newspapers," Lipsey adds. "I knew intuitively that Warren understood the importance of newspapers in our society. A new highway was about to pass through my plant, and I would have had to borrow a large sum of money to purchase a new press. I didn't like the Sun's business prospects, but I knew Warren had enough money to ensure that journalism would not suffer due to economic conditions. In twenty minutes, it was completed."

"I figured we'd pay a million and a quarter for it and take out a hundred thousand a year," Buffett tells me. This return was 8%, about the same as a bond—far less than he expected to earn from a business or stock. The long-term outlook suggested that return would decline rather than increase. But the partnership's money was lying dormant, and he desperately wanted to be a publisher. "Part of my deal," says Lipsey, "was that, even though the partnership was closed, he had to take me in." Buffett wanted the Sun so much that he agreed, despite the fact that he was considering ending the partnership.

Berkshire Hathaway acquired the Omaha Sun Newspapers January 1, 1969. Buffett aspired to be a national publisher, so this small neighborhood newspaper was just the beginning. Joe Rosenfield introduced him to West Virginia's Secretary of State, Jay Rockefeller, whom Rosenfield regarded as a rising political star. Soon, the Buffets were hosting the Rockefellers for dinner in Omaha. Rockefeller introduced Warren to Charles Peters, an idealist whose start-up magazine, the Washington Monthly, appeared to be the right national voice to express views on important issues. Buffett spoke with Gilbert Kaplan, who ran Institutional Investor magazine, to learn more about magazine publishing. Then he wrote to Rockefeller, "You've discovered my Achilles heel. I am a pushover for publishing deals, especially when I like the product. I might add that my enthusiasm for publishing ventures is exactly inverse to my calculated assessment of their financial viability."

Buffett introduced Fred Stanback and Rosenfield to the concept of investing in the Washington Monthly, cautioning them that it was unlikely to be a financial success. But imagine the scandals it could uncover, the ideas it could spread, the minds it could awaken, and the exposés it could reveal! They contributed a little money.

The Washington Monthly rapidly depleted its initial capital stake. Buffett mentioned the possibility of another $50,000. Then he and Peters had a 50-minute phone conversation. "Oh God," Peters exclaims. "As an investment, it reeked of potential failure. There was his hard-working business instinct and his philanthropic, good-citizen instinct, and they were clearly at odds. He was concerned about his business reputation and would almost pull out, but I would slowly try to pull him back. Warren kept finding new plausible escape routes, while I attempted to block the exits. But the best part was that he ended up staying inside." Buffett added the condition that the editors contribute some of their own money while Peters raises some from outside sources, which Buffett said he would match eighty percent.

Peters was a more talented journalist than an accountant. They raised the funds, the checks were issued, and the Washington Monthly remained silent for months. "They just vanished," Buffett claims. "Fred Stanback complained that he was getting IRS forms late, and had to amend his tax returns." Although the Washington Monthly was publishing compelling stories, as Buffett had desired, it was insufficient. He knew from the start that it would not make money, but he believed it should be held accountable for what money it did have. He was embarrassed to have dragged Stanback and Rosenfield into a bear hunt. Investors believed they were being treated like bank tellers. Buffett aspired to be a journalistic partner, a fellow newshound, rather than just a financier of idealism.

Despite the mixed results, Buffett was now pursuing the personal concerns mentioned in his October 1967 letter to his partners. Meanwhile, the market continued to dry up, depriving him of opportunity. Spending part of his time as a publishing magnate did not help him adjust to that reality. Whatever else he was doing, he remained completely committed to the partnership, and it turned out that a "less compulsive approach" to investing was not in his nature. So he began to consider the best way to end the partnership. He claims he received offers from a couple of people to buy the management firm, which would have allowed him to sell for a large profit, but he felt this was wrong. Even in those days, it was unusual for a money manager to turn down a large sum of money, and Buffett had shown no inclination to avoid becoming wealthier. But he had always sided with his partners, using his avarice for both their and his own benefit. Around Memorial Day 1969, Buffett wrote to his partners that lowering his goal did not reduce his intensity. He stated, "If I am going to participate publicly, I can't help but be competitive." I know I don't want to spend my entire life trying to outpace an investment rabbit. "The only way to slow down is to stop."15 And then he dropped the bombshell: he announced that he would give formal notice of retirement by the end of the year and close the partnership in early

1970. "I am not attuned to this market environment, and I don't want to spoil a decent record by trying to play a game I don't understand just so I can go out a hero."

What should he do now? "I don't have an answer to that question," he said. "I do know that when I am sixty, I should be attempting to achieve different personal goals than those which had priority at age twenty."

The partners howled with disappointment and, in some cases, fear. Many were naïfs, including his aunt Alice. They included ministers, rabbis, teachers, grandmothers, and mothers-in-law. His announcement was essentially a market call on stocks. He didn't believe the game would be worth playing soon. He had taught even the inexperienced to avoid an overheated market. Some people trusted no one but him. Nonetheless, "he just didn't want to operate in an environment where he didn't feel comfortable with the opportunities," recalls John Harding, "especially when it was something that he felt he had to devote all his time to."

Susie Buffett was relieved Warren was ending the partnership, if only for the sake of the children. They cared deeply about what their father thought of them. Susie Jr. had always received the majority of Warren's limited attention, and Peter felt rewarded for remaining quiet and in the background. But fourteen-year-old Howie, who had always sought an emotional connection with his father that had never materialized, had grown wilder as he grew older. Susie Jr. would discover a pair of mannequin legs covered in fake blood sticking out of her closet. He climbed the roof dressed as a gorilla to spy on her when she returned home from dates and drenched her with the sprayer from the kitchen sink when she appeared in her prom dress. When their parents were in New York City, Howie took advantage of the opportunity to experiment with anarchy.18 Warren, who was still reliant on Susie for everything, assumed she would look after Howie and the other kids. However, Susie had given up trying to control her children by this point. She had long let go of any idealistic expectations for her marriage. Her attention was increasingly drawn to an increasing number of "vagrants," as one friend put it, who wandered through the house, sought her assistance, and occupied her time.

Because she almost always accepted people unconditionally, some of her "clients" had histories as felons, con men, addicts, or, in one case, the alleged proprietor of a bawdy house. These people occasionally conned her out of money. She didn't mind. Buffett was furious at the prospect of being cheated himself, but he eventually accepted it as part of Susie's giveaway budget and even accepted it as part of her allure. Her circle of female friends grew to include Bella Eisenberg, Eunice Denenberg, Jeannie Lipsey, Rackie Newman, and others. Warren recognized most of them, but this was Susie's circle, not his. Other connections of hers, such as Rodney and Angie Wead, came from the activist community, while another group of friends gathered around the tennis courts at Dewey Park. And there was always the family: Leila, especially now that Roy Ralph had died and she had reclaimed the Buffett name; Fred and Katie Buffett and their son Fritz, who had married Warren; and Susie's former babysitter, Pam—who was now a friend of hers. Her nephews, Tom and Billy Rogers, were frequently present, as was David Stryker, a guitarist from the local music scene whom she met through Billy. Susie's friends, like the Rogers boys and Dave Stryker, were young. She was close to Renee and Annette Gibson, the daughters of baseball player Bob Gibson and his wife, Charlene. Russell McGregor, Pat Turner, and Duane Taylor, son of jazz legend Billy Taylor, were among the black students she had given scholarships to, and they would occasionally visit her. So it went.

Even though Susie was the driving force behind all of this generosity, she was beginning to crave some attention. According to her friends, all that was required was an ounce of effort on the part of her husband. She didn't believe making money was the ultimate goal of life. She felt impoverished, having to forgo travel, museums, theater, art, and most other forms of culture due to his lack of interest. Warren lavished her with praise in public, but when at home or at work, he reverted to his usual preoccupied state. It would make a difference if he made an effort to accompany her to an art gallery on occasion, or took her on a trip simply because she wanted to go, she stated. But, while he did occasionally show up when asked, she had to ask for a favor, not a gift.

Susie realized Warren was never going to take off to Italy for weeks on end, so she started traveling on her own or with her female friends, sometimes to visit family—such as Bertie, who now lived in California—and sometimes to attend personal-growth seminars.

One day at the Chicago airport, she was sitting on a bench when a man stopped in front of her. "Are you Susan Thompson?He asked. She looked up, embarrassed at being caught with her mouth full of hot dogs. It was Milt Brown, her high school sweetheart, who she hadn't seen in years. He sat down, and they began to reacquaint themselves. Susie, who was always looking for emotional connections, later stated that her husband wasn't devoid of emotion; he was simply disconnected from his own feelings. And it certainly appeared that his strongest emotional bonds were with his friends and partners, to whom he felt an intense obligation and had formed a de facto family. The other Buffetts couldn't help but notice how he lit up in their presence, as opposed to the dutiful but preoccupied demeanor he displayed while attending his own family events.

Thus, even as he prepared to end the partnership that had consumed the majority of his waking hours for the previous thirteen years, he remained fully engaged with his partners and appeared hesitant to let go of his connection to them. He went to great lengths to ensure their money was in good hands, writing them another letter outlining their options in detail.

Explaining his dedication to them, he says, "Finding other advisers is a difficult task. When I ended my partnership, I had these partners who relied on me, and I was going to distribute a lot of money. I felt obligated to at least offer some alternatives to them."

This was unusual behavior for a money manager. Even Ben Graham had only said, "Oh, buy AT&T," when asked, and mentioned Buffett casually to a few people. But Buffett made elaborate efforts to guide his partners through their future investing careers. Some were already part of the Munger partnership, and Buffett sent one or two more to him. But Munger was uneasy about the market. "Who wants to be around someone who is disappointing them?" he says. "Especially since you sucked them into the relationship?" He also lacked Buffett's knack for promotion.

"I recommended two people to the partners who I knew were extremely good and honest: Sandy Gottesman and Bill Ruane. I'd been in the investment world for a long time and had grown to know many of the people involved. So I not only knew their results, but I also knew how they'd achieved them, which was extremely important." So the wealthier partners would go to Gottesman at First Manhattan. But Sandy didn't want the small fry, so Buffett sent the rest to Ruane, who was leaving Kidder, Peabody to form his own investment advisory firm, Ruane, Cunniff & Stires, with two partners, Rick Cunniff and Sidney Stores, and establishing the Sequoia Fund specifically to handle the smaller accounts. They hired John Harding, who would be out of work when the partnership was dissolved, to run the new company's Omaha office. John Loomis, Carol Loomis' husband, and Buffett's trusted researcher Henry Brandt also visited Ruane, Cunniff, effectively giving it a full staff. These connections also kept Harding, Loomis, and Brandt within Buffett's extended "family."

Buffett brought Ruane to Omaha and pitched the Sequoia Fund to the partners. He praised Ruane in typical mathematical terms. Despite knowing Ruane for years, he left a small escape hatch to avoid blame in case things didn't work out. He wrote: "There is no way to eliminate the possibility of error when judging humans…[but] I consider Bill to be an exceptionally high-probability decision on character and a high-probability one on investment performance."22

However, as Buffett planned to end the partnership, the market's sparks began to fade. By July 1969, when US troops began withdrawing from Vietnam, the Dow had dropped by 19%. Even though the successful moon landing that summer gave the country a boost, Wall Street did not feel it. Exotic stocks like National Student Marketing and Minnie Pearl's Chicken System, Inc.—which had garnered a huge following in a market where half of the money managers and brokers had only been in the business for seven years— were starting to collapse.

Blue Chip Stamps, the trading-stamp stock painstakingly accumulated by Buffett, Munger, and Guerin, has now become a notable exception to the general trend. The three had been betting on the company's ability to settle its antitrust lawsuit with Sperry & Hutchinson. When a settlement was reached, this stock—which the Buffett partners had no idea they owned—showered them with nearly $7 million in profit in exchange for a $2 million investment less than a year ago.24 Now Blue Chip decided to have a public offering, and Buffett chose to sell the partnership's shares as part of that deal.25 It appeared that the partners were going to have a splendid final year in 1969. That October, Buffett convened another meeting of the Grahamites, including those who had met in San Diego the previous year, but without Ben Graham. This time, the wives were also invited, and while they did not attend the meetings where the men discussed stocks, their presence added to the festive atmosphere, making it feel like a vacation. Buffett delegated the planning to Marshall Weinberg, who lived in New York City and enjoyed traveling. But Weinberg, who liked to shave a dime and had no more experience with the jet-set life than Buffett, asked around and ended up at the Colony Club, a Palm Beach, Florida, resort where they were treated like rubes and snooted at even by the bellboys.

Ruane reported at the first night's dinner that the bellhop had returned his five-dollar tip with a sneer, saying, "You need it more than I do." Bill Scott had given his bellhop a handful of the dimes he always kept in his pocket to make phone calls for Buffet. On his way out, the bellhop threw the change all over the hallway floor.

For the next five days, as the group endured bad food, cramped quarters, high winds, and torrential rains, the men sat classroom-style, with Buffett most often in his usual spot at the front. "Charlie told some horror stories," Buffett wrote later, and "I drew the same gloomy conclusions, [while Walter Schloss] said that two mislocated steel companies with obsolete plants were still below book value, so all was not lost."

Buffett proposed the Desert Island Challenge. He asked, "If you were stranded on a desert island for ten years, what stock would you invest in?" The trick was to find a company with the strongest franchise, one that was less vulnerable to the corrosive forces of competition and time: Munger's concept of the great business. As Henry Brandt took copious notes on the various responses, Buffett announced his own choice: Dow Jones, the owner of the Wall Street Journal. His interest in newspapers was growing and would only grow stronger, but curiously, he did not own this stock.

The gathering ended much as it had begun, with more rude displays from the hotel staff, who had no idea they were hosting anything other than a third-rate group of stockbrokers at a time when the market was falling. The staff had officially shooed the Grahamites away from the hotel mezzanine's jewelry cases. On the final day, as the group was leaving, Ed Anderson approached the front desk and asked how to get to the airport. Most of our guests use limousines, he was told, but for you, we'll call a taxi.

Buffett went on to describe the Colony Club as "a friendly family hotel—that is, friendly if you were the Kennedy family." It was a "low-class performance by a high-class place," says Anderson. Later, when a Fort Lauderdale businessman who held the Colony Club's mortgage asked Buffett to advise him on a financing deal, Buffett told the man that he would gladly do it for free, but "if you ever have a chance to foreclose on them, do it."

Buffett invited Louis Kohn of Hochschild-Kohn to the Colony Club. Buffett had grown fond of Kohn and his wife, and he and Susie had spent a vacation with them in Cozumel. However, inviting them to the Colony Club gathering proved awkward, because no sooner had the meeting been scheduled than Buffett and Munger realized Hochschild-Kohn was not going to work for them.

"Retail is a very tough business," explains Charlie Munger. "We realized we were wrong. Almost every great chain-store operation that has been around for a long time eventually runs into problems that are difficult to resolve. The dominant retailer in one twenty-year period is not necessarily the dominant retailer in the next." Their experience had instilled in them a deep skepticism about retailing, which would only grow, not fade, with time.

They desired businesses that would lavish them with money, businesses that had some sort of sustainable competitive advantage and could outwit the natural cycle of capital creation and destruction for as long as possible. Not long after the meeting in Florida, Munger and Buffett sold Hochschild-Kohn to Supermarkets General for roughly what they had paid for it. Buffett wanted to move quickly to unload the company before dissolving the partnership and distributing its assets. With the company, the Kohns disappeared from the Buffetts' lives.

Diversified Retailing issued unsecured debt ("debentures") to fund the Hochschild-Kohn acquisition. Buffett had taken special care with his first public offering, insisting to his underwriters that the bonds have several unique features. The bankers had argued that a novel structure would make the bond harder to sell.

"I said, 'Well, but bonds should have this in there.' That was the first bond issue I ever sold, and I included a few things that the underwriters had no interest in at all. But I'd thought a lot about bond issues over the years. And I had considered how bondholders had been taken advantage of."

Bondholders have historically earned less than stockholders because they sacrificed the potentially limitless opportunity of a shareholder in exchange for lower risk. However, Buffett understood that in the real world, it was not always so.

"One of the things I put in was that if we didn't pay the bond interest for any reason, the bondholders took over voting control of the company, so they didn't have to get Mickey Moused by bankruptcy and all that kind of stuff." Ben Graham wrote about this in Security Analysis, with as much passion as he could muster on any subject, describing how courts rarely allow bondholders to seize the assets that back those bonds unless the assets are nearly worthless. Unsecured bondholders' interests were worked over in receivership through a strangling process that pushed payment almost to the point of insignificance. Thus, DRC's debenture also stated that the company could not pay dividends while the debentures were outstanding, preventing equity investors from siphoning off profits while interest on the bonds was deferred.

The second unusual provision was that the debentures paid eight percent but, depending on the company's earnings, could pay up to one percent more.

Buffett added a third provision. Because he believed the bonds would be sold primarily to people who knew him or his reputation, he wanted the bonds to be redeemable if he sold enough stock in DRC to no longer be the majority shareholder.34

"And no one had ever included anything like this in a covenant. I said, 'You know, they're entitled to this. They may choose not to redeem them, but they have the right to do so. When his own banker, Nelson Wilder, objected that such clauses were unprecedented and unnecessary, Buffett overruled him.35

Now that interest rates had risen and banks were reluctant to lend, debentures suddenly became a valuable source of low-cost financing, a powerful consolation prize. Nonetheless, because Buffett viewed a dollar today as the fifty or hundred dollars it could become someday, it was as if he had lost millions of dollars on Hochschild-Kohn due to the missed opportunity to put the money to better use. He reached a conclusion, which he later stated as:

Time is the friend of big business and the enemy of mediocrity. I had to learn this principle the hard way, even though it seems obvious. After ending our corporate marriage with Hochschild-Kohn, I had memories similar to the husband in the country song 'My Wife Ran Away with My Best Friend and I Still Miss Him a Lot.'It is far preferable to purchase a wonderful company at a fair price than a fair company at a fantastic price. Charlie realized this quickly; I was a slow learner. But now, when we buy companies or common stocks, we look for first-class businesses led by first-class executives. This leads directly into a related lesson: Good jockeys perform well on good horses but not on broken-down nags.

Even as Buffett and Munger were negotiating the sale of Hochschild-Kohn in the fall of 1969, Forbes published an article about Buffett titled "How Omaha Beats Wall Street." The article began in such an arresting manner that subsequent writers covering Buffett would copy it for decades.

"$10,000 invested in his Buffett Partnership in 1957," the magazine reported, "is now worth $260,000." The partnership's assets had grown to $100 million, with an annual compounded rate of 31%. In the twelve years it has existed, "it hasn't had one year in which it lost money.... Buffett has accomplished this through following consistently fundamental investing principles." The anonymous Forbes columnist then wrote one of the most insightful statements ever made about Buffett:

"Buffett is not a simple person, but he has simple tastes."

This is not simple. Buffett, who had simple tastes, insisted on complete secrecy in his stock dealings while running his partnership, and he was never profiled in any interviews. However, now that secrecy was no longer an issue, he had agreed to a high-profile article about himself. The article did not print or even mention his net worth. The reporter had no idea that since Buffett closed the partnership to new partners in 1966, his fees, reinvested, had quadrupled his net worth to $26.5 million in just three years—or that, with no money coming in from new partners to dilute him, his share of the partnership's assets had increased from 19% to 26%. The story mentioned his "rambling old Omaha house" 38 and the lack of computers and a large staff in his unimpressive office. True, the man with simple tastes still drank four or five bottles of Pepsi per day, requested it instead of wine at dinner parties, and ate only the dinner rolls if anything more complicated than a steak or hamburger was offered. As a helpless captive of whoever happened to be doing the laundry at home, he occasionally appeared in public looking little better than a hobo and barely noticed the state of his clothes. He would have been content in a two-room garage apartment; money was just a scorecard. Susie was concerned about living comfortably, and she believed that money was useless unless it was used for something.

Nonetheless, the Buffetts had for some time lived the life of a wealthy couple—though not as luxuriously as they could have afforded. Susie had even upgraded Warren to a Cadillac similar to her own, but only the most stripped-down version with no extra features, after calling every dealer within a mile to get the best price. People found the contrast between his simple tastes and his growing fortune refreshing. His friendly demeanor, self-deprecating wit, and calm demeanor put them at ease. He had lost some of his earlier gracelessness and arrogance, and the more obvious signs of insecurity—but his tolerance for criticism had not improved. He was learning how to hide his impatience. He was extremely loyal to longtime friends. His fundamental honesty particularly impressed people. Those who were in his presence for an extended period of time found the unleashed whirlwind of his energy exhausting. "Insatiable," they whispered, and occasionally felt guilty relief when his attention wandered. He inhaled information and was prone to bombarding his friends with mountains of clippings and reading material that he thought would be of interest to them, only to discover months later that they had fallen months behind him. His conversations weren't as casual as they appeared. They always appeared to have a purpose, no matter how obscure it was to those on the receiving end. People sometimes realized he was testing them. Buffett exuded an inner tension that belied his outwardly casual demeanor.

It was difficult to imagine what he would do with all that energy and intensity without the partnership. Many partners had trouble imagining what they would do without him. Many of them had become his train bearers and were unwilling to let go. Their reluctance struck an ironic note given the fate of Buffett's other family. Concurrent with its centennial, Fred Buffett threw his hands up in the air and abandoned the Buffett grocery store. Neither of his sons wanted to take over, and despite annual sales of half a million dollars, he couldn't find a buyer. The grinding wheel of capitalism had spoken. The Buffetts were not socialites and had never thrown a particularly large party. However, with both the store and the partnership closing, they celebrated with a party one night during the final weekend of September 1969. Nearly 200 people of various ages and races poured into their home. Businessmen, society matrons, poor adopted "clients" of Susie's, teenagers, friends who had become wealthy as a result of the partnership, Susie's female friends, assorted priests, rabbis, and ministers, and local politicians made their way through a string of flashing lights, past the three-foot Pepsi bottles in the windows. Susie had chosen a New York theme—Stage Door Deli food and decor—and instructed attendees to dress in "casual kosher." They appeared in various outfits, including culottes and cocktail dresses. A half-cut beer barrel overflowed with chrysanthemums in her favorite color, sunshine yellow. In keeping with the theme, a table was set up like a deli cart, with pastrami sandwiches and cheeses on top and sausages and a real plucked chicken hanging from it. A piano player near the beer keg in the sunroom encouraged guests to sing along. A popcorn machine outside the racquetball court beckoned visitors into an impromptu basement cinema. The court's ceiling bobbed with giant helium balloons, and films starring W. C. Fields, Mae West, and Laurel and Hardy played throughout the evening. In the solarium, the elderly Fred Buffett "protected" two bikini-clad models while the guests covered them in body paint. "I had such a good time that I hate to think it's over," Susie said afterwards.

PART FOUR

SUSIE SINGS

NEWSHOUND

Washington, D.C. - 1973

Nearly two years later, the Post was deep into reporting on the Watergate scandal, while the Sun's reporters in Omaha were basking in the glow of the Boys Town exposé. Reporting on Watergate, which began in June 1972 with the break-in, gained traction after Woodward and Bernstein linked a check made out to one of the burglars to Nixon's re-election campaign. The scandal unfolded over several months . As a secret FBI informant, Mark Felt—code-named "Deep Throat" and known only to Bob Woodward until thirty-three years later—funneled information to them about CREEP, the Campaign to Re-elect the President, and various CIA and FBI officials involved in funding and assisting the burglars. However, other newspapers and the public largely ignored the scandal. Nixon was re-elected with a massive majority that fall, despite vehemently denying any knowledge of or involvement in the break-in. The Nixon White House, which was already actively hostile to the Post following the Pentagon Papers scandal, dismissed Watergate as "a third-rate burglary attempt" and continued to threaten and harass the paper. Attorney General John Mitchell, who had managed Nixon's election campaign, warned Woodward and Bernstein that "Katie Graham's gonna get her tit caught in a big fat wringer" if the Post continued to report the story. A Wall Street friend with administration connections advised her "not to be alone."

In early 1973, a Republican fundraiser and friend of Richard Nixon challenged the renewal of the Post's two Florida television licenses. The challenge, which was most likely politically motivated, threatened half of the company's earnings, an attack on the core of the business.1 As a result, WPO stock fell from a high of $38 to as low as $16 per share.

Despite having a Pulitzer, the Watergate burglars convicted and imprisoned, and a growing body of evidence linking top Nixon administration officials to the break-in, Graham continued to question whether the paper was being set up or misled.2 The majority of her time and attention was now spent fighting these fires. Her chairman, Fritz Beebe, was ill with cancer and rapidly declining; still in need of an authority figure to rely on, she increasingly turned to another of her board members, André Meyer, senior partner at the investment bank Lazard Frères.

Meyer "crushed other people's personalities." He was known as "the Picasso of Banking" and a man with "an almost erotic attachment to money," and he was called the greatest investment banker of the twentieth century, "a genius of the art of acquisitiveness," according to his colleagues.4 He was also the well-connected man who warned Graham not to be alone during Watergate. He "had an ability to relate to people in times of distress in a way that created loyalty and exposed him to grand opportunities in the future," said a former Lazard executive.5 He soon took up Graham socially and was seen with her at restaurants, parties, and the theater.

Beebe died on May 1, 1973, and a week later his lawyer, George Gillespie, who also served as Graham's personal lawyer and one of her advisers, began settling his estate. Gillespie learned that a large investor in Omaha was buying Post stock, so he called Buffett from his summer home in Maine and offered a block of 50,000 Beebe shares that needed to be sold. Buffett snapped it up.

Buffett would have bought almost any newspaper for Berkshire Hathaway if he could have afforded it. When the bankers from Affiliated Publications, the publisher of the Boston Globe, were struggling to place their deal, Buffett broke his unwritten rule of not buying public offerings and purchased 4% of Affiliated at a discount. Berkshire ended up being its largest shareholder. He acquired stock in Booth Newspapers, Scripps Howard, and Harte-Hanks Communications, a San Antonio-based chain. The Sun's elevated status as a Pulitzer Prize winner allowed him to network his way through the newspaper industry, speaking with publishers as one of their peers. He approached the owners of the Wilmington News Journal, hoping to acquire the paper. Unfortunately, while newspaper stocks were cheap because investors failed to recognize their value, newspaper owners were not so naive. Buffett and Munger's efforts to acquire entire newspapers had failed in the face of competition.

Nonetheless, by late spring 1973, Buffett had accumulated more than 5% of the Washington Post stock.6 He then wrote a letter to Graham. She had never lost her fear that her company would be taken away from her, despite the fact that Beebe and Gillespie had divided the Washington Post's stock into two classes, making it impossible for an unfriendly buyer to do so.7 Buffett's letter informed her that he owned 230,000 shares and planned to buy more. Instead of legalistic boilerplate, he sent a highly flattering, personal letter that emphasized their shared interest in journalism and the Sun's Pulitzer. The letter started:

This purchase is a significant commitment to us—and an explicitly quantified compliment to the Post as a business enterprise and to you as its CEO. Writing a check separates conviction and conversation. I admit Graham controls and runs the Post. That suits me fine.8

Nonetheless, Graham panicked. She reached out for advice.

"At times," Jim Hoagland, one of her reporters, wrote, Graham was "capable of being taken in by mountebanks of the moment," and "particularly if they were adroit at a certain kind of kidding flattery."9 She was a "pretty dreadful snob" and "too easily impressed by people with big titles," according to another reporter.10 Moreover, while she instinctively pursued women's equality—she had given the seed money to Gloria Steinem for Ms. magazine—she was known to chide men f Thus, when André Meyer was "irate" and told her that Buffett meant her no good, she took him seriously11, as did another of Graham's acquaintances, Bob Abboud, a fellow trustee at the University of Chicago, who warned her away.

"André Meyer really wanted to believe he was in control of everything. And it was simple when he got a woman like Kay—he'd make her feel as if she couldn't go to the bathroom without first checking with him. He had that style. André kept referring to me as her new boss after I purchased this stock. You had all these guys who were worried that if I got into the inner circle, their power would diminish.

"She was understandably concerned about the possibility of being manipulated for political or journalistic purposes. She was used to having everyone in the world try to take advantage of her. But you could play on Kay's fears. If you wanted to manipulate her, you could make her feel insecure. And she was aware that you were doing it to her, but she couldn't resist."

"She would second-guess herself," says Arjay Miller, a Post board member. "She fell in and out of love with people. She could be bullied. She would become overwhelmed by certain people in business. She'd meet someone, be dazzled by them for a while, and believe they knew all the answers. She believed men knew everything about business and women knew nothing. That was ultimately the real issue. Her mother told her that, and her husband told her that repeatedly."12

Graham tried to learn all she could about Buffett. She barely remembered him from their brief encounter two years prior. She and her colleagues purchased copies of Supermoney and devoured the chapter on him, curious as to what the Nebraska man had in store for them. Those opposed to Buffett made certain she saw an unsigned article in the September 1 issue of Forbes about Buffett's purchase of stock in San Jose Water Works, casting a pall over the sunny portrait that Supermoney had painted of the mystery man.

This Forbes article had a very different tone than the glowing article the magazine had published two years before. It described a San Jose Water Works stockholder who wanted to sell his shares. He approached a company director, who referred him to Buffett. The article implied that Buffett must have been aware that a deal was being negotiated for the city to take over the water works at a higher price than he was paying for the stock—simply because a director had referred a seller to him. He had connections, so he must have known something. Right? The piece came to an end: "…the American Stock Exchange and the San Francisco office of the Securities Exchange Commission are making inquiries and asking questions." 14

However, it was not illegal for a director to refer a stock seller to a buyer.15 In fact, no transaction occurred. However, aside from Supermoney, this would be the most recent public mention of Buffett's name.16 Buffett felt like a cat's scratching post. If this cascaded into a series of expanding stories, it could tarnish his newly gilded reputation, even if the story contained no substance. He was not the type to storm and shout, but rather to brood and plan. Thus, while enraged, he was too astute to confront the magazine and denounce its anonymous reporter. He wanted retribution and vindication, so he used the opportunity to bring himself to the attention of magazine publisher Malcolm Forbes, writing him an artfully worded letter in which he talked of the pitfalls of journalism, complimented him on the magazine's good "batting average" in investigative reporting over the years—to which the article on San Jose Water Works was some kind of unfortunate exception—and mentioned the Sun's Pulitzer. On the same day, he wrote a

Sure enough, Forbes issued a correction. Buffett understood, however, that corrections were rarely read and had no impact compared to the original story. So he sent one of his proxies, the loyal Bill Ruane, to speak with the editors, not to complain, but to position Buffett as an expert who could write an article on investing.18 The attempt failed, at least initially.

Buffett now had a new cause—outrage at bias in news reporting—that centered on his sense of justice and interest in journalism in general. He was outraged that a reporter could lie by inference or omission without being held accountable. He knew that even well-intentioned news organizations would go into a frenzy and defend their reporters' questionable behavior on the grounds of newsroom morale and press independence. This stance, he would later learn, was referred to at the Washington Post as the "defensive crouch."19

He eventually helped fund the National News Council, a nonprofit organization that heard complaints about journalistic malpractice. The council's position was that media had become dominated by monopolies and concentrated in a few hands; this lack of competition meant that the First Amendment's right of freedom of the press gave publishers "power without responsibility." The council offered redress to victims who had been "traduced, misquoted, libeled, held up to unjustified ridicule, or whose legitimate views have been ignored in a one-sided report." Unfortunately, those very monopolies and the few The News Council eventually folded after its findings were repeatedly skewed by the supposed free and independent press.

The National News Council was a worthy crusade, perhaps ahead of its time, like many of the causes on which Buffett focused his efforts. However, by 1973, Susie Buffett had witnessed him expend a tidal wave of energy on each new crusade or obsession, sometimes altering entire coastlines in his wake. While most people's interests change over time, the shy, insecure man she married became obsessed with one thing after another. From his childhood hobby of collecting license plate numbers to reforming journalism's shady practices, three roles piqued his interest. The first was a relentless collector who grew his empire of money, people, and influence. The second was the preacher, who sprinkled idealism from the lectern. The third was the cop who thwarted the bad guys.

The ideal business would allow him to do everything at once: preach, play cop, and collect money to ring the cash register. The ideal business, therefore, was a newspaper. That was why the Sun had been a sliver of something he wanted a lot more of.

However, he and Munger had unsuccessfully attempted to acquire major city newspapers. Now here was Katharine Graham, unsteady on her feet in business, manipulated by those around her, flailing and seeking a lifesaver ring from anyone she could find. Despite her insecurities and vulnerabilities, she had become one of the most powerful women in the Western Hemisphere due to her leadership at the Washington Post. Buffett had always had a strong attraction to powerful individuals.

Graham was afraid of him. She asked George Gillespie if he was crooked. She couldn't afford to make mistakes. For several years, the Nixon administration waged an all-out war to discredit the Post. The Senate Watergate Committee was conducting hearings. Woodward and Bernstein discovered Nixon's "enemies list." A series of newly discovered tapes implicated the President, who had refused to turn over information he claimed was privileged, information that could answer the question of what happened and who was involved. Graham worked daily on the Watergate story. In a way, she had bet the Post's franchise on it.

She relied heavily on the opinion of the devoutly religious and completely respectable Gillespie. He had served the Graham family ever since, as a twenty-eight-year-old trust lawyer at Cravath, Swaine & Moore, drafting Eugene Meyer's final will and witnessing the fading old man's signature. "He's going to take over the Washington Post," she said of Buffett. "Kay, he can't take over the Post," Gillespie explained. "Forget it. It is not possible. It makes no difference how much B stock he holds. He possesses no rights. All he could do was elect himself to the board if he owned the majority of the B stock."

Gillespie had spoken with a San Jose Water Works director and was assured Buffett had no inside information. He made it clear that he disagreed with the powerful André Meyer, which was a bold move given Meyer's position and connections. He told her to talk to Buffett because he would be good to know.21

Graham wrote to Buffett, quaking as she dictated the letter, suggesting that they meet in California, where she would be traveling late that summer for business. He eagerly agreed, and when she arrived at an office provided by the Los Angeles Times, the Post's West Coast news-service partner, she looked exactly the same as she had two years before: impeccably tailored shirtdress, pageboy hairdo lacquered into place, lips pursed in a small smile. Graham said when she first saw Buffett, his "very appearance surprised" her.

"The great blessing and curse in my mother's life," says her son Don, "was that she had extremely high taste standards. She was accustomed to traveling in high-falutin circles. She believed that there was only one correct way to dress and eat, as well as one circle of people to whom attention should be paid. Warren violated all of her standards when it came to these things, but he didn't care."22 Wearing a suit that appeared tailored for another man, his hair no longer crew-cut and beginning to float up slightly at the ends, "he resembled no Wall Street figure or business tycoon I'd ever met," she later wrote. "Rather, he came across as corn fed and Midwestern, but with that extraordinary combination of qualities that has always appealed to me: brains and humor. I liked him from the beginning."

However, this was not apparent at the time. Instead, she came across as terrified, uncertain of both him and herself.

"When I first met Kay, she was wary and scared. She was terrified and intrigued by me. There was one thing about Kay you could tell. She wasn't the poker-faced type."

Buffett could tell Graham knew nothing about business or finance. She believed her board and managers outperformed her in running the company despite having a decade of experience. He told her he believed Wall Street did not see the Post's value. Graham let down her guard slightly. In her patrician accent, she invited him to meet her in Washington a few weeks later.

Warren and Susie arrived November 4, the night before meeting. They drove up in a taxi to the Madison Hotel, which was directly across the street from the Post headquarters, and discovered that the newspaper was in the midst of a printers' union work stoppage. Despite rumors that pressmen were armed, federal marshals were evicting the mutinous printers. Commotion, glaring lights, and television cameras lasted until dawn. Given what was going on in politics, there couldn't have been a worse time to shut down a newspaper, which was exactly what the union intended. Vice President Spiro Agnew was under criminal investigation but abruptly pleaded "no contest" to a tax-evasion charge less than a month ago, then resigned. The Watergate scandal had escalated into an explosive crisis. Two weeks following Agnew's resignation, U.S. Attorney General Elliot Richardson and Deputy Attorney General William Ruckelshaus resigned in protest rather than carrying out President Nixon's order to fire special prosecutor Archibald Cox, who had been appointed to investigate the scandal, and abolish his office. Nixon did so anyway, in what became known as the "Saturday Night Massacre." The President's interference in the supposedly independent judiciary branch of government marked a watershed moment in the Watergate scandal, decisively shifting public opinion against him over the last two weeks. Congress faced mounting pressure to impeach.

The morning after the Buffetts' arrival, Graham, exhausted from working with most of her managers until six a.m. to get the paper out, was embarrassed by the introduction her new shareholder had made to her paper, and was concerned about how the meeting would go. But she had planned a lunch for Buffet with Ben Bradlee, Meg Greenfield, Howard Simons, and herself.

Graham considered Meg Greenfield her closest friend, but referred to her as "a lone fortress...no one ever really got to know Meg." Greenfield, the editorial-page editor of the Post, was a short, chunky woman with cropped dark hair and a plain no-nonsense face. She demonstrated humor, honesty, toughness, good manners, and modesty.

Howard Simons, the Post's managing editor, was well-known for his sharp wit with Graham. "Howard Simons once said that you don't have to be dead to write obituaries. He was a wonderful person, but he was wicked. He used to tease Kay a lot.

Howard Simons, the Post's managing editor, was well-known for his sharp wit with Graham. "Howard Simons once said that you don't have to be dead to write obituaries. He was a wonderful person, but he was wicked. He used to tease Kay a lot.

"We were eating lunch, discussing acquisitions and media properties. I could tell she was afraid of me, although she had all A's. I mean, they had spent their entire lives devising and constructing defenses around the stock. So I mentioned how the amortization of intangibles made it difficult for media companies because they paid so much for goodwill, which caused issues if they were aware of valuation." Buffett was attempting to reassure Graham that it was difficult to acquire media companies because the accounting burdened would-be acquirers. "And Kay was bragging. She stated, 'Yes, the amortization of intangibles caused us a problem,' or something similar. Howard asked her directly, "Kay, what is the amortization of intangibles?"And at the time, I loved it. She was just frozen. She was paralyzed. Howard was enjoying it. So I jumped in and explained what amortization of intangibles meant to Howard. And when I finished this description, Kay said, 'Exactly!'."

Buffett enjoyed outthinking Simons, short-circuiting the game, and indirectly and subtly defending Graham. Graham's tight little smile softened. "From that point forward, we were best friends. I was Sir Lancelot. That was one of the highlights of my life. Turning defeat into victory for her."

Buffett met Graham about an hour after lunch, then texted to comfort her. "I said, 'Kay, George Gillespie arranged for you to gain control of the A shares. But,' I continued, 'I also know that it is so important to you in this world that you will worry about it regardless of what you have. It's your entire life. And so I said, 'I'm telling you that even though these teeth resemble Little Red Riding Hood's wolf fangs, they're actually baby teeth. But we'll simply take them out. Just have the orders come in this afternoon, and we'll white out some things. I'll never buy another share of stock unless you're okay with it. I knew that was the only way she'd ever be comfortable." That afternoon, Buffett, who had spent $10,627,605 to acquire 12% of the company, signed an agreement with Graham not to purchase any additional Post stock without her permission.

In the evening, the Buffetts were scheduled to attend one of Graham's famous dinners, this one for forty guests in honor of Warren and Susan. Despite her personal insecurity, Graham was regarded as Washington's greatest hostess, owing primarily to her ability to help people relax and enjoy themselves. Despite her exhaustion and the temptation to cancel, she had a small party for me tonight. That was her way of reciprocating. And when she hosted a party, she could invite anyone she wanted. Anybody—the President of the United States, anyone."

"She traveled widely in the world, so found occasions to give dinners," said Don Graham. "If she had gone to Malaysia, she would have prepared a dinner for the prime minister when he visited town. The ambassador would look up what they did the previous time, and there was always a meal at Mrs. Graham's house, so there would be another one. Someone would publish a book, someone would celebrate a birthday, and she'd host a dinner because she enjoyed hosting dinners. Graham used the dinners to make new friends and introduce people to one another. "She would sort of adopt people in different administrations," Don recalls. However, Richard Nixon led this administration. Graham had made few friends there, aside from Secretary of State Henry Kissinger, and he had to justify socializing with her.

"So all of a sudden I'm at the Madison Hotel with Susie, and around five o'clock, someone slips something under the door that describes the party I'd been invited to weeks before. The bottom says 'black tie.' I didn't have that, needless to say. So here comes this pathetic Nebraska guy in a business suit. He is attending a black-tie dinner in his honor, and he will be the only one who does not wear a black tie. So I called her secretary in a panic.

"Her secretary is a very nice lady. She says, "Well, let us put on our thinking caps." While I was trying to cross the street to find a store that was open to rent me something, and nothing was open," Graham's assistant, Liz Hylton, called another local store and found something suitable.

The Buffetts left the Madison Hotel and were driven down Embassy Row, passing mansion after mansion. The taxi turned onto Q Street, passing the historic Oak Hill Cemetery, where Phil Graham is buried. Around the corner, they saw a row of historic nineteenth-century townhouses with tiny manicured gardens. It was early November, and the leaves glowed with russet, amber, and gold. The taxi ride into Georgetown was like crossing the border into a Colonial-era town. Dumbarton Oaks, the ten-acre Federal estate where the United Nations conference was scheduled to take place, was tucked into the cemetery's corner and sprawling down its tree-swagged hill.

The taxi turned left at the corner, between two stone gateposts. The view ahead was breathtaking. As the taxi began to crunch its way up the wide sweep of white pebbled drive, the Buffetts noticed in the distance a dignified three-story cream-colored Georgian mansion with a green mansard roof. The broad lawns that surrounded it extended all the way to the top of Georgetown's Rock of Dumbarton, allowing the house to look down on the cemetery. To the right, down the hill past a deep colonnade of trees, were the neighborhoods that led to the old Buffett house in nearby Spring Valley, and just beyond that, Tenleytown, where Warren had delivered papers at The Westchester and stolen golf balls from Sears.

The Buffetts were led through Graham's front door to join the other guests, who were enjoying cocktails in the living room. Asian art from her mother's collection hung everywhere on eggshell-white walls draped in blue velvet curtains, alongside a Renoir painting and Albrecht Dürer engravings. Graham began introducing the Buffetts to her other guests. "She told them nice things about me," Buffett says. "Kay went to great lengths to make me feel at ease. [Yet] I was very uncomfortable."

He had never been to a gathering of such formality or grandeur. When cocktail hour was over, Buffett felt no more at ease crossing the hallway to the massive dining room where Graham hosted her famous parties, its paneled walls lit by the glow of tapered candles in bronze sconces. This setting was more intimidating than the living room. Crystal candlesticks and armorial porcelain gleamed on the round walnut dining tables, but the guests Graham had invited overshadowed the beauty of the setting. At any given time, the room could be filled with a variety of U.S. Presidents, foreign leaders, diplomats, administration officials, Congressional members of both parties, senior lawyers in town, and people chosen from her group of perennial friends—Ed Williams, Scotty Reston, Polly Wisner,31 Roy Evans, Evangeline Bruce, Joseph Alsop, as well as people like the Buffetts who, for one reason or another, suited the occasion or were interesting to her.

Buffett found himself seated next to Edmund Muskie's wife, Jane, an obvious dinner companion given that the Buffetts had entertained her husband in Omaha. On his opposite side was Barbara Bush, whose husband was the US Ambassador to the United Nations but would soon become the Chief of the US Liaison Office in Peking, with the important task of guiding the US through the delicate process of renewing diplomatic relations with China. Graham pressed a button to signal the kitchen, and waiters began to circulate among the antique Georgian tables, serving. Warren attempted not to gape at the protocol. "Susie is over there sitting next to a senator. And he's trying to make out with her, putting his hand on her leg and all that. But I'm dying because I have no idea what to tell these people. Barbara Bush couldn't have been nicer. She could tell I was uncomfortable."

The waiters began to follow an American version of service à la russe, serving the first course, then a fish course, and finally the main course, all on trays from which diners served themselves. Classes continued as wine was poured to the sounds of Washington chatter. The waiters added and removed unfamiliar sterling implements, such as fish knives. As they served him food he would never eat and wines he would never drink, the meal became more complicated and intimidating. Graham's other guests were relaxed and at ease, but Buffett was completely intimidated by the time dessert arrived. Then came the coffee he did not drink. His discomfort turned to terror when, as she did at the end of each evening, Graham stood up and read an articulate, witty, polished, personal, and original toast to her guest of honor, which she had obviously put a lot of thought into writing but delivered with a lack of confidence. The guest of honor was expected to stand and toast his hostess in kind.

"I didn't have the courage to stand up and offer a toast, as you are supposed to do. I totally blew it. I was incredibly uncomfortable. I even considered throwing up. I couldn't stand up in front of half the cabinet and speak. I wasn't up for it. All he wanted to do was escape. As he and Susie said their goodbyes, they had the impression that the hicks from Nebraska would be the talk of Georgetown long after they left.

"This Senator was still attempting to score with Susie as we were leaving, and he was so focused on explaining how she should come down to the Senate and see his offices that he opened the door to a closet and walked inside. That was my introduction to Washington."

While the formal, glittering society that surrounded the powerful Mrs. Graham unnerved and made him uncomfortable, Buffett had never been one to hide his enthusiasm. Susie Buffett must have realized quickly that her husband wanted more of this world.

THE GIANT

Omaha and Los Angeles, 1973–1976

Howard Buffett was one of the few people who prospered in the wake of the 1929 stock market crash. His son's star was rising as the century's second great crash occurred.[1] However, the world had changed; even in business, stardom had become synonymous with fame. Buffett had ended his partnership during a media boom in the United States, when cable had transformed television, newspaper companies were going public, and advertising was still in a golden age of selling to a monolithic audience, with nearly the entire country sitting down together on Tuesday nights to watch Happy Days.

Buffett had entered the media business as an investor with a natural affinity for it. However, as he entered a new, post-partnership phase of life, the publicity he received from the Forbes story in 1969, followed by the Supermoney profile, allowed him to reap the benefits of the discreet use of profile-raising press. He was now a subject of media interest, not just a media investor, and no less a figure than Katharine Graham was paying attention and taking him seriously, bringing him into the orbit of one of the most important newspapers in the United States.

Graham, as she often did with powerful men, sought his assistance. Buffett required little encouragement.

"The first time she was going to speak to the New York Society of Security Analysts, I went over to her apartment in New York on a Sunday morning to assist her with her speech. She was a basket case. She was terrified that all these men would be there, and she would have to stand in front of them. She always struggled with public speaking. The funny thing was that she had a great sense of humor and was very intelligent, but she would freeze up in front of a large crowd. Especially if she thought they were going to ask her about numbers."

According to Robert Redford, who met Graham for the first time to discuss the Watergate film All the President's Men, she had a "tight-jawed, blue-blooded" quality that demanded her privacy not be violated. Why, Redford wondered, "did she keep making speeches and accepting awards?"2—especially because she was terrified to do it.

Buffett sat in the living room of Graham's large apartment, which is on the upper floor of the modern UN Plaza and overlooks New York's East River. They began working while surrounded by Agnes Meyer's collection of Asian art and antiques.

"She kept imagining the questions they would ask, such as how much you pay for your newsprint per ton. She assumed it was a quiz. And I said it makes no difference. So you're paying the same as everyone else for newsprint. But that was a big deal. She was simply convinced. I kept trying to steer her away from trying to remember facts. "Just have a theme." Graham wanted to emphasize that good journalism generates good profits. Buffett snorted as he refocused her. "You know, good journalism does not conflict with good profits, or something." Forget about everything else. I just tried to convince her that she was far smarter than all those dumb males out there. That was what initially bonded us.

In an ironic turn of events, Buffett became Kay Graham's personal Dale Carnegie instructor. He, of all people, could empathize with someone who would freeze in front of a crowd. Furthermore, Susie's gentle tutelage over the years had taught him a more subtle way of dealing with people. He understood how to anticipate their reactions and phrase things in a nonthreatening manner. His letters, which had always been self-conscious, were now more eloquently written and compassionate. He had learned to listen, show interest in others, and converse about topics other than stocks. It helped that Graham truly fascinated him.

Graham announced after they had finished preparing and rehearsing that she would be attending a party at the Agnellis' that night. "You might find the sightseeing entertaining," she told me. "Why don't you come with me?" Buffett was always open about how uncomfortable and out of place he felt at glamorous events, and how uninterested he was in attending them. So he told Graham, "Yes, I'll go." That evening, he left his Plaza room to pick up Graham and take him to the Upper East Side.

"We were this very improbable couple—her in her mid-fifties, me in my early forties—and we arrived at this apartment, which was more than an apartment; it was like a triplex, and it was enormous. And everyone was bowing and scraping at Kay. There were all the characters from La Dolce Vita's party scene. I was the designated walk-on, the potted plant. You wanted it to move in slow motion so you could see everything. Gianni Agnelli, the Fiat chief, and his wife, Marella, were absent. It almost felt like a costume party, but it wasn't."

Buffett returned to Omaha after discovering Graham's new side. As he got to know her on a more personal level, he realized she was a bundle of contradictions. "Fearful, but determined. Patrician, but democratic. Wounded by those she cared most about." He was surprised at how much she still talked about her ex-husband a decade after his suicide.

"When you first met her, she would frequently get off on the subject of Phil, much like Charlie would. And she described him in terms that were difficult to believe, given how badly he treated her. But as I got to know her better, she told me everything about him and their relationship. She couldn't see herself in the same league as him. She felt like a fraud, pretending to be in the same room as him. They spent a lot of time with the Kennedys, and she felt like she didn't belong there. Anything he said was funny, and everything he did was correct. He used to chop up the children right in front of her, and she wouldn't stop him—the whole thing."

Given Buffett's own childhood experiences, it seems almost inevitable that he and Graham, who suffered the consequences of a cruel, neglectful mother and years of abuse at the hands of a sadistic husband with untreated bipolar disorder, would be attracted to one another. He knew how to behave around her in a non-threatening manner. By the spring of 1974, she had begun to shift her allegiance from her other advisors to him. In turn, he seized the opportunity to teach business to the CEO of the Washington Post Company, as if he had always wanted to play Pygmalion: his very own Eliza Doolittle. He was more patient than Henry Higgins and gently coached her while sending Kay and her son Don helpful, interesting articles.

As Buffett's influence grew, Graham noticed that the phrase "Warren says" made some of her board members shudder. However, Buffett hoped to be invited to join that board. When Tom Murphy approached him about joining the Cap Cities board, Buffett declined, saying he was waiting for the Post. Murphy dutifully informed Graham, who "felt dense" because she hadn't figured it out herself.

***

Susie proposed that instead of taking on additional business responsibilities, her husband would sell some of their stock and donate the proceeds to a worthy cause. While riding in a taxi with him in Washington, D.C., she pointed out philanthropist Stewart Mott, who ran the Stewart R. Mott Charitable Trust, which donated funds to causes such as peace, arms control, population and family planning. The Buffetts were now wealthier than Mott, who began with $25 million. "Why don't you quit?" Susie said. "Stewart Mott is doing all these other things now and he doesn't have to work every day." But Warren was unable to give up; he relied on his belief that $50 million today would be worth $500 million someday. Nonetheless, he was not completely estranged from his family or insensitive to his wife. He had detected some vibrations from Susie, indicating that she desired more from her life. With Peter progressing through high school, Warren told her, "Susie, you're like someone who lost his job after 23 years. "Now, what are you going to do?"

The answer, she said, was to sing. Her nephew Billy Rogers had made her some instrumental guitar tracks so she could record herself and listen to her performances. Rogers had been playing jazz guitar at Mr. Toad's, Spaghetti Works, and other Omaha clubs, and Susie, like him, had become a fixture in the local music scene. But when she started practicing, "I was scared, really scared," she admitted. "I was bad." She had last performed in public ten years ago at a fundraiser at Central High. So she sought coaching and focused on contemporary love songs and ballads. Susie made her debut as a chanteuse in July, in front of a friendly crowd at a private party in Emerald Bay. "People seemed to like it pretty well," she said.6 Her husband was overjoyed to see his friends praising his wife's abilities.

While the Buffets were in Emerald Bay that summer, Warren invited Graham to pay her a visit as part of a trip to Los Angeles to speak at an analyst meeting. Buffett had been dancing around his office at Kiewit Plaza for days ahead of time, happy and excited as a child on Christmas Eve, sensing Graham would approach him about joining the Post board.7

The Buffetts' house at Emerald Bay, down a steep driveway set well back from the beach, still had the feel of a modest rental house, with few personal touches that spoke of a family. Warren had no idea what kind of impression the place would make on Graham, who owned several massive, impeccably decorated and maintained mansions, including the farm at Glen Welby and a vast, shingle-style waterfront estate in Martha's Vineyard.

Apparently, he must have convinced his wife that they would have to make an extra effort for Graham. The first morning after Kay arrived, Susie awoke at an unusual hour and pretended to be domestic: she cooked a full breakfast for the three of them, which both Buffetts pretended to consume. Her husband spent the rest of the day engrossed in Graham, discussing newspapers, journalism, and politics, and urging her to invite him to the board.

At some point, he set down his newspapers, put on a bathing suit purchased specifically for the occasion, picked up a brand-new beach umbrella purchased in Graham's honor, and left the house with Graham to walk the hundred or so yards down a steep path to the shore to join the family. Previously, his attitude toward the ocean was as follows: "I think having the ocean nearby is an attractive feature, and it's fun to listen to at night, and so on. But actually getting into it—I think I'll save that for my old age." But now, after sitting on the sand for a while and looking at the water, he waded gamely into the Pacific. According to all reports, Susie and the Buffett children "went into convulsions of laughter" at the odd sight.

We don't know what Susie thought about this extraordinary gesture. But Warren's explanation is on record: "Only for Kay," he says. "Only for Kay."

On Sunday morning, they dropped their business manners, and Susie sleep walked through cooking bacon and eggs for Graham, eating nothing herself, while Warren sat nearby spooning chocolate Ovaltine from a jar.8 After breakfast, he and Graham resumed their conversation. Graham eventually told him that she wanted him to join her board but needed to wait for the right time. She was aware that some of her board members, including André Meyer, would not welcome Buffett. But he asked, "When is the appropriate time?"This forced her to make a decision. So, in short order, they agreed that Buffett would join the board of the Washington Post Company. He felt elated.

Buffett drove Graham to the Los Angeles airport that afternoon after dropping off his family at Emerald Bay. "On the way, she suddenly looked at me like a three-year-old child. Her voice and eyes changed, and she said, basically pleading, 'Just be gentle with me, please don't ever assault me.' I later learned that Phil and some people at the paper would push her buttons just to watch her fall apart, either for their own ends or for pure entertainment. Phil's behavior was cruel, the rest was manipulative. It was simple to do; the button still worked."

Buffett officially joined the board at the end of the summer, on September 11, 1974, propelling him from a star investment manager in Omaha to an official adviser at one of the world's most important media companies. Even at the first meeting, he could tell Graham was constantly pleading with the board for help. Buffett reasoned, This won't do. You cannot put yourself in that position as CEO. But he still didn't know her well enough to say anything. Instead, he learned about the Post board, which was full of prominent and influential people, and began to tiptoe his way past the powerful, jockeying men who were used to dominating Graham. He was a quiet board member who used his skills behind the scenes.

At the time, Buffett was preoccupied with much more than Kay Graham and the Washington Post. Investors had expected the market to rally in 1974, but instead it was in full collapse. Pension fund managers had reduced their share purchases by over 80%. Berkshire's own portfolio appeared to have undergone a severe hedge trimming, with nearly one-third lost in the second Great Crash, which occurs only a few times per century.

Munger kept his partnership open after Buffett closed his. Now its value is plummeting. His performance had always been more volatile, both up and down, than the market's. For the past few years, he had produced decent but unspectacular returns. But by 1974, Munger was in trouble, with his partners losing nearly half of their money.9 Like Ben Graham half a century before, he felt compelled to recoup their investment.

"If you're put together properly, you have a fiduciary gene like Warren and me," says the man, "and if you've told people, 'I think I can get you extraordinary results,' then you really hate the idea of not delivering for them."

As for himself, "Certainly, the quoted value of my capital decreased. I didn't like it, but think about how many years could pass—what difference does it make in the end if I have X dollars or X minus Y? The only thing that bothered me was that I knew how difficult it was for the partners. That was what killed me—the fiduciary aspect of my position."10

Munger still had approximately twenty-eight limited partners, including some family trusts. To recoup half of his capital losses, he would need to more than double the remaining stake. The value of Blue Chip Stamps would have a significant impact on his ability to accomplish this.

Bill Ruane's Sequoia Fund was also in trouble. It began with $50 million from Buffett's former partners and invested wisely by buying large positions in undervalued stocks such as Tom Murphy's Capital Cities Communications. This was not the type of stock that money managers who had piled into glamour television and electronics stocks a few years prior were now purchasing. They had galloped all at once straight the other way, into the arms of the "Nifty Fifty," a small group of the largest, best-known corporations.

"In this business," Ruane said, "you have the innovators, the imitators, and the swarming incompetents." The imitators and the swarming incompetents were now in charge, and the stocks that Ruane and his partner Rick Cunniff had bought in 1970 had been cut in half.

Compounding their problems, they had purchased a seat on the New York Stock Exchange just before seat prices plummeted. The timing of Sequoia's launch was obviously unfavorable—Ruane had agreed to start up just as Buffett was closing due to a lack of opportunities. Sequoia had consistently underperformed the market, cumulatively by a significant amount. The Sequoia Fund's worst year was 1973, when it lost 25%, compared to the market's loss of 15%. It was on its way to another disastrous year in 1974. Bob Malott, Ruane's largest supporter, was outraged. He was already known as a "ballbuster" in Ruane, Cunniff for calling to report minor discrepancies in his family's accounts. Now, he berated Ruane for purchasing a seat on the exchange and for his poor performance with such vehemence that Ruane feared he would withdraw his capital from the firm. Buffett, on the other hand, remained calm, knowing that Mr. Market's opinion of a stock's price at any given time had no bearing on its intrinsic value. He knew which stocks Ruane and his partners had purchased and was confident that they had made sound investments.

Buffett's 1969 meeting of the Grahamites at the Colony Club, while not exactly an ego boost due to the snooty staff, did provide mutual support in a difficult market. Since then, Buffett had given them the name Graham Group; Ed Anderson had planned the third outing in Williamsburg, and Charlie Munger the fourth in Carmel, California. Buffett instituted biennial meetings in 1971. Out of loyalty, he allowed Ruane to invite Malott—a favor that is normally prohibited—and Malott and his wife, Ibby, joined the next meeting in Sun Valley in 1973, which was organized by Rick Guerin.

Malott, who was deeply impressed by the entire situation, remained in Ruane's employ, although his complaints continued at a frequency and volume that made Ruane fearful of his defection. By the end of 1974, the market had fallen by more than 25%, but the Sequoia Fund had managed to produce a smaller loss than the market.

Nonetheless, the market's cumulative toll on the Sequoia Fund was such that Henry Brandt and John Loomis, Carol's husband, who had both gone to work there, feared the worst and abandoned what appeared to be a sinking ship.

Forbes captured Buffett's attitude in an interview that November, which began with a juicy quote: Buffett replied, "Like an over-sexed man in a harem," when asked how he felt about the market. "This is the time to start investing." He went on to say, "This is the first time I can remember that you could buy Phil Fisher [growth] stocks at Ben Graham [cigar butt] prices." He felt this was the most significant statement he could make, but Forbes didn't include it; a general audience wouldn't understand the references to Fisher and Graham.17 When Forbes asked for specific stock ideas, Buffett turned "A water company is pretty simple," he said. Blue Chip owns 5% of San Jose Water Works. The reporter fell for the bait; San Jose Water Works appeared in the story with no mention of the earlier piece implying that he had purchased it using insider information.

Despite his enthusiasm for the market so far in 1974, he had only invested a trickle of money, primarily into Studebaker-Worthington, Handy & Harman, Harte-Hanks Newspapers, and Multimedia, Inc., while also increasing his Coldwell Banker position. He increased some of his other holdings by ten to twenty percent. He also acquired 100,000 shares of Blue Chip from Rick Guerin. "He sold me at five bucks because he was getting squeezed," Buffett tells me. "That was a brutal period."

The "harem" comment had a double meaning. While now was the time to start investing, Buffett could mostly look but not touch. One of National Indemnity's business partners, an aviation broker, had gone wild, selling money-losing aviation insurance policies. The company attempted to stop the agent by revoking its authority, but was unable to do so for several months.18 The accounting records were in shambles, and the losses were unclear. National Indemnity had no idea how much the "Omni affair" would cost, but worst-case estimates ranged up to tens of millions of dollars. The hope was that they would be much lower, as National Indemnity did not have tens of millions. Buffett was sweating.

His problems worsened dramatically within a few months, by early 1975. Chuck Rickershauser, a partner at Munger's law firm, now known as Munger, Tolles & Rickershauser, called him and Munger to inform them that the Securities and Exchange Commission was considering filing charges against them for violating securities laws. What appeared to be a brewing but manageable problem had now escalated into a full-fledged emergency.

Rickershauser began doing legal work for Buffett and Munger during the See transaction. He had recently been fighting a rear-guard action after an SEC staff lawyer called and asked him a few questions.

Rickershauser, assuming the situation was routine, directed the man to Verne McKenzie, Berkshire's controller.

When McKenzie answered the phone in Nebraska, he found the head of the SEC's Enforcement Division, Stanley Sporkin, the much-feared "tough cop" of the business world, on the other end of the line. Sporkin appeared to spend his evenings hunched droopy-eyed under a desk lamp, personally drafting the charges against large corporations that, for the first time in American history, had scared a remarkable number of them into settling with the SEC without ever setting foot in court.[20] On the phone, he questioned McKenzie on a wide range of subjects, from Wesco to Blue Chip to Berkshire and beyond. His tone was not friendly, but McKenzie assumed this was his normal behavior. McKenzie, on the other hand, had the impression that Sporkin believed that if you were wealthy, you had done something wrong.

Rickershauser nearly died when he learned that Sporkin, rather than a staff lawyer, had personally called and grilled McKenzie for several hours. Sporkin's batting average had established his jowly profile as one of the most recognizable in American business. In practical terms, he had more power than his boss, the SEC chairman.

What appeared to have piqued the SEC's interest was a nearly two-year project in which Buffett and Munger attempted to delicately untangle the many strands of spaghetti that connected the various companies they owned. Their first attempt had been to merge Diversified, the smaller chunk, into Berkshire Hathaway. By 1973, Diversified had become little more than a vehicle for purchasing Berkshire and Blue Chip stocks. However, the Diversified transaction had been delayed due to the Securities and Exchange Commission's approval, which was required. Munger had assured Buffett it was nothing serious. He instructed Rickershauser to "invite anyone in the SEC" who had questions to contact him directly, "if this will expedite his work and clearance of our papers."

Instead, over the next eighteen months, the SEC staff appeared to have nosed around looking at Blue Chip Stamps and other investments, concluding that Buffett and Munger had deliberately smashed up the Wesco-Santa Barbara deal by offering a high price for a quarter of the stock with the intention of acquiring the rest. At least, that was how it appeared to Santa Barbara, because it had apparently turned into Blue Chip to the SEC.

For the first time, they all realized that Blue Chip was in trouble.24 No sooner had Buffett achieved the glory of joining the Post board than his and Munger's need for legal services was about to grow at breakneck speed. Rickershauser, who already knew what it was like to work with Buffett, once told a colleague, "The sun is nice and warm, but you don't want to get too close to it."25 He would spend the next few years testing what became known as Rickershauser's Law of Thermodynamics.

In February 1975, the SEC issued subpoenas and launched a full-blown investigation into Blue Chip's purchase of Wesco: "In the Matter of Blue Chip Stamps, Berkshire Hathaway Incorporated, Warren Buffet [sic], HO-784." The commission staff speculated that Buffett and Munger had committed fraud: "Blue Chip, Berkshire, Buffet [sic], singly or in concert with others...may have engaged in acts which have, directly or indirectly, operated as a device, scheme, or artifice to defraud."

The commission's lawyers zeroed in on a theory that Blue Chip had planned to take over Wesco Financial from the beginning but had not disclosed that fact; that Blue Chip's purchases of stock after the Santa Barbara deal dissolved must have been "tender offers" that were never registered with the SEC.26 This latter charge was most serious and carried with it the risk that the SEC would file civil fraud charges not only against Blue Chip

Sporkin had a choice when it came to taking action against a specific target. He had the option of going to court or reaching an agreement. A settlement allowed the target to apologize without officially admitting guilt. It neither consented to nor denied the charge of fraud, but agreed to accept a penalty. Further, when agreeing to a settlement, the SEC could choose whether to name the individuals involved or simply reach an agreement with the company without naming anyone. Being named in a settlement may not mark the end of someone's career, but there will be no elephant-bumping afterward. Buffett began a desperate fight to save his reputation after being elevated to the high and mighty by Supermoney, Forbes, and the board of the Washington Post.

Instead, the investigation expanded. Buffett was forced to open his files under subpoena, which, of course, represented a massive and comprehensive collection of documents, equal in size and scope to everything he had ever collected. Buffett felt persecuted after lawyers from Munger, Tolles sifted through trade tickets, information about recent stock purchases, memos to bankers, letters to See's Candies, notes to Verne McKenzie at the textile mill, and other documents and shipped them off to investigators in Washington, D.C. A massive, lumbering giant pursued him and Munger in a nightmare. To survive, they had to outrun it.

Munger, Tolles, and the SEC exchanged letters as if they were shuttlecocks. Buffett maintained a calm demeanor, but his back problems were bothering him. Munger did not conceal his agitation.

By March 1975, the investigation had led to command performance at the SEC. Betty Peters was hauled inside. "Is your lawyer here?"" they inquired. "No. Do I need a lawyer?"She replied. "Well, everybody comes with a lawyer," they explained. "Don't you want to know what happened?"" she asked. They interviewed Peters without a lawyer.

Munger was summoned. For two days—also unaccompanied—what additional legal counsel could Charles T. Munger possibly require?—he attempted to defend Blue Chip against allegations that it was attempting to derail the Santa Barbara merger, and explain why Blue Chip paid more than was strictly necessary for Wesco's stock. Yes, Blue Chip considered acquiring control, he admitted, but those plans were only "remote and contingent" until the Santa Barbara merger failed. Given his and Buffett's role in speaking with Vincenti, and their admitted "wooing" of Betty Peters and the Casper family's votes, the conversation became somewhat circular. Munger had a regrettable habit of interrupting and lecturing SEC staff lawyer Larry Seidman. "We wanted to look very fair and equitable to Lou Vincenti and Betty Peters," he said.27 However, the SEC lawyers had never met the intractable Lou Vincenti. They couldn't possibly understand. What about your blue-chip shareholders? Seidman asked. Seidman saw no reason for Blue Chip to be so generous to Wesco shareholders, as the company's stock was largely owned by arbitrageurs at the time.

These were investors who had purchased Wesco stock with the expectation that it would rise to the price Santa Barbara had offered once the transaction closed. They hedged their bets by shorting Santa Barbara stock, just as Graham-Newman had previously purchased Rockwood stock in exchange for cocoa-bean warehouse receipts. But when the Wesco deal failed, it was as if the price of cocoa beans had plummeted. Why would the Arabs benefit from keeping the price high?

Munger reached for his ultimate weapon: Benjamin Franklin. "We did not believe that our obligation to shareholders conflicted with our desire to be fair. We have Ben Franklin's idea that honesty is the best policy. It had a sort of shoddy mental image of us trying to reduce the price."

Seidman appeared perplexed by this argument, and even Munger admitted that the specifics of what had been done did not look promising. He begged Seidman to look at the big picture. "As you look at the overall records, we go way beyond any legal requirement in trying to be fair with people and observe the niceties of fair-dealing. I simply hope that you will reach the conclusion that this averages out as not an appropriate case for any sort of prosecution..." If there is any defect, it is not intentional."

When Buffett appeared, they asked him why he and Munger hadn't allowed Wesco to enter the tank so they could buy it cheaply. "I think the general business reputation of Blue Chip would not have been as good," Mr. Buffett said. "I think someone might have been sore about it." But why should he care? Because, according to Buffett, it was "important how Wesco management feels about us." You could argue that it makes no difference because we own the controlling interest. Lou Vincenti does not necessarily need to work for us... If he thought we were slobs or something, it wouldn't work."

Now Buffett, who, like Munger, surprised the enforcement lawyers by arriving alone, made himself useful by returning to Washington several times, patiently explaining how Blue Chip worked, expounding on his investment philosophies, and discussing his childhood in Washington. He made a good impression on Seidman, but not on the senior SEC staff lawyer in charge of the investigation, who was known as a "tiger" whose motto was "They shall not pass." He found these arguments unconvincing. The senior investigator's attitude was that nobody who did anything close to the line would ever get by him.

The SEC staff continued to investigate. It appeared to be fascinated by the complexities of Buffett's empire. It even began to investigate whether he had traded on inside information about San Jose Water Works. The staff began kicking around Source Capital, the closed-end investment fund that Munger had purchased a 20% stake in as a cigar butt and helped turn around. By then, the stock market had recovered. Ruane's Sequoia Fund had made a huge comeback in 1975, rising nearly 62% compared to 37% for the market. Munger had nearly repaid his partners' investments in 1975, with a 73% gain. He took no fees for himself and was dissolving his partnership. Explaining why their convoluted empire made sense based on the low prices paid for stocks at the time became more difficult as the market recovered. The investigation continued to grow hairy legs, much like a tarantula.

Rickershauser had been studying a chart depicting all of Buffett and Munger's complex financial interests. Buffett sat in the center, buying Blue Chip, Diversified, and Berkshire, putting them in so many pockets that Rickershauser shuddered. Everyone knew Buffett, the great white shark, couldn't stop himself from buying these stocks. If he found ten dollars and saw a share of Blue Chip, Berkshire, or Diversified, he charged, grabbed, and threw it into the nearest drawer. After he and Munger had purchased the first 25% of Wesco, Rickershauser finally advised Buffett to buy stock only through formal tender offers to avoid the appearance of impropriety. Buffett's complex cross-holdings made it appear as if he was attempting to hide something. Rickershauser looked at the crazy diagram and worried, "There's got to be an indictment in there somewhere." He didn't think the SEC would have enough evidence to convict, but it would be incredibly simple to accuse.

In the grand scheme of things, Munger was a two-bit player, with a fraction of Buffett's financial stake. He had been caught as a minor accomplice. However, because Blue Chip was his territory, he was a principal in the Wesco saga and thus played a central role in the SEC's questioning. He admitted to Seidman, "We do have a very complicated set of business affairs, and I believe we have learned, to our regret, that that may not be too smart. But we tried to keep all of the balls in the air, properly synchronized with the other balls, and handled them honorably."

Despite the pair's protests and the fact that it found nothing wrong with the San Jose Water Works or Source Capital transactions, the SEC continued. A prosecutor's tiger now advised Sporkin that the SEC file charges against Buffett and Munger individually. He was unconvinced by Buffett and Munger's testimony and concluded that they had purposefully scuttled the Santa Barbara merger by overpaying for Wesco stock. He was unconcerned about, "Who was harmed?'" explanation for paying more for the stock, and thought the pair's explanations of events were too fine-grained.

Rickershauser addressed Sporkin directly. He begged him not to prosecute Buffett and Munger, "individuals who value their good names and reputations as their most priceless possessions," because "many people, probably most people, assume evil conduct on the part of anyone civilly prosecuted by the commission." Even if Buffett and Munger agreed to a settlement without admitting or denying the charges, filing them would cause "terrible, irreversible damage" because "the good reputation of the commission automatically and inexorably destroys the good reputation" of the defendants. "A giant's strength should be used with great discretion," he told them. "The risk from inadvertent oversights in business should not become so onerous that people who value their reputations are deterred from participation." He begged to save Buffett and Munger reputations by agreeing to a consent decree on minor, technical disclosure violations on Blue Chip's behalf only, as long as no individuals were named.

Panic in Buffett's mind is only imagined. Within the office, he tried to maintain an imperturbable façade so as not to alarm his office staff, any of whom could be interviewed by the SEC.

Rickershauser worked like a stevedore to present his clients as upstanding citizens from ideal model families. He submitted biographies of Munger and Buffett to the SEC, emphasizing their charitable work, the numerous boards on which they served, Howard Buffett's tenure as a Congressman, and the millions of dollars in taxes that Buffett had paid to the government since filing his first tax return at the age of 14. Buffett had obviously been working on this document like his life depended on it.

Munger had resigned. "If a policeman follows you down the road for five hundred miles," he told Buffett, "you're going to get a ticket."

Rickershauser suggested to Sporkin that Mr. Buffett and Mr. Munger's complex financial interests may make it difficult to follow legal requirements, despite their efforts to do so. "They now wish to simplify their holdings as rapidly as they can."

In their talks, SEC lawyers had already discussed what simplifying meant. "Sometime in the future, it is certainly possible that we would merge Blue Chip with Berkshire," Buffett had responded to their question, "but Blue Chip has a lot of legal problems, and until some of those are resolved, it may be difficult to arrive at what we would feel reasonably certain would be a fair exchange ratio. If I had my way, they would eventually be merged. So, hopefully, we will have more or less the same businesses as we do now, but with fewer complications. I don't like the complications. It may appear that I prefer these complications. I don't have a great staff to handle everything. "It seemed simple while we were doing it," he said, "but it's not simple anymore."

When asked by an SEC investigator if Buffett had "contingency plans" to simplify things, Munger replied, "Oh, he does." "He has about twice as big a contingency plan as before this investigation started."

According to Sporkin today, Rickershauser was instrumental in reviewing the proposal. The guy "was one of those few lawyers that I've met in life that, whatever he told you, you could go to the bank on." Sporkin regarded Rickershauser as not only a brilliant lawyer, but also one who was honest, straightforward, and upright, incapable of deception. Rickershauser told Sporkin that Buffett was "going to be the greatest person that Wall Street has ever seen" and that "he was the most decent, honorable person you would ever meet." Sporkin would have dismissed this as rhetoric if it had come from anyone else, but when it came from Rickershauser, he saw it as both sincere and probably well-judged. Sporkin believed he had a greater duty to absolve than to convict. He believed that a prosecutor had to distinguish between a fundamentally honest person who had made a mistake and a criminal. When it came to criminals, his job was to put them away. His assessment of Buffett and Munger was that while they had made mistakes, they were not criminals.

So the giant gently tapped Blue Chip's wrist.

The company agreed to an SEC finding in which it neither admitted nor denied that it failed to notify investors that it was attempting to disrupt the Santa Barbara merger by purchasing Wesco's stock, and that Blue Chip artificially propped up Wesco's market price over the course of three weeks. Blue Chip promised never to repeat what it had not admitted to doing. The consent decree did not name any individuals. The event's publicity was trivial and would fade. Buffett and Munger's records and reputations remained clean.

Two weeks later, the SEC appointed Buffett to a high-powered panel to investigate corporate disclosure practices. It was forgiveness and, above all, a new beginning.

AND THEN WHAT?

Omaha, 1977

Susie's friends claimed she created a separate life for herself within her marriage to accommodate Warren's obsessions. As one person said, Warren's "real marriage was to Berkshire Hathaway." There was no denying that. Despite their discomfort, their routine had proven effective. At least, it worked for them until another of Buffett's obsessions, with Katharine Graham, became so strong that it pushed Susie off stage. That's when she finally acted.

Warren now spends a lot of time with Graham at black-tie events in New York and Washington, or at her house for Kay Parties. Despite his residual awkwardness and cackling laugh, he was introduced to Kay's circle of powerful, celebrated friends and acquaintances, who opened his eyes to a new world. "I met Truman Capote," he says of the author of Breakfast at Tiffany's and In Cold Blood, who had thrown the legendary Black and White Ball in Graham's honor at the Plaza Hotel in New York, which became known as the "party of the century." Capote had been a confidant of many rich international society women.

"He'd come down to her place and sit there, this little guy hunched down on the sofa, talking in this unbelievable voice. He did, however, know all of their secrets. He really knew them because they all spoke to him. He was extremely cunning. Kay was the only person he really liked. Unlike the others, he didn't think she was a phony.

Buffett was even summoned by former British ambassador Walter Annenberg, who owned Triangle Publications, which included the Philadelphia Inquirer and Buffett's childhood favorite, the Daily Racing Form.

"Walter read about me in the Wall Street Journal in 1977." I received this letter addressed to 'Dear Mr. Buffett,' and he invited me to Sunnylands, his California estate. Buffett was intrigued after hearing stories about the famously thin-skinned ambassador from Tom Murphy and Kay Graham, both of whom had reason to be aware of his sensitivity to offense. Annenberg's father appeared in several stories. Aside from the publishing interests he had left to his son, Moe Annenberg had also left a legacy of scandal and shame. He had been imprisoned for tax evasion in connection with a racing wire he ran that telegraphed horse race results to bookies across the country. It was of questionable legality, was linked to organized crime, and contributed to his reputation as a mobster. Moe Annenberg pleaded guilty and was led into jail wearing a homburg hat and chains, allegedly to protect his son from prosecution alongside him. Walter later claimed that his gaunt, pain-racked father, dying of a brain tumor in St. Mary's Hospital, whispered as his last words, "My suffering is all for the purpose of making a man out of you."1 Whether this scene was true or not, Walter acted as if he believed it.

Walter was consumed by a desire to restore his family's honor and was now responsible for the support of his mother and sisters. He learned the publishing business through trial and error and proved to be an exceptional entrepreneur. He created Seventeen magazine, followed by a booklet-sized magazine called TV Guide, which satisfied the public's desire for information about television schedules, shows, and celebrities. By the time he met Buffett, he had not only become a great business success story, but also attained the pinnacle of social respectability after Richard Nixon appointed him ambassador to England's Court of St. James's. Despite restoring the family name, he was unable to overcome the personal scars of his legacy.

Buffett arrived at Sunnylands eager to meet Annenberg. The two already had a connection: Annenberg was the brother of Aye Simon, the "spoiled, spoiled" widow of Ben Rosner's former partner Leo Simon—the same Aye Simon whom Rosner had decided to screw when he sold Associated Retailing to Buffett for too little because she was no longer his partner. Buffett had only met Aye Simon once, and she had entertained him in her vast, art-filled apartment in New York City. Maids tiptoed back and forth carrying silver trays of cucumber sandwiches. Aye explained to Buffett that her "Pop," Moe Annenberg, once had his goons, known as "the boys," "take a few shots at Leo" to improve his attitude toward him. She told Buffett that bullet holes can still be seen on a building on a certain corner of Michigan Avenue in Chicago. Aye asked her son to join the Buffett partnership. Warren, "envisioning bullets" if he turned in a year of bad results, "tap-danced" his way out of the situation.

Her brother, Walter, had spent decades cultivating a reputation for propriety that was as far from the image of bullets on Michigan Avenue as you could get. Sunnylands was a vast and opulent desert oasis in Rancho Mirage, California. In a garden adorned with images of Mayan sun gods, Rodin's bronze sculpture of Eve stood in a reflecting pool, her face covered in shame. Hundreds of floating bromeliads gazed at her from the water beneath her feet. Annenberg had entertained Prince Charles at Sunnylands, hosted Frank Sinatra's fourth wedding, and provided peace and quiet for his friend Richard Nixon to write his final State of the Union address.

"He had a courtly air about him and was very formal. We went outside by the pool and Walter sat down. He was immaculately dressed, and everything he wore appeared to have been purchased that morning. He was about seventy at the time, and I was around forty-seven. And he said, in a nice, kind tone, as if he were speaking to a young man he was attempting to assist, "Mr. Buffett, the first thing you should know is that no one likes to be criticized. That was setting the ground rules for getting along."

Nothing could be simpler for Buffet. "I answered, 'Yes, Mr. Ambassador. I got it. Don't worry about that one.

"Then he started on 'Essentiality.'

"'There are three properties in the world,' he said, 'that have the quality of 'essentiality.' They are the Daily Racing Form, TV Guide, and Wall Street Journal. And I own two of three.

"What he meant by 'Essentiality' was that, even during the Depression, he saw the Racing Form being sold for two and a half bucks down in Cuba."

The Racing Form was of such high quality because there was no better or more comprehensive source of information on handicapping horses. "It sold one hundred and fifty thousand copies per day for about fifty years. It cost over two dollars, but it was essential. If you were going to the racetrack and were a serious handicapper, you needed the Racing Form. He could charge whatever he wanted and people would pay it. Essentially, it is the same as selling needles to addicts.

"So every year, Walter would go in and say, 'Mirror, mirror, on the wall, how much should I raise the Racing Form price this fall?'"

"And the mirror would always tell Walter, 'Charge another quarter!'"""

Back then, you could buy the entire New York Times or Washington Post for a quarter. Nonetheless, Buffett, the New York Times, and the Washington Post were regarded as successful businesses! That meant the Daily Racing Form was a fantastic business.

Annenberg enjoyed owning two of the Essentials, but wished to own all three. The visit to Sunnylands marked the start of a recurring reel in which he and Buffett discussed whether and how they could jointly purchase the Wall Street Journal.

Nonetheless, "the real reason that he had me out there was to send a message to Kay."

The Annenbergs and the Grahams had once been friends.2 Then, during the confirmation hearing for Annenberg's appointment as ambassador to Great Britain, the Post's muckraking columnist, Drew Pearson, penned a column saying that Annenberg's fortune "was built up by gang warfare" and repeated an unsubstantiated rumor that his father had paid $1 million a year in protection money to mob boss Al Capone.3 Annenberg, enraged, accused Graham of using her paper as a political "President Nixon may have had his flaws," Annenberg said afterward, "but he paid me the highest honor that anyone ever paid the family." 4

The morning of his confirmation hearing, Annenberg read another Pearson column that detailed his editorial vindictiveness at the Philadelphia Inquirer. He clutched his chest as his face turned purple. His wife believed he was having a heart attack.5

Annenberg called Graham and asked for a retraction. She tried to console him, but claimed she never interfered with the editorial page. That evening, after a stressful day of hearings in which Walter had to defend himself one by one against the points raised in the Pearson columns, the Annenbergs reluctantly went to Graham's Georgetown mansion to attend a dinner party for fifty guests to which they had been invited several weeks before. Upon entering Graham's gilded splendor, Annenberg—who cared deeply about protocol and was well prepared to take offense that night—did indeed take offense when Graham seated someone else next to her and seated him between two of her friends, Evangeline Bruce, wife of the outgoing British ambassador David Bruce, and Lorraine Cooper, wife of a prominent senator.

Annenberg's prickliness toward anything he perceived as a slight resembled in many ways his friend Nixon's lack of perspective. He and Nixon also shared an unfortunate inability to charm and disarm.6 Thus, a feud that had been brewing between Mrs. Annenberg and Vangie Bruce over the decoration of the ambassadorial residence soon escalated and overshadowed the meal.7 Compounding this, Mrs. Cooper offended Annenberg by allegedly implying that he wasn't rich enough to be ambassador.8 Feeling set up, Annenberg stalked out of the party early and stopped speaking to Kay Graham.

"Kay was upset about it. She really wanted to hang with Walter. Kay wasn't looking for fights with anyone. This was not her style. She enjoyed being in charge, but she was not one to brag. She liked big shots, especially big-shot guys. So she was uncomfortable fighting him. But she also wanted Walter to know that she was not going to tell Ben Bradlee what to write in the newspaper.

"So by the time I went out to see him, he was thinking about having a book commissioned about Phil Graham, and how Phil's teeth were in a funny way."

Philip Graham's teeth.

Walter believed that having gap teeth indicated mental instability. And if Walter had a theory, you did not challenge it. Walter liked me, and one of the reasons was that I never disagreed. If Walter said black was white, I would say nothing.

"So I became the go-between with Kay." Annenberg expected Buffett to convey the message that publishing a book about Phil Graham's teeth would be show business.

"Meanwhile, he could not have been kinder to me. He put me in this luxurious guest room. And he led me into his office, where he had a small display in a glass case of a Prussian coin, a pocket knife, and another item. It was all his grandfather had in his pocket when he arrived in this country from Prussia. And he said, 'Everything you see here is a product of that.' Walter had rehabilitated his family within a few years. He made his father proud. And that was his main goal in life: to make his father proud.

Buffett understood Annenberg psychologically but failed to notice certain similarities between the ambassador and himself. This was most likely due to their significant differences in other areas. Annenberg's lack of humor, fondness for opulence and formality, and hostility toward the Grahams distinguished him from Buffett, and they were ideologically opposed. Nonetheless, beneath their similarly paper-thin skins, these two astute businessmen shared a strong desire to prove themselves—both professionally and socially— and a reverence for fathers whom they felt the world had unfairly treated.

They started a correspondence. Annenberg would come to regard himself, in an avuncular way, as training Buffett in philanthropy. He believed that rich people should give everything away before they died, lest their appointed stewards fail to fulfill their obligations.9 He wanted to warn Buffett about the potential pitfalls. Mistrustful by nature and always testing people—again, similar to Buffett in both respects—Annenberg had conducted extensive research on failed foundations and the perfidy of trustees. He sent Buffett examples of foundations that went wrong after their benefactors died, and stock market chit chat and formal correspondence. Buffett, a budding philanthropist and publisher whose newspaper had won a Pulitzer Prize for exposing a major charity's poor stewardship, read this material with interest. Annenberg expressed to him his fear of an imperial administrator for his money, one who would commit what he called "foundation rapings" after his death.

"Dear Warren," he wrote, thanking Buffett for sending an article about Mac Bundy, who ran the Ford Foundation in a way that Annenberg found abhorrent.10 "Henry [Ford II] once described McGeorge Bundy as 'the most arrogant son of a bitch in the country, who developed the lifestyle of an Arabian prince on Ford Foundation money.'"11

Annenberg spent a lot of time planning to avoid being double-crossed after he died. He informed Buffett about the Donner Foundation, whose executive director had changed the foundation's name to the Independence Fund, effectively erasing the founding donor.12 "I respectfully suggest you make sure that no one can tamper with the name of your foundation after you're gone," he wrote. "Remember Mr. Donner."

Buffett had a different perspective on the foundation he and Susie had established. "It should not have been named the Buffett Foundation," he added later. "It was foolish to name it the Buffett Foundation. But it would also be foolish to change it now, because it would be too obvious."14

He and Annenberg shared a fascination with media and publishing. TV Guide was Annenberg's most valuable asset. It had the same "essentiality" as the Daily Racing Form but reached a much larger audience. When Buffett learned that Annenberg was planning to sell TV Guide, he and Tom Murphy flew to Los Angeles to see if the imperious ambassador would sell it to them for fifty percent.

However, Annenberg preferred to be paid in stock rather than cash. "And we wouldn't give our stock away," Murphy says. "Warren never gave away his stock, and neither did I if I could help it. You don't get rich that way." Giving stock in exchange for TV Guide meant, literally, that they believed it would earn more in the future than the share of Berkshire Buffett traded for it. Paying with stock demonstrated contempt for your own business in comparison to whatever you were purchasing—unless you were paying with stock that had become wildly overpriced.15 As a rule, the way they ran their businesses and dealt with their shareholders ensured that this did not occur, so they did not purchase TV Guide.

Nonetheless, Buffett continued to serve as a liaison for Annenberg and Graham, who had been taking Buffett to etiquette school and preparing him for these elevated activities. She called him constantly to discuss the smallest details of her life. He paid a visit to her rambling shingle mansion on Martha's Vineyard, which overlooks Lambert's Cove, and they frequently traveled together to business meetings, including a trip to Niagara Falls. He took her to visit one of his totems, the Berkshire textile mills. As the flirtatious, fifty-nine-year-old Kay was spotted tossing the forty-six-year-old Warren her house key at charity benefits and the two were seen together ever more often in public, by early 1977 the gossip columns had taken note, and, as Graham put it, "eyebrows shot up."

Friends observed, as one put it, that the pair had "zero chemistry." Yet Graham discussed an affair candidly with her friends.17 She was obviously sexually insecure but tried to project the opposite, as illustrated in her memoir.18 Her mother, notably, was famous for pursuing (and flaunting) obsessive, flirtatious, but platonic relationships with powerful, brilliant men. Buffett would have a history of romanticized friendships with women. Whatever genuine romantic elements the relationship with Kay may have had at first, it was ultimately a friendship.

However, publicity disrupted Susie and Warren's delicate equilibrium. Whatever else was going on in her life, she still cared deeply about her husband. Furthermore, Susie needed the people in her life to rely on her. She now felt discounted and trivialized. But she would never let herself look like the rejected Daisy Mae in public. She remained at Kay's house when she traveled to Washington, smiling benevolently no matter how frequently her husband was seen with Kay. Susie's friends believed she was indifferent. Others believed she needed to be in control, or that Warren's relationship with Kay gave her permission to live her own separate life in peace. Nonetheless, she made it clear to several friends that she was angry and humiliated. Kay dealt with the situation by sending Graham a letter granting her leave to pursue a relationship with Warren—as if Kay had been waiting for such permission.19 Kay showed the letter to people as if it absolved her of any responsibility.20

Susie was now focusing on a serious singing career. In 1976, she approached the owners of Omaha's French Café, a formal restaurant housed in a renovated warehouse in the city's quaint, cobblestoned Old Market district, and asked to sing in their lounge, The Underground. They were astounded, but gladly agreed. Susie had previously hosted a benefit there for African relief, barefoot, in gingham, and wearing a bandanna.21 Advertisements appeared, confirming rumors that Susan Buffett would become a chanteuse. "This is very scary, but I've always wanted to live to the hilt,"22 she told a reporter ahead of her first performance.

She "lacked self-confidence," according to one reviewer, but her "Ann-Margret youthfulness," "stylized jazz," and desire to please won over the audience in the French Café's stone-lined basement cabaret. The audience was described as being made up of "uncritical friends" and people who attended out of curiosity to see a rich man's wife.23 Within weeks, Bill Ruane told her, "This is Broadway Bill. I've set you up with auditions in New York." She spent three weeks as an opening act at Yellow Brick Road, See Saw, Tramps, and The Ballroom. She replied, "I've been asked back, but I'm going to be flexible about the timing. Perhaps after the first of the year. First, I want to find a musical director and put together a package. Now I understand how difficult it is, but I'm hooked, and when I return, I want to go for six months without stopping."24 She signed with the William Morris talent agency.

That summer, both Buffetts traveled to New York. Warren played bridge in Kay's apartment, and Susie sang while Warren watched her from the audience. Her musical career brought them together; he was overjoyed by her success. They considered purchasing an apartment in a landmarked building just off Fifth Avenue in New York City, which would have provided them with a permanent base in the city—but decided to pass.25

Susie was indeed loose with the timing, and by the fall of 1976, she had made no plans to return to New York. She still spent more time in Laguna than Warren. Moreover, her "clientele" in Omaha was a distraction. Susie was besieged with hours of stories about Howard's 38½ years with Leila; Howie, who was running a backhoe outside Omaha; and Dottie, who seemed to be sleepwalking through her life, so passive that when she called and reported a big fire at her house, Susie had no sooner hung up the phone than she wondered whether Dottie had called the fire department. Susie called her sister back. Dottie said no; she had only considered calling Susie.26 And all these responsibilities came solely from the family; Susie's "vagrants," lonelyhearts, and local relationships outnumbered them by a long shot. Instead of making a commitment to sing in New York, she scheduled another round of performances at Omaha's French Café in the spring of 1977. As a result, the Omaha World-Herald magazine decided to do a cover story on the millionaire's wife who decided to become a cabaret singer in her middle age. The reporter, Al "Bud" Pagel, began with a routine story, approaching Susie's friends and asking them basic questions about her life. What makes Susie sing? He wanted to know. Like many people in Omaha, he had heard rumors about Susie's extracurricular activities.27 Susie's friends were "defensive" and "protective."

Eunice Denenberg "bristled" and declared, "Susie is one of those old-fashioned GOOD people that many people nowadays don't believe exist." So they attribute some of their own baser behavior to her because it bothers them." Worshippers formed a circle to protect the saint. Pagel admitted that, when confronted with such an aggressive pack of defenders, he felt compelled to throw a handful of mud at Susie's best white party dress.

Susie sat down with Pagel on the couch by the fireplace in the Buffetts' family room, which had a Ping-Pong table and posters on the wall reading "Love Is Here to Stay" and "Damn Everything but the Circus." She struck him as vulnerable.

"Being a performer is kind of the opposite of being a mother," she told him during the interview. "I am not used to caring for and feeding Susan Buffett. Maybe I'm a source of encouragement for someone who is about to say, 'I want to try something but I'm afraid to do it.' I'm just another person who tried something but was afraid to do it." She paused. "That's the only story I have." 30

The reporter indicated he was looking for a bigger story than that. Instead of muzzling his curiosity, her pit-bull defenders had piqued it. Susie opened up and talked about herself for five hours, without mentioning her personal relationships. Nonetheless, by the end, she expressed surprise at what she had done: the woman whose lips were sealed like mollusks when people tried to pry her open at dinner parties had given herself to Pagel. In the process, she won him as a friend.

When the story was published, the magazine's cover read: What Makes Susie Sing? and included a photo of her with the caption, "Who knows?"" expression, tentative smile, eyes tilted upward, avoiding the camera. In the photographs, Susie looked away from the camera, gazing down at Hamilton with a small smile and her hands on the piano keyboard. Something inward, an uncertain dream, had taken the place of the open-jawed grin that appeared in almost every photograph of her.

Susie showed up on Pagel's doorstep the morning the story was published, clutching a large box of See's Candies and as excited as a child about the portrait he had drawn of her. She added him to the guest list for her opening at the French Café and sent him an invitation.31 He and other guests recall her as looking young and radiant that night, wearing a brunette shag wig and a sequined dress that hugged her newly svelte figure. Raven-feather lashes fluttered around her bright eyes. The expression on her face suggested that she was discovering that caring for and feeding Susan Buffett wasn't so bad. By now, she had honed her craft as a performer, and she smiled seductively as the audience hooted and hollered between songs. Her guests saw the glow of a woman emerging from behind her role as a wife and mother onto the stage of her life. The audience enjoyed her tender delivery and smooth liquid styling of pop standards and sentimental favorites. Her medley repertoire includes "Daddy" songs like "My Heart Belongs to Daddy" and cabaret classics like "What Are You Doing with the Rest of Your Life?"" and her personal favorite, Sondheim's "Send in the Clowns"—moisturized eyes. Susie's torchy side emerged as she sang, and she opened up emotionally. Buffett, standing in the back with his arms crossed, watching his wife vamping, flirting, and romancing her audience, remarked in good humor, "This is pretty good of me to let her do this."

However, by the summer of 1977, Susie had not followed up on her New York opportunities. Warren assumed it was because his spontaneous wife refused the structured time commitments required of a professional singer. Some of the Buffetts' friends questioned whether Susie's pretty voice and appealing stage presence could compete with established singers of higher caliber. While Susie enjoyed performing, Warren hoped his wife would become a singing star with a recording career. Her ambitions had always been directed toward others rather than herself. Meanwhile, Susan Buffett's care and feeding were handled separately and in private.

That was the issue. Being the wife of a wealthy man provided her with opportunities to pursue a successful singing career. However, it also opened doors that allowed others to peer into her personal life, which she would rather keep closed. Warren could stay at Kay Graham's house and be seen as her date in public with complete freedom, while the gossip columns did nothing but wink. Susie, by contrast, lacked such freedom because she was married. The women's movement had altered many aspects, but not that. With her privacy eroding, the question of how to deal with her increasingly conflicting emotions was tearing her apart.

Stan Lipsey, their Sun publisher friend, was also struggling with his marriage. He and Susie sat on park benches in the mornings, sharing secrets. Both of them were interested in Eastern thought and the human-potential movement, which had originated at the Esalen Institute in Big Sur, California.34 They persuaded Warren, Stan's wife, Jeannie, and Susie's sister, Dottie, to attend a weekend workshop in a Lincoln hotel. The goal was to contact myself. The workshop began with an exercise to encourage people to open up to one another without judgment, which is one of Susie's skills. Warren's reaction to such an outpouring was unlike his wife's.

"There were five hundred people who had traveled from up to a thousand miles away. And they started doing all these crazy things. First, we had to find a partner. And one of them was to begin talking, and the other person, no matter what, just kept saying, "And then what?"

"So I paired up with this nice woman from Oklahoma, and she began talking. Then she pauses, and I ask, "And then what?"' Within ten minutes, she is sobbing uncontrollably. I've destroyed her simply by saying, "And then what?"' It felt like I was bored with her. I felt like I was running a torture facility or something."

Buffett eagerly left his tear-stained companion, having misinterpreted this exercise in every way imaginable. The leader told participants to find another partner. "Now, when I hear the leader say, 'I want you to choose a partner of the opposite sex,' Lipsey says, 'I'm looking for someone attractive.'" Buffett stood looking around, as if unsure what to do. "The next thing you know," Lipsey tells me, "he's paired with this very heavy woman."

"She was wearing a muumuu and weighed around 400 pounds. My job was to get on the floor. The leader then instructed this woman to give me the "gift of her weight," which meant she flopped right down on top of me. There was a whale coming straight at me. I was just--back! It proved to be the gift that never stopped giving.

"In the other room, people were barking like dogs. I could hear Dottie—who was so nervous she couldn't say hello to anyone—trying desperately to bark."

After being blindfolded and led through the streets of Lincoln to experience sensory deprivation, Susie and Stan gave up. They all ran away to a movie theater to watch Annie Hall—"a nervous romance"—and "spent the rest of the weekend gorging ourselves on fried food and ice-cream sundaes," according to Lipsey.

During the summer of 1977, while Buffett continued to run bridge marathons at Kay Graham's apartment in New York, Susie stayed away from home at all hours.

That August, Howie married Marcia Sue Duncan, despite her father's warnings that she wouldn't be happy with a guy who dug basements for a living and drove a pickup truck around with a couple of big shaggy dogs in the cargo bed. After sending the newlyweds a gift, Kay Graham called Buffett to express her disgust that Howie had misspelled three words in the thank-you note.

Susie gave her final performance in Omaha over Labor Day weekend, opening for singer-songwriter Paul Williams at the Orpheum Theater. In a pink chiffon gown, she smiled and beguiled as her smooth contralto oozed romantic jazz ballads like warm honey, "languorous and sensual." She greeted the audience with "Let's feel like we're in love, okay?" But in a small, gossipy city like Omaha, that announcement could have gone unnoticed.

Susie appears to have realized how disorganized her life had become that autumn. She stayed out until four a.m., driving all the way to Wahoo—where she had spent her wedding night—and blasting music from her Porsche's radio before returning to her lonely home at dawn.36

Susie's best work involved sharing a piece of her soul with others. She panicked and reached out to others, who took on her problems. Friends listened to her agonize in parks, on walks, and during long drives. She accumulated small sums of money and gave them to friends to hold, as if planning an escape. She entered Berkshire Hathaway's office through the doorway of her tennis friend Dan Grossman, sobbing and seeking advice, while her husband sat in his office next door.

Susie appeared to understand on some level that she was endangering many people by telling them more than her husband about his troubled marriage and his disillusioned wife's secret yearnings. "You can't tell Warren," she told one person. If you love him, you will not hurt him this way. If he ever found out, he would commit suicide.37

Susie was so powerful, so beloved, and so evident in Warren's devotion to his wife, and Susie had trained everyone to believe that he was helpless without her, that people accepted this burden. Some did it instinctively, some out of loyalty, and some reluctantly, half aware of the flaws in her reasoning. But they all felt responsible for keeping her secrets under the guise of Warren's vulnerability.

However, nothing seemed amiss at Gardiner's Tennis Ranch in Arizona, where the Graham Group was meeting that fall. The majority of the group—now commonly known as the Buffett Group—had long accepted the notion of "Warren-o" and "Susan-o" as an affectionate couple who lived separate lives. This year proceeded as usual, with Susie and the other wives in attendance. Bill Ruane presented Warren's Fortune article "How Inflation Swindles the Equity Investor."38 Buffett explained that stocks, especially stocks of companies that can raise prices as their costs increase, are the best protection against inflation—but their value is still eroded by severe inflation, a problem he referred to as a "giant corporate tapeworm."39 During a social break, Marshall Weinberg told Warren and Susie about his niece, who was living and working on a "Oh!" Susie gushed. "I'd love to do that! It would be fantastic to live so simply and help those poor people on a reservation in this way." Warren looked at her. "Sooz, I'll buy you one," he said, deadpan 40.

At age 47, Warren had already accomplished everything he had ever desired. He was worth $72 million. He ran a $135 million company, and his newspaper had won two major journalism awards. He was one of Omaha's most influential men, and his national profile was growing. He was on the boards of the largest local bank, the Washington Post, and several other companies. He had been the CEO of three companies and had successfully bought and sold more stocks than most people could recall in a lifetime. Most of his original partners were now extremely wealthy.

All he wanted was to continue making money for the thrill of it, without changing anything else in his life. He knew Susie thought he was obsessed with money, but she had always been, and they had managed to live their lives in such a way that they respected their differences while remaining a cohesive team for twenty-five years. Or so it appeared to him.

Later that fall, after the Buffet Group meeting, Susie visited a high school friend in San Francisco. She stayed about four or five weeks. One relationship after another appeared to bind her to California. Billy Rogers, her nephew, had moved to the West Coast to pursue his musical career. Susie had promised to help him kick his heroin addiction, but she was concerned about him alone in California. Bertie Buffett, who was now married to Hilton Bialek, lived in both San Francisco and Carmel. Jeannie and Stan Lipsey were considering moving to San Francisco. Rackie Newman, Susie's widowed friend, now lives there. Susie Jr. and her husband lived in Los Angeles. Peter, on whom she had relied, was now a sophomore at Stanford in Palo Alto. She and Warren had already settled in California, with a vacation home in Emerald Bay, south of Los Angeles. With fewer and fewer ties, she returned to Nebraska. The house in Omaha was eerily empty: as soon as Peter left for college, Hamilton the dog ran away and moved in with one of his friends.

Susie discovered San Francisco to be a beautiful, creative, and spirited city during her extended stay there. From every angle, the bay and ocean, bridges and sunsets, and rickrack rows of Victorian houses beckoned, "Come look at me." A delirious mosaic of people, neighborhoods, architecture, culture, art, and music declared, "You'll never be bored in San Francisco." The San Francisco thermometer never read 110 degrees. The city air raced through your lungs, fresh and liberating. In the 1970s, San Francisco was the epicenter of mind-expanding, hedonistic spirituality, a magnet of tolerance where people didn't judge one another.

Susie looked at several apartments. She returned to Omaha and went to the French Café, where she had been singing. She spoke with Astrid Menks, the maître d' on Monday nights, and a sommelier and occasional chef. She and Menks got along well; Astrid served her tea between sets at the French Café and catered a dinner at the Buffetts' earlier that year when Peter Jay, the new British ambassador to the United States, came to Omaha. Knowing the Buffetts' preferences, Menks had either delighted or irritated Jay with the carb count of Warren's favorite meal: fried chicken, mashed potatoes, gravy, corn on the cob, and hot fudge sundaes.

Susie now asked Astrid to check in on Warren and cook him an occasional meal. Then she spoke with him and told him she wanted to rent a funky little cubby hole in Gramercy Tower on Nob Hill as a base in San Francisco.

Warren's proclivity to not listen, to hear only what he wanted to hear, worked in Susie's favor when she explained that she would not leave him. They weren't "separating." They would remain married. Nothing would change if she had her own room, a place to be herself in San Francisco. She simply wanted to surround herself with a city rich in art, music, and theater, she assured him. Their lives were already taking such different paths, and they both traveled so much that he would barely notice the difference. With the children grown, it was time for her to focus on her own needs. She repeatedly reminded him, "We both—we both—have needs." That part was undoubtedly true.

"Susie wasn't completely leaving, that was the thing. She simply wanted a change."

In all of Susie's travels, in her talk of buying this or that place, he had never imagined she would leave, because he would never abandon her. "Wanting a change" and "not totally leaving" were ambiguous Buffett Esque statements they both used to avoid feeling like they were disappointing anyone.

Then she left.

Susie traveled to Europe for several weeks with her friend Bella Eisenberg. She returned to Emerald Bay for Christmas with her family before leaving to return to Europe, where she met Tom Newman, her friend Rackie's son, in Paris. Susie and Tom, who would soon join his mother in her new San Francisco home, became fast friends.43 It became clear that for Susie, having her own place in San Francisco did not imply renting a pied-à-terre to escape to for a week every now and then. Warren struggled to care for himself, so Susie Jr. returned to Omaha for a few weeks to help. Since the Quicksilver wedding, she had spent much of her marriage crying to her mother. Big Susie was gently guiding her out of the marriage while also freeing herself from many of the conventions that had tied her to her own marriage. Susie

Jr. tried to explain to her father that, given how much time he and her mother had spent apart, his life would not be significantly different from before. However, Warren had not previously considered himself and Susie to be living virtually separate lives. Susie, in his mind, was his everything. She certainly acted like she did when they were together. So it was difficult to accept that Susie wanted her own life and would not always be available to him.

Susie and Warren spoke for hours by phone. Now that he understood, Warren would have done anything she asked to get her back, including moving to California and learning to dance. Unfortunately, it was too late. He couldn't give her what she desired, whatever it was. She explained it in terms of her freedom, her need to be separate, and her desire to fulfill her needs and discover her true identity. She couldn't do it while caring for him full-time. So he wandered aimlessly through the house, barely able to feed or clothe himself. He usually arrived at work with a raging headache. He maintained his composure in front of the staff, although he appeared to be having trouble sleeping. He called Susie every day, weeping. "It was as if they couldn't live together and they couldn't live without each other," according to one individual.

Susie was torn when she saw her husband helpless and devastated. She mentioned to a friend, "I might have to go back." However, she didn't. They both had needs. One of her needs was for her tennis coach to relocate to San Francisco. She moved him into a small, separate apartment down the street from her own. His understanding was that this was only temporary, and that once Susie divorced, they would marry.44

While Susie rambled, she made no move to divorce. "Warren and I don't want to lose anything," she explained to a friend who asked about her plans. She wasn't talking about money; she already owned enough Berkshire stock. Susie was the type of person who never took away from her life, but rather added to it, and she never considered acting differently now.

Meanwhile, she called Astrid Menks at the French Café repeatedly. Have you called him yet? Have you called him yet?45

Susie was very familiar with her target. Astrid Beaté Menks, born in West Germany in 1946 after her parents "walked out of Latvia when Russia took it," emigrated to the United States at the age of five with her parents and five siblings aboard a converted, broken-down battleship. Her first sight of America as they entered the harbor was a massive object approaching through a fog bank—the Statue of Liberty.

The Menk's family was assigned sponsors in Verdell, Nebraska, where they lived on a farm with a pot bellied stove but no electricity or indoor plumbing. When Astrid was six, the family relocated to Omaha. When their mother was diagnosed with breast cancer, Astrid and her two younger brothers enrolled in the Immanuel Deaconess Institute of Omaha, an all-purpose facility run by Lutheran sisters that included a retirement home, an orphanage, a hospital, a church, and a recreational hall. Her father, who spoke little English, worked as a groundskeeper while the children stayed at the orphanage. Astrid's mother died in 1954. When Astrid was thirteen, she was moved to three different foster homes. "I can't say I had wonderful experiences in foster care," she tells me. "I felt more secure at the children's home."

Menks attended the University of Nebraska after high school, but she dropped out due to financial constraints. Following a stint at Mutual of Omaha, she worked as a buyer and manager for a women's clothing store, albeit dressed in thrift-store finds. She eventually ended up working as a garde manger in restaurants, slicing fifty pounds of zucchini and preparing cold foods. She lived in a small apartment downtown in the Old Market near her workplace, which was convenient because the rusted-out floor of her Chevy Vega had holes through to the street.[46]

She was always broke, but she knew everyone in the warehouse district, which was constantly gentrifying. She was part of a restaurant crowd that would help organize the area's would-be artists, stray singles, and gay men to put on a meal or holiday feast. Astrid, a small-boned, fair-skinned woman with ice-blonde hair and refined features, exuded Nordic beauty with a hint of hard work. At times, she appeared younger than her thirty-one years. She always made light of her personal struggles, but when Susie Buffett met her, she was depressed, empty, and unfulfilled. Nonetheless, when it came to caring for those in need,[47] she could outperform Susie Susie any day.

Menks was terrified because she didn't know where Susie was going with all this insistence on calling Warren. But eventually, she made the call.[48] When she arrived at the door to prepare a home-cooked meal, she discovered a cave full of books, newspapers, and annual reports. Warren, who could not function without female companionship, was desperate for affection; he had tried to fill the void by taking Dottie to the movies and spending time with Ruthie Muchemore, a divorcee and family friend. Nonetheless, he was clearly a lonely, unhappy man who had been emotionally reduced to an eleven-year-old boy. He required feeding. His clothes were a mess. Astrid was the least pushy woman imaginable. But, as Susie had expected, when confronted with a problem, she knew what to do.

Warren later explained why Susie left this way: "It was preventable." It should not have happened. That was my biggest mistake. "Whatever I did regarding Susie's departure would be the biggest mistake I ever made."Some parts are difficult to understand. It was unquestionably 95 percent my fault. It could have been as high as 99%. I wasn't attuned enough to her, whereas she was always perfectly attuned to me. Almost everything had always gone in my favor. My work became more interesting over time. When Susie left, she felt less needed than I had intended. Your spouse will come second. She kept me together for many years and contributed 90 percent to raising the children. Strangely, I believe I had roughly the same amount of influence. It simply wasn't proportional to the time spent. After the children were raised, she effectively lost her job.

"In some ways, it was time for her to indulge in her favorite activities. She did a lot of volunteering along the way, but it never really worked out. She did not want to be Mrs. Big, as many wives of prominent men in town do. She did not enjoy being a prominent woman because she is the wife of a prominent man. She enjoys connecting with others, and everyone connects with her.

"She loved me, and she still does, and we have a wonderful relationship. However, this should not have happened. And it's completely my fault."

Warren discovered that he was still alive with each passing day, regardless of how large the wound was or why it had occurred. So he eventually returned to the one role that suited him best: teacher/preacher. People would listen to him as long as he possessed intelligence and a good reputation.

Buffett resumed writing his annual letter in winter 1978. The previous letter had provided a brief, informative update on how the businesses were doing. He began writing a lesson on how to measure management performance, an explanation of why short-term earnings are a poor criterion for investment decisions, a lengthy dissertation on insurance, and a tribute to his friend Tom Murphy's management skills at Cap Cities. His neediness at the time was almost unfathomable. He reached out to Carol Loomis for companionship, with the intention of making her the letter's official editor. She spent the hours on trips to New York, where they discussed how he wanted to convey these lessons to the people who had stuck with him throughout, those who had put their trust in him: Berkshire Hathaway shareholders.

PART FIVE

The King Of Wall Street

PHARAOH

Omaha, 1980–1986

Five hundred grateful rich people, dressed in black tie and ball gowns, walked up the red carpet to New York's swanky Metropolitan Club for Buffett's fiftieth birthday celebration. With Berkshire Hathaway trading at $375 per share, the Buffetts' net worth has more than doubled over the last year and a half. They could easily afford the space. The Buffett Group included semi-celebrities like Gary Cooper's daughter. Susie had ordered a cake shaped like a six-pack of Warren's favorite Pepsi-Cola. He had asked Don Danly, his old pinball partner, to bring him the balance sheet for Wilson's Coin-Operated Machine Company. Buffett was beginning to collect materials from his early business ventures, treating these objects as totems and showing them to people with a hint of reverence. They seemed tangible proof of himself, reassuring artifacts.

Susie brought her band from San Francisco and took center stage to perform a version of "Shuffle Off to Buffalo" for her husband:

Warren became fed up with candy.

He lacked proficiency with stamps.

The song went on for verse after verse about Buffett's latest caper: packing his duffel and heading to Buffalo to buy an undervalued paper.

Susie's star turn, corny but sweet, marked the start of a new trend. Buffett's family and friends had begun to recount in his presence the list of companies and investments he had amassed like beads on a rosary. The man himself, with brows sprouting like ivy tendrils over the frames of his glasses, appeared less awkward in black tie. He had created a modern Berkshire Hathaway, which churned out new rosary beads like clockwork. Buffett's search for things to buy had become more ambitious, free of the cigar butts and lawsuits of the previous decades. The great engine of compounding worked as a servant for him, at exponential speed and with the approval of a public gaze. The method was the same: estimate an investment's intrinsic value, factor in risk, buy with a margin of safety, concentrate, stay within the circle of competence, and let compounding do the work. These simple ideas are understandable to anyone, but few can put them into action. Even though Buffett made the process appear simple, the technique and discipline behind it required a significant amount of effort from him and his employees. Kiewit Plaza remained at the heart of his business empire as it expanded from coast to coast, from the shores of Lake Erie to the suburbs of Los Angeles—a quiet but never-endingly busy temple of commerce furnished with dinged, scuffed steel-frame furniture and linoleum floors. With each new investment, there was more to do, but the number of people at headquarters remained relatively constant. Buffett remained behind closed doors, protected by Gladys. Bill Scott, who was extremely wealthy, now worked part-time and spent his days playing with his polka band. A new manager, Mike Goldberg, has joined headquarters. Verne McKenzie handled the finances. Except for the occasional meeting in the conference room, which could only accommodate four people, the employees rarely left their cramped offices. There were no conversations around the water cooler. Regarding a period of ease following the scuffle at the Buffalo Evening News, McKenzie stated, "There was never such a time."3 Those who tested Rickershauser's Law of Thermodynamics discovered that the sun was indeed nice and warm, but Buffett was so focused and his mind worked at such a rapid pace that extended conversations with him left them sunburned. "My mind was so tired," one friend admitted. "I had to recuperate from seeing him," said another. "It was like being pounded on the head all day long," said a former employee.

Buffett had the energy and enthusiasm of a restless adolescent; he seemed to remember every fact and figure he had ever read; he persuaded people to volunteer for difficult jobs, then assumed they could perform miracles; and, while remarkably tolerant of others' quirks and flaws, he was less so of quirks and flaws costing him money. He was so eager for results, so confident in others' abilities, and so unaware of how far behind his own they were, that he consistently underestimated people's workloads. Buffett, the sun around whom everyone revolved, was unaffected by Rickershauser's Law of Thermodynamics.

"They say I put pressure on them. I never intend to. Some people enjoy applying pressure. I never do. It's the last thing I want to do. I don't think I'll ever do it, but enough people have told me I do it, so it must be true.

The managers in the hinterlands who ran the businesses that Berkshire and Blue Chip owned were fortunate because Buffett largely ignored them, his management trick being to find obsessed perfectionists like himself who worked incessantly and then ignore them except for occasional "Carnegizing"—attention, admiration, and Dale Carnegie's other techniques. Most would not have wanted it otherwise.

Buffett's stock-picking decisions in the 1970s were defiant bets against pessimism during the great bear market, which was plagued by rampant unemployment and consumer prices rising at an intolerable 15% per year. That bet has finally paid off, thanks to a desperate President Carter, who appointed Paul Volcker as the new Federal Reserve Chairman in 1979. To keep inflation under control, Volcker raised the central bank's discount rate to 14 percent. In 1981, new President Ronald Reagan began sharply cutting taxes and deregulating business, all while supporting Volcker despite the howls of pain his policies were causing. The economy and markets had been in foreclosure for two and a half years. Then, in late 1982, the 1980s bull market began its stampede as stock prices began to catch up with corporate earnings growth.4

Buffett's late-70s spending spree was fueled in large part by a windfall from insurance and trading stamp sales. While National Indemnity thrived, Blue Chip stamp sales continued to fall, but investments made with the slowly dwindling pool of float from prepaid stamps paid handsomely.

The Buffalo Evening News' turnaround eliminated the need for Buffett and Munger to debate whether Blue Chip's largest asset was worth more dead than alive. The News would survive; it now generated a consistent stream of profits. In 1983, they finally agreed on a price for Blue Chip, and Berkshire swallowed it whole—the final step in the great untangling.6 Buffett and Munger were now full partners for the first time, despite Munger being the junior partner by far.

Buffett appointed Munger, who now owns two percent of Berkshire, as the company's vice chairman. Munger also took over as president and chairman of Wesco, a small company compared to the now-bloated Berkshire, but Munger's own. It dangled like a tiny strand of spaghetti from the corner of Berkshire Hathaway's mouth, the only morsel Buffett had yet to swallow. Wesco's shareholders eventually realized that he would get to it someday, and they began to value Wesco's stock at a prohibitively expensive price.

Munger's influence on Buffett's thinking had always surpassed his financial power. They thought so much alike that the main difference in their business behavior was Munger's occasional veto of deals that the more easily enraptured Buffett might have struck. Their attitudes toward their shareholders were identical. With the merger completed, the two men outlined a set of operating principles to Berkshire's shareholders in the 1983 annual report. They referred to them as "owner-oriented principles." No other management told the company's owners these things.

"Although our form is corporate, our attitude is partnership," they declared. "We do not view the company as the ultimate owner of our business assets, but, instead, view the company as a conduit through which our shareholders own the assets." 7

This deceptively simple statement represented a throwback to a previous generation of corporate governance. The modern corporate chief saw shareholders as a nuisance, a noisy or quiet group that could be appeased or ignored. They were definitely not his partners or boss. We don't play accounting games, Buffett and Munger stated. We do not like having much debt. We run the company for the best long-term results. All these sounded like simple truisms, except that so few managers could honestly make all these claims.

In addition, Buffett also wrote that year, "[r]regardless of price, we have no interest at all in selling any good businesses that Berkshire owns, and are very reluctant to sell sub-par businesses"—even if that hurt performance—"as long as we expect them to generate at least some cash and as long as we feel good about their managers and labor relations."8 That was a warning in the guise of a hint to Gary Morrison, who took over from Ken Chace at Berkshire in 1982 after By then, Buffett had shut down the Manchester mill and reduced production in New Bedford by one-third.

"The textile industry would generate revenue for about ten minutes per year. We made half of the men's suit linings in the country, but no one went to a tailor and said, 'I'd like a pin-striped gray suit with a Hathaway lining.' A square yard of cloth from our mill cost more than a square yard from somewhere else, and capitalism is frugal in that way. We'd get supplier of the year awards from Sears, Roebuck, and we'd take them fishing and supply them during WWII, and I was personal friends with Sears' chairman, and they'd say, "Your products are wonderful." And we'd ask, "How about another half-cent per yard?" And they would say, "You're crazy." So, it was a terrible business."

Instead of "generating cash," Morrison begged Buffett for cash so he could upgrade the mills. Buffett said no.

Nevertheless, he clung to the beleaguered mills. As a result, selling one of the company's most profitable businesses, the Rockford Bank, was even more difficult, similar to having a root canal without novocaine. But he had to do it because the Bank Holding Company Act required it in order for Berkshire to continue its non banking interests (particularly in insurance).9 Even so, he kept money with Gene Abegg's picture on it in his wallet afterward.

He was also reluctant to lose Ben Rosner, who had finally retired from Associated Cotton Shops. Rosner's subordinates had made fun of his toilet-paper-picking habits. Once they took command, Associated fell into the tank. For months, Verne McKenzie slogged back and forth to New York's garment district, peddling its soggy carcass.10 Finally, he found a buyer willing to pay half a million dollars to haul away the remains of a business that had only recently earned Berkshire up to $2 million per year.

A few of the Berkshire companies were so self-sufficient that it was difficult to distinguish between a well-run business and one guided solely by the wind. Lou Vincenti, who resisted being managed at Wesco, managed to keep his Alzheimer's disease hidden from Buffett and Munger for several years.

"We didn't see him that often," says Buffett, "so he would get himself psyched up to try to get past that. Also, we didn't want to see it. Charlie and I adored him so much that we didn't want to face it."

"Lou Vincenti was decisive, he was intelligent, and he was honest and shrewd," according to Munger. "And he ran the last savings and loan in California to transition to a computer-run system for depositor accounts, because it was still cheaper to do it manually with community college students working part-time. You can see how that would entice Warren and me. He was cranky, independent, and a wonderful human being. And we loved him so much that, even after we found out, we kept him at his job until the week he was transferred to the Alzheimer's home. He enjoyed coming in, and he was not causing us any harm."11

Buffett and Munger turned this story into a humorous parable, claiming that they wanted more businesses that could be successfully run by an Alzheimer's patient.

Buffett was sensitive to the issue of Alzheimer's. He was very proud of his strong memory; however, his mother began to forget. Her mental state could have been obscured by Leila's tendency to live in the past and create her own ideal reality—her version of Buffett's bathtub memory, in which—whoosh—the plug popped up and bad memories drained away. Her son's success was her greatest joy now that she was in her late seventies, but Warren trembled whenever he had to spend time with her. It was unsurprising, given that old rages flared up occasionally. By now, almost every member of the family had had the experience of picking up the phone and hearing her wrath erupt over the line. Her victims all ran to Susie for comfort, who told them, "You must understand that this happens to other people, not just you. Warren and Doris went through it for years. So don't focus on what she said, because it's false."12

Leila had always left one of her grandchildren: Peter. She occasionally mentioned that he resembled Howard and walked like Howard, which could explain why. The resemblance was only in appearance. Peter had dropped out of Stanford shortly before graduation and married Mary Lullo, a recently divorced woman six years his senior with four-year-old twin daughters, Nicole and Erica. Peter treated them as if they were his own daughters, and they began using the name Buffett, becoming Big Susie's favorites. Warren had been trying to interest Peter in Berkshire for some time and eventually sent his protégé, Susie's former tennis buddy, Dan Grossman, to talk to him about working in the business, but Peter was uninterested; his future lay in music. He cashed in $30,000 of his Berkshire stock to finance Independent Sound, a recording and music production company that scored commercials out of his San Francisco apartment with Mary as his business manager and promoter.

Susie remained close to Peter through his music, while she experimented with the idea of reviving her career, collaborating with producers Marvin Laird and Joel Paley. She took them to Omaha and showed them around the Old Market jazz clubs. They felt as if they were writing an act for "their favorite English teacher." Susie showed no signs of wealth, but because they had heard about a newspaper and See's, they reasoned, "Maybe she'll pay us with candy."

Finally, they decided on an act that Susie would perform at Delmonico's in New York as a benefit for New York University. She wanted them to create an act that reflected her personality: a bohemian, gypsy soul with a wicked, sly sense of humor. In the end, she sang a conventional medley, replacing 1977's soulful, passionate songs with standards: "String of Pearls," "I'll Be Seeing You," "The

Way You Look Tonight," "Satin Doll," "Take the A Train," and "Seems Like Old Times."

Warren smiled as he watched his wife interact with the audience at the benefit. Laird and Paley realized that showcasing his talented, beautiful wife made Buffett proud and happy. It appeared to them that, unlike most show business performers, Susie's performance was not about her ego. Performing allowed her to connect with the audience while also giving something to her husband.15

Laird and Paley, who jokingly referred to themselves as "musical gigolos," became a part of Susie's singing life, meeting Peter and going down to the Laguna house to work with her on her music for the next few years as she considered whether she could make a career out of singing. They never met Susie Jr., who had relocated to Washington, where Katharine Graham became interested and arranged for her to work as an editorial assistant, first at the New Republic and then at U.S. News and World Report. She married again in November 1983, in a lavish ceremony at New York's Metropolitan Club, this time to Allen Greenberg, a public-interest lawyer for Ralph Nader. Greenberg possessed her father's cool analytical bent and resembled someone who lived in a library. Susie's parents took to their new son-in-law right away, and people commented on how much Allen resembled Susie's father—rational, dispassionate, and good at saying no. The newlyweds moved into a Washington townhouse, but rented out the majority of it to other tenants while living in a small apartment. By this point, Susie Jr. had sold all of her Berkshire stock, which was trading for less than $1,000 per share.

Howie's first marriage, like his sister's, did not last. Despondent, he spoke with his father, who told him that a change of scenery would be beneficial and suggested that he work for one of Berkshire's businesses. Attracted to California, Howie accepted a position at See's Candies in Los Angeles. Big Susie sent him to live with Dan Grossman, whom Buffett had installed at one of Berkshire's small insurers in Los Angeles when it ran into difficulties. Howie began mopping floors and performing maintenance before progressing to ordering boxes and getting into various adrenaline-charged scrapes. Buffett informed him that he had to stay at See's for two years. Howie had planned to resign and wait it out, but he did not last long at Grossman's. He moved into the house in Laguna, where he felt more at home.16

By chance, Howie was paired in doubles tennis at Emerald Bay with Devon Morse, a sweet, unhappy married blonde with four daughters. To impress her, he shimmied up a post to change the time on a clock near the tennis court, then fell off and broke his foot. She helped him get home and then came home with some food. They started talking, and he discovered she was attempting to leave her wealthy husband. The marriage that resulted from their relationship was the culmination of a series of Howie-style adventures; the couple removed the children from Devon's husband's home, a gun collector with hundreds of weapons. In 1982, Howie persuaded Devon to relocate to Nebraska, where they were married by a judge, with Buffett and Gladys Kaiser as witnesses.17

Buffett now had six step-grandchildren and was soon joined by a grandson when Howie and Devon had their own child, Howard Graham Buffett Jr., also known as Howie B. Buffett liked children but was awkward and stiff around them, with no idea how to play with or engage them. So he did what he had done with his own children: he left them to Susie, who enthusiastically took on the role of grandmother at family gatherings and quickly added trips to see grandchildren in Nebraska to her already extensive travel schedule.

Buffett took a more active role in Howie's career. Howie initially worked in real estate, but his true ambition was to become a farmer. Buffett agreed to buy a farm and rent it to his son, similar to the arrangement he had with his sharecropper when he was still in high school. Howie trudged through Nebraska, inspecting over a hundred farms and making offers on behalf of his father, who was adamant that a farm be a cigar butt and would not pay a dime more than necessary. Finally, somebody bit into Tekamah, and Buffett put down the necessary $300,000.18.

Despite taking Howie's rent checks, he never set foot on the farm. Like Susie's art gallery, he was only interested in money, not experience. He compared farming as a commodity business to men's suit linings. "No one goes to the supermarket to buy Howie Buffett's corn," he explained.

Buffett's attempt to control his children with money while never teaching them about money may appear odd, but it was the same story as with his employees: he believed any smart person could figure it out. He handed the kids their Berkshire stock without emphasizing its importance to them in the future, explaining compounding, or mentioning that they could borrow against it without having to sell it. Carol Loomis had polished his shareholder letters to a fine sheen by this point, and he undoubtedly believed that these, combined with his own life experience, provided adequate lessons. It probably did not occur to him that his children might require more personal tutoring than his partners.

Buffett was very concerned about what they did with their stock, though, because he and Berkshire were one. Selling the stock meant selling him too. Despite this, he did not want his children to live on Easy Street due to Berkshire Hathaway. Rather, he believed that the futures of his children and Berkshire Hathaway would eventually be linked not through company ownership, but through philanthropy— their stewardship of the Buffett Foundation's stock.

Buffett expressed his feelings about inheritance and philanthropy in a tribute he wrote for the Omaha World-Herald following the death of Peter Kiewit, a near-mythical figure in Omaha. Kiewit's company, Peter Kiewit Sons, Inc., was reportedly the most profitable construction company in the world, once dubbed the "Colossus of Roads."[20] Buffett and Kiewit never did business together, but Kiewit owned the Omaha World-Herald and Buffet served on its board.

Kiewit, a childless workaholic, lived in a penthouse apartment in Kiewit Plaza, Berkshire's headquarters, and commuted to work by elevator. Buffett envied him for this arrangement.[21] Kiewit was another Buffett prototype, a strict taskmaster and penny-pincher in the office who instilled his values through catchy little sayings. The company was his labor of love, and he was often "pleased, but never satisfied." "A reputation is like fine china," he said, "expensive to acquire, and easily broken." When making ethical decisions, therefore, "If you're not sure if something is right or wrong, consider whether you'd want it reported in the morning paper."[22] Kiewit, like Buffett, was obsessed with managing other people's weight.

The main distinctions between them were three: Kiewit was a hands-on manager. He avoided publicity. And he only appeared to be a cheapskate. While in Omaha, he drove a four-year-old Ford and lived like a Spartan to set an example for his employees, but at his Palm Springs vacation home, he drove a Cadillac and led a more-than-comfortable lifestyle.[23] Nonetheless, in many ways, Peter Kiewit exemplified Warren Buffett's ideas about how a life should be lived. When Kiewit died, Buffett's tribute not only honored the man, but also expressed—more than anything Buffett ever wrote—how he wanted to be remembered himself. 24

Kiewit established one of the world's leading construction companies from scratch. Although not the largest, it may be the most profitable business of its kind in the country, a feat made possible only by Kiewit's ability to instill an unwavering commitment to excellence and efficiency in a workforce of thousands.

"Kiewit was overwhelmingly a producer, not a consumer," he claimed. "Profits were used to increase the organization's capacity rather than to provide opulence to the owner.

"In essence, someone who spends less than they earn is accumulating 'claim checks' for later use. At a later date, he may reverse the procedure and spend more than he earns by cashing some of his accumulated claim checks. Alternatively, he may pass them on to others—either during his lifetime through gifts or after his death through bequest."

Buffett wrote that William Randolph Hearst spent many of his claim checks on the construction and maintenance of his castle in San Simeon. He arranged for ice to be delivered daily to the bears in his private zoo, much like pharaohs used their claim checks to build the pyramids. Buffett had pondered the pyramid economy. If he hired a thousand people to construct a pyramid for himself, he says, "It would all go into the economy." Each dime. Many different types of giving and spending are simply variations on that. It's crazy, and it's probably also morally wrong. However, some people believe it is fantastic that you are employing those who are tugging the slabs for the pyramid. And they are making a mistake. It's not productive. They are thinking in terms of input, not output.

"If you want to build pyramids for yourself and take a lot of resources from society, you should pay like hell for it. You should pay a perfectly appropriate tax. I would force you to give back a significant portion of your wealth to society in order to build hospitals and educate children."

Instead, he noted in this article, some who earned the claim checks passed them on to their heirs, allowing hundreds of descendants to "consume far more than they personally have produced; in effect, their whole lifetimes have been spent at the withdrawal window of the bank of societal resources." Buffett found the results ironic.

"I love it," he says, "when I'm around the country club and I hear people talk about the debilitating aspects of a welfare cycle, where some woman had a child at seventeen and now gets food stamps, and we're perpetuating a cycle of dependency. And these same people are leaving their children with a lifetime of food stamps and other benefits. They do not, however, have a welfare officer, but rather a trust fund officer. And instead of food stamps, they have dividend-paying stocks and bonds.

Peter Kiewit left approximately 5% of his wealth to his family, despite making significant contributions to society. The remainder went to a charitable foundation for the benefit of the people in the region where he lived, the same causes Kiewit had supported while alive. Kiewit had ensured that his employees could only sell to one another, so the majority of the company remained in their hands. "Peter Kiewit could not have better served his community and his compatriots," he said.

Buffett admired Andrew Carnegie and John D. Rockefeller as original thinkers in the philanthropic world. Carnegie had established public libraries in impoverished communities across the United States. The Carnegie Foundation sent Abraham Flexner as emissary to study medical education in the United States. When his 1910 paper exposed the shocking state of medical schools, Flexner persuaded the Rockefeller Foundation to donate enough money to revolutionize medical education. Rockefeller also wanted to address issues that lacked a natural funding source. He discovered that poor black colleges, lacking wealthy alumni, had no way of improving themselves. "In effect, John D. Rockefeller became their alumnus," Buffett explains. "He tackled problems without concern of which among them was most popular, and he backed them up big-time."

At this point, the Buffett Foundation had a token $725,000 and gave away less than $40,000 per year, almost entirely to education.26 Susie ran the Buffett Foundation, which reflected their shared belief that money should be returned to society. If Susie had had access to them, she would have distributed large sums quickly. But Buffett was in no hurry. He believed that by allowing the money to compound over time, there would be more to give away later—after he was gone. By 1983, he had a solid argument in support of this idea. Between 1978 and the end of 1983, the Buffetts' net worth increased dramatically, from $89 million to $680 million.

As he became wealthier, requests for money from friends, strangers, and charities flooded Kiewit Plaza. Some were heartfelt pleas from those in genuine need. Others seemed entitled to his money. The United Way, universities, cancer, churches, heart disease, the homeless, the environment, the local zoo, the symphony, the Boy Scouts, and the Red Cross were all worthy causes, but the response was the same: if I did it for you, I would have to do it for everyone. Some of his friends agreed with him, while others were perplexed that a man who was so generous with his time, advice, and wisdom could be so frugal with his money. They said it wouldn't kill him to peel off a few dollars. Why didn't he find joy in giving?

But as long as Buffett was still building the snowball, promising to give it all away after his death was akin to Alice in Wonderland's White Queen's "jam tomorrow". "After he died" was the same as never; another safeguard against mortality, one of Buffett's major concerns. In some strange way, the "White Queen" form of denial reinforced itself. The Buffetts now knew of at least nine friends or relatives who had attempted or committed suicide, or whose family members had done so. Recently, one of his friends' sons drove his car off a cliff on Christmas Eve. Ann Guerin, Rick Guerin's wife, had shot and killed herself just days before their son turned eight. Buffett's preoccupation with suicide was understandable given the circumstances. Nonetheless, he was determined to live as long as possible—and to earn money until the end.

As his fortune grew, Buffett's often articulated and unwavering determination to continue making money at a rapid pace while withholding it from his family and foundation sparked a revolt among his friends. Rick Guerin had written to Joe Rosenfield about Buffett's potential as the world's richest man: "What will Warren do when he becomes No. 1 sled dog and realizes there's more to the world than hair and a small target?" (He believes it's a bull's-eye, but we know better.)"27

When the Buffett Group met in Lyford Cay, Bahamas, between snorkeling and deep-sea fishing, George Gillespie sparked a heated debate by organizing a talk on "The Children (and Charity) Will Have to Wait." Years earlier Buffett had said he gave his kids a few thousand dollars for Christmas each year and told them to expect half a million dollars when he died.28 That, he thought, was "enough money so that they would feel they could do anything, but not so much that they

"Warren, that's wrong," Larry Tisch, one of his former partners, said. "If they aren't spoiled by age twelve, they won't be spoiled." Kay Graham, tears streaming down her cheeks, inquired, "Don't you love your children, Warren?"

Carol Loomis prompted Fortune to address the issue in a cover story titled "Should You Leave It All to the Children?"Many people said that family comes first.

"My kids are going to carve out their own place in the world and they know that I'm for them, whatever they want to do," Buffett told reporters. But "just because they came out of the right womb," setting them up with a trust fund—which he considered "a lifetime supply of food stamps"—could be "harmful" and a "antisocial act."31 Buffett was the rational one. When his children were toddlers, Buffett wrote to a friend that he wanted to see "what the tree has produced" before deciding whether to give them money.

Nonetheless, Buffett had made a decision that showed newfound—if minor—flexibility. In 1981, he established an innovative program under which Berkshire Hathaway would donate $2 per share to a charity of the shareholder's choosing. Berkshire did not pay a dividend, but this program gave shareholders control over how the company spent its charitable dollars, rather than allowing top management to donate to their preferred causes and receive credit. The program did not allocate much money, but Buffett's participation was a sign of weakness. The shareholders loved it. The program's participation rate was consistently close to 100%.

Buffett, the information collector, discovered that the contributions program was also a small gold mine. It provided him with information about each shareholder's philanthropic interests that he would not have obtained otherwise. Collecting this information served no purpose, much less than collecting nuns' fingerprints. Buffett, on the other hand, was insatiably curious and had a strong desire to learn about his shareholders as individuals, as if they were members of an extended family, which he considered them to be.

Buffett, who had already "retired" twice, was contemplating philanthropic and inheritance issues at age fifty-three. Retirement was clearly unsettling to him. He joked about working after his death and made a point of mentioning elderly managers such as Gene Abegg and Ben Rosner. But they had retired, and Lou Vincenti had Alzheimer's. Perhaps it was not surprising, then, that Warren's next move would be to make a deal with an eighty-nine-year-old woman who would outlive everyone he had ever met.

THE LOTTERY
Halfway Around the World, 1991–1995

Buffett's testimony in Congress as the reformer and savior of Salomon transformed him from a wealthy investor to a hero. Salomon was more than just a white hats versus black hats story. The success of his unconventional approach to scandal—embracing regulators and law enforcement instead of hunkering down—tapped into many people's desire for nobility: the dream that honesty is rewarded, that the besmirched can be redeemed through honor. Even as the crisis subsided, Buffett's star rose. Berkshire stock surged past $10,000 per share. Buffett was now worth $4.4 billion. Susie's stock alone was valued at $500 million. His original partners would now receive $3.5 million for every $1,000 they had invested in 1957.

When Buffett entered a room, the electricity was palpable. People felt a sense of greatness around him. They wanted to touch him. They either became speechless in front of him or made inane remarks. People listened without question to everything he said.

"I was at my best at giving financial advice when I was twenty-one years old, but no one listened to me. I could have stood up there and said the most brilliant things and received very little attention. And now I can say the dumbest things in the world and a lot of people will think it has some great hidden meaning or something."

He moved in a haze of fame. Reporters are constantly calling. He was followed and asked for an autograph, and photographers began to shadow him. Zsa Zsa Gabor wrote and requested a signed photo. As writers began working on books about Buffett, those who saw him every day—his supporters—found the frenzy incomprehensible. A woman arrived at Berkshire's office and began bowing and scraping with him. Gladys Kaiser was overcome with annoyance. "Do not bow to him!" she stated.

Many Salomon employees and ex-employees were, naturally, less impressed with Buffett than the rest of the world. He had curtailed their free-spirited culture, ruined their bonus day, and despised their business, which they were well aware of. Many employees had unhappy stories. The contrast between Buffett's affable demeanor and his coldly rational side quickly drew national media attention. How do you explain the contrast between Buffett figuratively sitting on a front porch with a glass of lemonade, telling folksy stories and teaching through homilies, and his long history of sophisticated business accomplishments? What was he doing as interim chairman of an investment bank while describing Wall Street as a gang of con artists, sharpies, and cheats?

What he was doing was attempting to align Salomon's pay practices with the interests of shareholders, but his concern about compensation was only one aspect of his fundamental objection to a company in which almost every department had an inherent conflict of interest with its customers. And without decimating Salomon by abandoning everything except proprietary trading, he couldn't do much about it. However, by 1991, the Wall Street Journal and the New Republic1 had taken note of his straddling of two worlds and published stories highlighting the differences between them. The discrepancy between Buffett's portrayal of himself as a middle-class Midwesterner who had awoken in Oz and the elephant-bumping in which he routinely engaged with his collection of jumbo-dumbo celebrity friends fueled the press's eagerness to debunk. The Wall Street Journal's article, "Buffett's Circle Includes the Moneyed and Powerful," included a sidebar that named people such as Walter Annenberg.2 Several of those mentioned in the story later claimed they were misquoted. Among them were Tom Murphy and a new friend, Bill Gates, CEO of Microsoft Corporation, who had had a casual conversation with Murphy about how he was being "ripped off," as Charlie Munger put it, by the cost of making television commercials. The Journal portrayed this conversation, which took place at a Buffet Group meeting, as musing over where the price of advertising was going and what advertising rates should be, which might fall into a "gray area of antitrust."3 Buffett and his friends sparred with the Journal's editors with little effect. Meanwhile, Gates, who might have been annoyed at finding himself entangled in this public-relations mess involving antitrust issues less than a year after the Federal Trade Commission launched a probe into possible collusion between Microsoft and IBM in the PC software marketplace, instead wrote Buffett an earnest letter apologizing for embarrassing him.4 At the time, Gates had known Buffett for less than five months.

The two had met that summer during the Fourth of July holiday, when Kay Graham and her Washington Post editorial-page editor and friend Meg Greenfield had dragged Buffett to Greenfield's Bainbridge Island home for a long holiday weekend. To Buffett, a weekend on an island a half-hour ferry ride from Seattle that could only be reached by boat, seaplane, or hitching a ride across the bridge by car was a "anything for Kay" experience. Greenfield had also invited him to spend the entire day at the nearby four-house compound on the Hood Canal that Bill Gates had built for his family. Gates, Buffett's twenty-five-year-old junior, appealed to Buffett primarily because he was known for his brilliance and the two were neck and neck in the Forbes race. But computers looked like Brussels sprouts to Buffett, and he didn't want to try them just once. Greenfield, on the other hand, had assured him that he would welcome Gates' parents, Bill Sr. and Mary, and other notable guests. Buffett had reluctantly agreed to go.

Kay and Warren drove down the dirt and gravel road to Meg's glass-walled contemporary home, where silky pink and purple sweet peas waved like pocket squares near the front door. The weekend began inauspiciously when Buffett learned that Graham, journalist Rollie Evans, and his wife would be staying in Greenfield's two guest rooms, which faced Puget Sound. He would, however, be staying in a small guest house located some distance away. When he arrived, he discovered that the owners had set up a temporary bed in a downstairs sitting room for him because all of the other rooms were already booked.

Buffett, who didn't care about his surroundings, was a good sport in this situation. To make himself more comfortable, Greenfield stocked his room with Cherry Coke, See's Candies, and honey-roasted peanuts. The bathroom he was supposed to use, however, had a sign in it that said, "No TP." Perplexed, he enlisted Graham and Greenfield, who had accompanied him to the bed-and-breakfast, as interpreters because no one was available to explain. Neither could understand what "No TP" meant either. They concluded there was likely a plumbing problem. Except for daytime visits, Buffett was unable to use the facilities at Greenfield's house. Greenfield suggested using the nearby gas station bathroom as an alternative.

Buffett sat in his room that evening, eating honey-roasted peanuts and drinking Cherry Coke. Memories differ as to whether he visited the gas station facilities in the early hours only to discover that the door was locked.5 In any case, the next morning, at Greenfield's house, they were all perplexed again about what "No TP" meant.

After breakfast, Greenfield led her guests into town to watch the Fourth of July parade from the roadside, among a small crowd of people sprawled out in lawn chairs. Uncle Sam, dressed in a blue tailcoat and a Stars and Stripes top hat, presided over a small brass band; fire trucks, an ambulance, and antique cars idled by; dogs trotted past in homemade costumes led by their couturiers; high-kicking high school cheerleaders preceded a troupe of dozens who struggled to control a massive U.S. flag raised overhead. Another antique car or two passed by, followed by a group of strawberry-dressed people, and finally the Kiwanis Citizen of the Year. Greenfield then hosted her annual garden party, where guests dressed in summer dresses, sport coats, and ties competed in a fierce croquet match against a vibrant backdrop of flowers rising from the lawn to her house.

The next morning, Buffett put on a cardigan and tidied his wild hair into a neat gray comb-over. Greenfield packed all five of them into her small car for the 90-minute drive to the Gates compound. "While we were driving down there, I thought, 'What the hell are we going to do all day with these people?'" How long should we stay to be polite?'" Gates had similar feelings. "I had a constant dialogue with my mom," he says. "Why don't you come to the family dinner? No, Mom, I am too busy; I am working. So she told me Katharine Graham and Warren Buffett were coming." He was interested in meeting Graham, a seventy-four-year-old legend who had softened into an older but still patrician—and imperious—figure, like a witty version of Queen Elizabeth, but, "I told my mom, 'I don't know about a guy who just invests money and picks stocks.'" I don't have many good questions for him; that's not my thing, Mom.' But she insisted." Gates arrived in a helicopter to make a quick getaway. When a small car drove into the driveway, he was surprised to see a group of famous people— Greenfield and her guests—pop out like a gang of circus clowns.6

Graham was led over to meet Gates, who appeared to be a recent college graduate dressed in a red sweatshirt over a golf shirt with his collar turned up in a small saucer around his neck. While Gates was arranging for Graham to take a seaplane ride, Buffett was introduced to Bill Gates Sr. and his wife, Mary.7 Bill III, also known as Trey, was brought around to meet Buffett.

Observers kept a weather eye on this introduction. Gates was well-known for expressing his impatience on topics that did not interest him. Buffett no longer left to read a book when he was bored, but he could quickly disengage himself from conversations he wanted to leave.

Buffett skipped the small talk and instead asked Gates whether IBM would do well in the future and if it was a competitor of Microsoft. Why did computer companies seem to appear and disappear? Gates began explaining. He advised Buffett to buy two stocks: Intel and Microsoft. Then he inquired about the economics of newspapers, to which Buffett responded that they had deteriorated due to competition from other media outlets. Within minutes, the two were deep in conversation.

"We talked and talked and talked without paying attention to anyone else. I began asking him a series of questions about his business, not expecting to understand any of it. He's an excellent teacher, and we couldn't stop talking."

The day began to go by. The croquet games started. But Gates and Buffett talked on, even as many of Seattle's best-known people circulated around them: Speaker of the House Tom Foley; chairman and CEO of Burlington Northern Jerry Grinstein; former EPA administrator Bill Ruckelshaus; Arthur Langlie, son of a former three-term governor, his wife, Jane, and their son Art; and Joe Greengard, a close friend of Greenfield's, plus a local doctor, judge, newspaper owner, and art collector.8 Gates and Buffett took a walk They were beginning to attract attention. "We were sort of ignoring all these important people, and Bill's father finally said, gently, that he'd like us to join in with the rest of the people a little more.

"Bill began trying to persuade me to get a computer. I said, "I'm not sure what it will do for me." I don't care how my stock portfolio is performing every five minutes. And I can calculate my income taxes mentally. Gates said he would choose the most attractive woman at Microsoft and send her to teach me how to use the computer. He'd make it completely painless and pleasant. I told him, 'You've made me an offer I almost can't refuse, but I'll decline.'"

During cocktail hour, Buffett and Gates continued to talk as the sun set over the water. At sunset, the helicopter had to depart. Gates did not agree with it.

"Then, at dinner, Bill Gates Sr. asked the table what factor they felt was most important in getting where they were in life. I said, 'Focus.' Bill said the same thing."

It's unclear how many people at the table understood "focus" the way Buffett did. This level of innate focus could not be replicated. He mentioned intensity, which is the price of excellence. It referred to the discipline and passionate perfectionism that made Thomas Edison the quintessential American inventor, Walt Disney the King of Family Entertainment, and James Brown the Godfather of Soul. It referred to Jeannette Rankin's deep commitment and mental independence in standing alone as the only representative in Congress to vote against the United States' entry into both World Wars, despite widespread ridicule. It referred to a single-minded obsession with an ideal. "Focus" referred to the type of person who could earn billions by allocating capital but was perplexed by a sign that read "No TP."

Sometime during the weekend, a less focused guest realized that "No TP" meant touchy plumbing that couldn't handle toilet paper. Finally, the mysteries of the indoor facilities were revealed, and Buffett was released from the gas station. However, some traitorous member of the party—Graham, Greenfield, or one of the Evanses—had found the story so amusing that Buffett's introduction to the Gates family included a recounting of "No TP."

A day later, Buffett escaped the island and returned to Omaha's normal plumbing. He could see Gates was brilliant and had a thorough understanding of business. But, since telling Katie Buffett not to invest in Control Data and passing up the opportunity to invest in Intel's start-up, Buffett has never trusted technology companies as investments. Technology companies came and went, and their products were often obsolete. With his interest piqued, he purchased a hundred Microsoft shares, which he compared to eating a single Cheerio. He couldn't bring himself to buy any Intel stock, even though he would occasionally buy a hundred shares just to keep track of the company. Grinnell College had made a lot of money from its Intel stock, but it had already been sold.10 Buffett himself would never buy stock that relied so heavily on future growth and that he didn't fully understand. However, he did invite Gates to the next Buffett Group meeting. Soon after, he received a phone call from Don Feuerstein and Tom Strauss, and for the next two months, he thought only of Salomon's misery.

In October, after being released from the conference rooms of 7 World Trade Center and the browbeatings of Congressmen and regulators for a few days, he traveled to Vancouver, British Columbia, for the Buffett Group's most recent meeting. The organizers, FMC Chairman Bob Malott and his wife, Ibby, valued Native American culture and planned a "potlatch dinner" and Native American dance one evening. The person who introduced the dancers explained that the ceremony had been shortened from its usual length of three days. For the next few hours, the Buffett Group twitched and yawned on hard wooden benches, with no refreshments or way out. Roxanne Brandt leaned over to Buffett at one point and asked, "Which is worse, this or Salomon?""She whispered." "This is worse," Buffett responded.11.

Bill Gates avoided the dancers' evening and attended the meeting for only one session that piqued his interest. The Buffett Group planned to examine the ten most valuable companies in 1950, 1960, 1970, 1980, and 1990—and how the list had changed. What gave a company a sustained competitive advantage? What gave companies an advantage, and why didn't they maintain it?—because the majority didn't.

Bill and his girlfriend, Melinda French, entered the room unobtrusively from the back, having arrived late due to a fog delay on his new seaplane. Melinda had assumed they would leave fairly early. However, after about the fourth slide, she realized that they might stay.12 Tom Murphy and Dan Burke, both members of IBM's board of directors, began discussing why IBM, the hardware leader, hadn't progressed to the software leadership. Buffett said, "I think we've got somebody here who can add a little something to this discussion." Everyone turned to see Bill Gates. The discussion continued. If you were Sears in 1960, why couldn't you keep hiring the smartest people and selling at the best prices? What did you fail to see that prevented you from remaining the leader? The majority of the proposed answers, regardless of the company, revolved around arrogance, complacency, and what Buffett referred to as the "Institutional Imperative"—the tendency for businesses to engage in activity for its own sake and to copy their peers rather than try to stay ahead of them. Some companies don't hire young people with new ideas. Sometimes management was not aware of tectonic shifts in their industry. Nobody said these problems were easy to fix. After a while, Buffett asked everyone to choose their favorite stock.

What about Kodak? Asked Bill Ruane. He returned his gaze to Gates, anticipating his response.

"Kodak is toast," Gates stated.14

Nobody else in the Buffett Group anticipated that the Internet and digital technology would render film cameras obsolete. In 1991, even Kodak didn't realize it was toast.15

"Bill probably thinks all the television networks are going to get killed," said Larry Tisch, whose company, Loews Corp., owned a stake in the CBS network.

"No, it's not that simple," Gates replied. "Nothing will fundamentally change the way networks create and expose shows compared to camera film. There will be some falloff as people seek more variety, but the networks own the content and can repurpose it. The networks face an interesting challenge as we shift TV transport to the Internet. But unlike photography, where you get rid of film, knowing how to make film becomes completely irrelevant."16

Everyone wanted to talk to Gates, who could explain the new digital world and its significance to them. "The next thing we knew, we were going on the boat that afternoon," Gates says. "And Kay was making sure that I didn't just talk to Warren." That was fortunate, because Buffett—who liked to stick close to certain people—would have liked to be Bill Gates' Siamese twin. They set out on Walter and Suzanne Scott's massive boat, the Ice Bear. Graham introduced Gates to Tisch, Murphy, Keough, and the rest. Within a half-day, he and Melinda had become de facto Buffett Group members. A group of people dropped in and out of a come-and-go discussion about a variety of topics, including Gates complaining to Murphy about the high cost of his television advertising. A month later, the Wall Street Journal story appeared, portraying Buffett as a hypocrite rather than the complex personality he was, and making everyone regret—not the conversation about ad prices, but responding after the meeting to questions from a reporter who didn't have a working tape recorder in his hand.

By 1993, Berkshire stock had nearly doubled, thanks in part to Salomon's salvation. By the time Warren Buffett began his way through arbitration with John Gutfreund, the stock had broken through $18,000 per share. Buffett was now worth $8.5 billion, while Susie's stock was worth $700 million. The original partners had $6 million for every $1,000 they had invested in 1957. Buffett was now the United States' richest man.

Over the holidays, he and Carol Loomis began the annual ritual of writing and editing his chairman's letter, this time with the knowledge of a much larger national—even international—audience. Buffett held his annual shareholder meeting in May 1994, the same month that Gutfreund's arbitrators awarded him zero, and over 2,700 people attended at the Orpheum Theater. Buffett instructed See's, the shoe companies, and the World Book Encyclopedia, which the company also owned, to set up booths in the lobby. See's sold 800 pounds of candy and over 500 pairs of shoes.18 World Book also sold well, but Buffett had no idea that it, like Kodak, would be toasted by the Internet. Buffett was pleased with his shareholders' purchases, so he drove over to Borsheims and made an appearance before heading to the Furniture Mart. "He goes out to where we have the mattresses displayed," said Louie Blumkin, "and he's selling, man."19 Buffett began to seriously consider the idea of hawking products at shareholder meetings. He promised to move the meeting to the Holiday Inn, which had more room for sales booths. Next year, he decided to sell Ginsu knives.20

His rising celebrity swept the rest of the family along with it. Buffett's charitable foundation would now be one of the five largest in the world, and his and Susie's decision to leave almost all of their money to it ensured that it would be Berkshire's largest shareholder after he died. Reflecting on this, he recently appointed Susie, president of the Buffett Foundation but with no business experience, to the Berkshire Hathaway board. The foundation had been giving away about $3.5 million per year, which had doubled by 1994 but remained small in comparison to families of similar wealth. Its future riches, however, were widely known. The Buffett Foundation and its president were suddenly in the spotlight.

When Susie moved to San Francisco and decided to stay married to Warren while going her own way, she imagined being able to keep the two halves of her life separate, quiet, and balanced. She was never a thinker, so she was taken aback when her husband rose to prominence in the business world, taking her with him. First, she wanted privacy and freedom. On the other hand, she wanted to please Warren, enjoyed running the foundation, and was drawn to the high-profile aspects of public service. Nonetheless, her position as president of the Buffett Foundation and now member of the Berkshire board made her a public figure. Susie was trapped. To avoid attention, she minimized her role and explained that she was merely an accessory to Warren's fame. Nobody should be interested in her, so no one should write about her or her life. To maintain her privacy, she had to strike a delicate balance between keeping a low profile in San Francisco and declining opportunities as her husband's status rose. Susie occasionally expressed resentment toward Warren to various people, as if it was his fault that her life had become so difficult.

Her routine with Warren now included the celebrity Sun Valley scene every July, the biannual Buffett Group meetings, which were held in different locations every other year, family Christmas and New Year's in Laguna Beach, and two weeks in New York with the entire family each May. In between these trips, Susie counseled a long list of "clients," visited and hosted her grandchildren in Emerald Bay, and accompanied son-in-law Allen Greenberg on Buffett Foundation business, which took them as far as Vietnam. She also entertained, attended parties, concerts, museums, spas, had pedicures, shopped, continued the never-ending renovation of the Laguna house, maintained her other relationships, wrote hundreds of cards and sent hundreds of gifts, and traveled frequently with friends. And she would gladly drop everything to be by the side of anyone who was dying or sick.

However, painful bouts of adhesions in 1987 slowed her progress, as did more adhesions and a hysterectomy in 1993. Kathleen Cole found herself taking her friend and boss to the ER too often. She tried to get Susie to exercise and wean her off her steady diet of Tootsie Rolls, cookies, and milk by stocking the kitchen with low-fat SnackWells. However, the Pilates equipment gathered dust downstairs, in a second apartment that Susie had convinced Warren to buy for her, and some friends noted that Susie routinely over extended herself with commitments to care for others.21 The family seemed strangely unperturbed each time Cole called Nebraska to say that Susie had been hospitalized, as if they had adopted her serene attitude.22 "Thank God I have my health," she often remarked, and continued to view herself as the well

By now, she was running a hospice from her apartment. Her first patient was an artist friend dying of AIDS, whom she invited to move in and spend his final weeks with her. Cole found herself administering IV drips to a terminal patient while Susie's other employees walked in and out of the room, questioning her about foundation issues or the renovations and redecoration of the Laguna Beach house, which was still evolving after a decade.23 After that, whenever one of Susie's gay friends dying of AIDS approached the end of his life, she invited him to live with her. She and Cole took some of her dying friends on dream trips, one to Japan and another to Dharamsala, where she arranged for him to meet with the Dalai Lama—an almost unimaginable spiritual experience for a man on the verge of death. After he died, she threw a La Cage aux Folles-style masquerade party instead of a memorial service, as requested by one friend. She kept her friends' ashes on her mantle so that others would remember them. Peter started calling his mother the Dalai Mama.

Howie, who had always absorbed so much of his mother's energy, was now stepping out from under her wing, just as his father's growing fame began to have an impact on him. In 1989, he was appointed chairman of the Nebraska Ethanol Authority and Development Board. Through this position, he became acquainted with Marty Andreas, an executive at Archer Daniels Midland, a large Illinois-based agricultural company heavily involved in ethanol. Marty Andreas was the nephew of ADM's CEO, Dwayne Andreas, who served on the Salomon board alongside Warren. Two years later, Howie, then thirty-six, was asked to join the ADM board as the youngest member.

Dwayne Andreas had been charged, but acquitted, of making illegal political campaign contributions during Watergate. He also made huge and sometimes controversial donations to politicians of both parties while Congress was repeatedly passing the tax subsidies for ethanol that benefited ADM. Buffett's view that rich people and powerful business interests were far too able to buy access and influence with politicians clashed sharply with the way that ADM did business.

Six months after Howie joined the board, Andreas hired him for a position in public affairs. Howie had no experience in public relations or finance, but he did have a basic understanding of money and business, making him the most Buffettesque of his siblings. At a school bake sale for the local junior high kids, he worked the checkout line. When people handed him five bucks for a fifty-cent brownie, he looked them in the eye and said, "We don't have change." He told the principal, "This is how you raise money." All afternoon, people donated whatever was in their pocket because Howie refused to give them change.24 Similarly, he was shrewd when it came to calling his father to talk about the job at ADM. He knew better than to What happens to the donations I can make through the Sherwood Foundation if I accept this position? He inquired. Buffett said he would not remove it. Okay, said Howie, perhaps understandably concerned about the impact of a desk job on his waistline; what about the farm's rent? Buffett swapped fixed for floating by allowing Howie to begin paying a flat seven percent rent on the farm's cost. After settling on another point or two, Howie agreed to relocate to Decatur, Illinois, where ADM was headquartered. The company placed him in charge of working with analysts.26

On the surface, Howie's position at ADM had nothing to do with his surname or his father's recent reputation as a model of corporate ethics. He would not have taken the job unless he thought it was a good fit, and his knowledge of ethanol made it seem plausible. His father had instilled in him disdain for special privilege. However, despite his many years of experience with people attempting to exploit his father's wealth, Howie was naive about large corporations, and he saw nothing unusual in a major corporation hiring a member of its board of directors to work as a public-affairs spokesperson.

Buffett, who would never invest in a company like ADM or hire someone who mixed business and politics in the same way Andreas did, said nothing to stop his son from serving on a board and working for a company so reliant on government subsidies. This unusual reticence reveals his desire for his son to gain business experience and, to some extent, follow in his footsteps.

Andreas was tough and demanding, according to Howie, and assigned him tasks such as purchasing flour mills in Mexico and working on the North American Free Trade Agreement. However, Howie remained the same person he had always been: adrenaline-fueled, energetic, painfully honest, and vulnerable. During family trips and gatherings, he continued to surprise his relatives by jumping out of closets in his gorilla costume.27 He wrote his mother letters filled with tears. His office resembled a teenager's bedroom, crammed with company tchotchkes such as toy trucks with ADM and Coca-Cola logos and Coca-Cola bottles that played the company theme song. Nonetheless, Howie felt he was getting years of business education compressed into a short period of time.

Buffett invited Howie to join Berkshire Hathaway's board in 1992, promising that his son would become non-executive chairman after his death. Howie's business experience was limited; he had never completed college, and he was more interested in agriculture than investing. He now had the beginnings of a credible resume. Buffett had every right to do this because he was the largest shareholder in what amounted to a family corporation. He reasoned that Howie would oversee the culture after he was gone. He recognized that his son was maturing and was a principled individual.

Buffett now had to do some mental backflips to reconcile all of the statements he had made over the years—denunciations of the evils of the "divine right of the womb," dynastic wealth, and advantages based on parentage rather than merit—with his decision to appoint his relatively inexperienced son as chairman of Berkshire Hathaway after his death. It was unclear how Howie's role would complement that of Berkshire's next CEO. That may have been the point. Every sign indicated that Buffett would ensure that power did not concentrate in the hands of a single individual after his death. This may or may not limit Berkshire's potential, but it would protect the company from the gruesome Institutional Imperative, which he saw as the most serious threat. Buffett desired a degree of control from beyond the grave, and this was his first step toward achieving it.

In a second step, he appointed Susie Jr., then Peter, to the board of the Buffett Foundation, with the understanding that Susie Jr. would head the organization after her mother died. Everyone involved assumed it would not happen until Warren was gone. Buffett's attitude toward the foundation, as with so many other things, was that "Big Susie will take care of it." Susie Jr.'s assumption of foundation responsibilities was presumably many years away; in the meantime, he was coming to rely on her in other areas. She was a budding philanthropist who contributed significantly to her father's civic and social life in Omaha. She had looked far and wide that year for a hail-damaged car that was affordable to her father. She was assisting him in organizing volunteers for the first Omaha Classic, a charity golf tournament he had founded his fellow CEOs would attend primarily but also by some celebrities. As her father's celebrity grew, Susie Jr. became his most frequent elephant-bumping escort, now that Kat Graham, in her seventies, was not getting out as much. Astrid, who only occasionally attended events with him, volunteered at the zoo and had no desire to serve on committees or chair events. Buffett's newfound fame had little impact on her life, except for the occasional gawker in the driveway.

Peter, too, remained on the ground as his father's celebrity soared above him like a speeding hawk. He had relocated to Milwaukee, the headquarters of his record label, where he and Mary had purchased a showy house to use as a recording studio. Warren Buffett's son's mansion was featured in the papers, making Peter the family member who had transgressed and embarrassed his father by appearing ostentatious. After a stressful marriage, he separated from Mary in May 1991, just before the Salomon affair began, and has since been going through a messy divorce. His father, who had long observed difficult divorces among friends and family, understood this. Following his divorce, Peter formally adopted his twin stepdaughters, Erica and Nicole. Big Susie had always welcomed them as her granddaughters, but Warren was more reserved. Later, in retrospect, it became clear that he saw the adoption as a new postmarital bond formed between Peter and his ex-wife—one to which Warren did not feel bound.

Peter, who is naturally introspective, found the end of his marriage to be catalytic and revelatory. He was doing inner work to establish a solid identity after so many years of being overshadowed and submerged by others. Despite this traumatic period in his personal life, his career had advanced. He had previously released several solo New Age albums. After reading Son of the Morning Star, a best-selling book about the Battle of Little Bighorn, his music began to incorporate Native American elements that he found deeply meaningful. That led to a job scoring the Fire Dance scene for Dances with Wolves, and a live performance at the film's premiere. He was now working on a film score for The Scarlet Letter and a CBS miniseries, and developing a multimedia show based on the Native American theme of identity loss and reclaiming.

Peter was respected but not famous, a working musician but not a celebrity. In the music industry, Buffett's name meant nothing. His father was proud of his son's film scoring and other accomplishments. But Warren's artistry, divorced from fame or commercial success, flew past him just as Peter's investing and business passion flew past him; their worlds did not intersect. Surprisingly, Warren and Peter were the most similar; both shared a passionate devotion to a vocation for which they had been destined since childhood; both became so engrossed in their work that they expected their wives to be their conduit to the outside world.

Buffett now had, indeed, a third son: Bill Gates.

At first it was what Gates calls "a tiny bit of 'Warren's the adult and I'm the child.'" Gradually this evolved into "Hey, we're both in this learning at the same time." Munger often attributed much of Buffett's success to the fact that he was a "learning machine." Although he wasn't going to learn to code software, and Gates wasn't going to learn to cite the statistics of every business for the last seventy years, their shared intellect, interests, and way of thinking had the same intensity. Buffett taught Gates how to invest and served as a sounding board for his business ideas. The way Buffett learned to think in models impressed Gates the most. Buffett was as eager to share his insights into what makes a great business with Gates as Gates was to hear them. If Buffett could have discovered more great businesses, he would have purchased them all. He never stopped searching for them. However, the town where the Graham-and-Doddsville Superinvestors lived was becoming increasingly crowded. Wall Street as a whole had been overrun, with fewer and fewer odd pockets of missed opportunity. Buffett had freed up more time and achieved greater balance in his life. He no longer wandered off to read American Banker during dinner parties, and he genuinely enjoyed socializing. While his business focus remained constant, as the 1990s progressed, the deals grew larger—but more sporadic. Meanwhile, a new interest developed. It would not lessen his enthusiasm for Berkshire, but it would shift his social priorities, travel plans, and even friendships.

Buffett now wanted to spend his spare time playing bridge. He had been playing a casual social game for nearly 50 years, and while in New York to deal with Salomon, he began playing a more serious and competitive game. In 1993, while playing in a simultaneous international bridge tournament with George Gillespie, he met Sharon Osberg, who was partnered with Carol Loomis.

Osberg grew up holding a deck of cards in her hand. She was a former computer programmer who began playing bridge in college. She had won two world team championships by the time she took over Wells Fargo's new Internet venture. It didn't hurt that she was a petite, sweet-faced brunette in her mid-40s.

"The next time she's going cross-country," Buffett told Loomis, "have her stop in Omaha. Let her call me."

"Where is Omaha?"", Osberg said. It took her three days to gather enough courage to pick up the phone, "scared to death." I had never spoken to a living legend before."31

Osberg, who lived in San Francisco, was on her way to Omaha about a week later. "I've never been so scared, breathing in and out," she tells me. Debbie Bosanek, Buffett's new secretary, showed her into the inner sanctum. He greeted her by reaching into a box and giving her three dice. These were covered with an odd set of numbers, such as seventeen and twenty-one, or six and zero. "Now you can look at these for as long as you want," Buffett said. "Then you pick any of them, and I'll pick, and we'll roll to see who wins." Osberg stared at the dice. She was so terrified that the numbers merged into a blur. After a few minutes of no response, Buffett said, "Well, let's just throw 'em." Three minutes later, Osberg was crawling on her hands and knees rolling dice on his office floor. That cracked the ice.

The secret of Buffett's "nontransitive dice" was that each die could be beaten by another; it was similar to the game "rock, paper, scissors," except that the players went one at a time. Whoever chose first automatically lost—because the other player could simply choose whichever die beat the one chosen first. Bill Gates and philosopher Saul Kripke figured it out, but no one else ever did.

Following that, Buffett treated Osberg to dinner at Gorat's, his new favorite steakhouse. He drove her through a residential neighborhood before pulling up next to a pharmacy and an AutoZone in the parking lot of what appeared to be a 1950s ranch house with metal steer heads near the front door. A big blue globe traced with black continents highlighted the sign, "Gorat's finest steaks in the world." Sitting in a room full of families eating at Formica tables, Osberg decided to play it safe and declared, "I'm going to have whatever you're having." Minutes later, she found herself looking at "a piece of raw meat the size of a baseball mitt." Afraid of offending a living legend, she ate it. Then they went to the local bridge club to play, and at ten o'clock, Buffett drove her around Omaha to show off his collection. She saw the Nebraska Furniture Mart parking lot, his house, the house where he grew up, and Borsheims, all while driving in the dark. Then he dropped her at the hotel. Both were leaving early the next day.

When Osberg checked out the next morning, the front desk clerk told her, "Someone came in and left a package for you." Buffett had arrived at the hotel at four-thirty a.m. and left her a compilation of his annual reports to shareholders, which he had privately printed and bound into a book.34 She had just become one of Buffett's people.

Soon after, Buffett arranged for Osberg to meet Kay Graham while she was in Washington on business. She served as a fourth bridge player alongside Graham and her friends Tish Alsop, widow of her friend Stewart Alsop; Cynthia Helms, wife of former CIA director Richard Helms; and Teeny Zimmerman, wife of Warren Zimmerman, who had recently been recalled as ambassador from the suddenly former Yugoslavia. Osberg soon began staying at Graham's house and regularly playing bridge in Washington with people such as Sandra Day O'Connor. She called Buffett from the guest bedroom. "Oh, my God!" she stated. "There is a real Picasso in the bathroom!"

"I never noticed it and I've stayed there for thirty years," Buffett later said of the Picasso sketch. "All I know is she leaves shampoo out."

Buffett began scheduling his trips to coincide with Osberg's business trips to New York. They played bridge at Graham's apartment with Carol Loomis and George Gillespie. "We liked each other," says Buffett, "although—she wouldn't say this, but—she was appalled at how badly we all played." Osberg was so gentle that she could correct him without hitting the hair-trigger button in him that reacted to criticism—Buffett always avoided or limited his time with anyone he feared would criticize him. After a few hands, she'd ask Buffett why he'd played a specific card. "Now, we have a learning opportunity," she would say, explaining what he should have done.

Soon the two had become close friends. Osberg felt it was a shame Buffett could only play when he was in a room with other bridge players. He needed a computer. They debated this for months. "You know, I think you might." I really don't." "You know, you could play bridge." "Uh, not really." Finally, Osberg said, "Warren, you should just try it." "Okay, okay," he said. "You come to Omaha and set up the computer, you stay at the house."

Bridge and Osberg accomplished something even Bill Gates had not. Buffett had the Blumkins send someone from the Furniture Mart to set up a computer. He stopped the Indefensible in a Midwestern city where Osberg was competing in a tournament and took her to Omaha. When they arrived home, she introduced Buffett to Astrid before teaching him how to use the Internet and a mouse. "And he was fearless, just fearless," Osberg claims. "He only wanted to play bridge." "Just write down the things I need to know to get in to play bridge," he suggested to her. "I don't want to learn about anything else. Don't try to explain to me what this thing is doing."36 Buffett adopted the moniker "tbone" and began playing on the Internet four or five nights a week with Osberg ("sharono") and other partners. Astrid would prepare an early dinner for him before he began playing bridge. Buffett quickly became so engrossed in Internet bridge that nothing could distract him. When a bat entered the house and flapped around the TV room, banging into the walls and becoming entangled in the curtains, Astrid screamed, "Warren, there's a bat in here!" Sitting across the room in his frayed terry-cloth bathrobe, staring at his bridge hand, he never moved his eyes from the screen as he said, "It's not bothering me at all."37 Astrid called the pest-control people, and the bat was removed without disturbing his bridge game.

Buffett felt his skills had improved significantly under Osberg's tutelage, and he wanted to compete in a serious tournament. "Why not start from the top?" she stated. They registered for the World Bridge Championships' mixed pairs event. The Albuquerque convention center was packed with people sitting around bridge tables and kibitzers watching the players. Murmurs and stares filled the room as the richest man in the United States and two-time world champion Sharon Osberg entered the World Bridge Championships together. Buffett's lanky frame and thatch of gray hair had become well-known by this point, causing quite a stir. It was unusual for an unranked amateur to attend the world championships as his first tournament. Warren Buffett's decision was shocking.

Osberg expected to lose quickly, so the goal was to have fun and gain experience. Instead, Buffett sat at the table and appeared to block everything. It was like nobody was in the room. His bridge abilities were not up to the level of most other players, but he was able to concentrate as calmly as if he were playing in his living room. "My defense is better with Sharon," he informs me. "It's almost as if I can feel everything she does. And you can be confident that everything she does is meaningful." His intensity overcame his game's weakness. Osberg was astounded when they qualified for the finals. "We were just good enough," she explains.

But after a day and a half of playing, Buffett was exhausted and drained. The only breaks had been an hour here and there to sneak out for a hamburger. He looked like he'd completed a marathon. In the break before the finals, he told Osberg, "I can't do it."

"What?!" she stated.

"I can't do it. Tell them we're not going to play in the final. Tell them I had a business emergency," he explained. Now Osberg had to explain this to the World Bridge Federation.

Nobody who had qualified for the finals had ever chosen not to compete. The representatives of the World Bridge Federation were outraged that Warren Buffett would attend their tournament, endorse it with his famous and important presence, qualify for the finals, and then attempt to leave. "You cannot do that!" they stated. When Osberg insisted, they threatened to deprive her of her rank and credentials. "I am not the one who refuses to play!"She insisted, saying he had a business emergency. Finally, they conceded that she was just Buffett's proxy, relented, and let the two of them leave without punishing her.

Naturally, Buffett encouraged Bill Gates, who had dabbled in the game, to take bridge more seriously. He also sent Osberg to Seattle to set up Bill Gates Sr. on the computer to play bridge, which began to integrate her into the Gates family.

Until this point, he and Bill had mostly seen each other at football games, golf courses, and Microsoft events. However, their relationship was gradually becoming more intimate. Bill and Melinda got engaged over Easter weekend 1993. Bill had the pilot give fake weather reports from Seattle on the way back from San Diego to trick Melinda into thinking they were flying home. She was taken aback when the aircraft door opened after they landed. Warren and Astrid were waiting on the red carpet at the bottom of the stairs. Warren took them to Borsheims, where Susan Jacques, CEO, helped them choose an engagement ring. Buffett flew to Hawaii nine months later for their New Year's Day wedding, which was to be held on the twelfth tee of the Four Seasons Manele Bay golf course on Lanai. Buffett had never visited Hawaii, although his sister Bertie owned a house on the Big Island. He was as excited about the Gates wedding as if it were one of his own children's weddings, though it could have been held anywhere, including Dubuque, Iowa. He believed Bill Gates was making one of the best decisions of his life by marrying Melinda French. However, Bill and Melinda's wedding clashed with Charlie Munger's seventieth birthday celebration, which took place the same weekend. The famously loyal Buffett never abandoned his old friends, but he did occasionally have to play Twister to manage his relationships. If a disagreement arose, he tended to resolve it by appeasing whoever he thought was most likely to be upset with him—which usually meant snubbing the most loyal and trustworthy of his friends, the ones he could rely on not to criticize or be angry with. This left the rejected person with the paradoxical comfort of knowing that he was the person Buffett most trusted and felt closest to. People who loved him understood, so they tolerated it.

Munger, Buffett's longtime friend, would tolerate almost anything, including missing his seventieth birthday party. Gates was the newer friend; in fact, Buffett came in second only to Melinda in terms of falling in love with Gates. So he decided to attend the wedding and brought Kay Graham with him. Graham, now seventy-six, travels less frequently these days, but she still attends state events like this. Furthermore, Gates had recently surpassed Buffett, who was now ranked second, to become the leader in the US money race. Together, they transformed the tiny island of Lanai into the world's wealthiest resort on New Year's Day. Meanwhile, Warren sent Susie to Los Angeles for Munger's party, where she sang.38

Susie, Warren's chess queen for many years, was used to such situations. She had her own definition of what he needed from the women in his life, categorizing each of them as utilitarian. She looked around the table one night while having dinner at Gorat's with Warren, Astrid, and Sharon Osberg, whom she had just met. Only Kay and Carol Loomis were absent from the harem. She laughs and shakes her head. "Someone for everything," she explained. She had placed Osberg in the "bridge" category. But Susie always downplayed the others' roles, and all of Warren's female friends shared Daisy Mae's loyalty.

Buffett soon began calling Osberg several times a day, taking her with him on trips, and making her one of his closest confidantes. She, like Astrid, preferred to remain in the background rather than disrupt the perceived order of Buffett's other relationships, which he had always kept separate. By the mid-1990s, the public's perception of how he spent his time differed significantly from how he actually spent it. Buffett continued to play Twister to avoid hurting anyone, but as usual, conflicts were resolved to appease whoever might erupt on him. The shrieking wheel received the grease.

Sharon, like Astrid, did not shriek. She was quietly invited to Susie Jr.'s Thanksgiving dinners and played bridge with Bill Gates. On January 1, 1995, a year after their wedding, Bill and Melinda Gates celebrated their first anniversary at their San Diego home. Buffett invited Bill, Charlie Munger, and Sharon to join him for a New Year's Day bridge game. Susie, who had grown accustomed to Warren choosing his own pursuits even during a family gathering, spent the day with family and friends, while Gates, Osberg, and Buffett sat at the bridge table waiting for Munger. Buffett, who was always punctual, noted that it was time to start but otherwise ignored Munger's tardiness because no one else seemed to care.

Gates was in a good mood, but as they talked, Buffett became irritated that they were kept waiting. When Munger did not appear after a few minutes, Osberg proposed a game of three-handed bridge to keep the others entertained, partnering with Buffett and Gates while maintaining her end of the conversation.

Buffett, who was acting as the polite host, cracking jokes and making conversation in an attempt to make everything okay, had become noticeably jumpy and restless after 45 minutes of three-handed bridge. He suddenly jumped out of his chair. "I know where he is," he explained. He picked up the phone and dialed the Los Angeles Country Club.

Whoever answered the phone searched. Within a few minutes, he had found Munger in the golf grill, sitting with his buddies, as he did every day when not at work. He was about to bite his sandwich.

"What are you doing, Charlie?"" Buffet asked. "You're supposed to be playing bridge with us."

"I'll be there in a few minutes," Munger said.

He hung up the phone, set down his sandwich, and walked to his car without saying anything.

Half an hour or so later, Munger walked into the Buffetts' house at Emerald Bay, sat down at the table as if nothing had happened, as if he hadn't noticed that he'd kept Bill Gates waiting for an hour and a half on his first anniversary, and said

"Happy new year. "Let us play."

The other three were stunned and sat in silence for a brief moment.

Then Gates replied, "Okay. "Let us play."

They played.

Another group of Buffett's loyal friends joined him for their biennial ritual in September 1995, when the Buffett Group met at the Kildare Club in Dublin. Because Bill Gates was present (Gates straddled all of Buffett's worlds, as Buffett aspired to be his Siamese twin), the Irish government treated them as emperors. They were greeted at the airport by official government limousines and guarded by security agents in helicopters. They dined with the chairman of Guinness, the Taoiseach and his wife, and the US ambassador, walked the cobblestones of Trinity College to the Book of Kells, and clapped their hands in admiration of the Irish National Stud's sleek hunt stallions in County Kildare. They had never experienced such luxury before, not even in Williamsburg under Kay Graham's direction. The K Club, which is filled with incredible artwork and antiques, raises all of its own food on-site and prepares it with European staff and chefs.

The gloss and glamour of the surroundings belied the fact that the Buffett Group members, many of whom were already fabulously wealthy, remained largely unchanged. Warren saw some of these people only once a year or so, but he remained completely committed to them. Bill Ruane remained gregarious and told long, funny stories. Walter Schloss continued to live in a tiny apartment and pick stocks the same way he had always done. The Stanbacks, among the group's wealthier members, would still refuse to fly anything other than coach. Sandy Gottesman remained skeptical of everything and demanded an override on all transactions. Tom Knapp had finished buying up large chunks of Maine's coastline and was now focusing on Hawaii. Jack Byrne was as full of energy as ever. Roy Tolles continued to keep his thoughts to himself, except for occasional one-liners. Ed Anderson and Joan Parsons poured money into human-sexuality research, but Ed continued to pick up pennies on the street, unless they were particularly dirty. Marshall Weinberg remained an irresistible flirt. Lou Simpson was still a great stock picker, and he had become one of Graham-and-Doddsville's Superinvestors. Carol Loomis had made enough money from Berkshire stock to fly in a private jet, but she couldn't buy a jar of pickles without remembering the luxury of pickles during her Depression-era childhood.39 Walter Scott, who had retired from building massive dams and bridges, now builds gigantic houses. Instead of taking a cab after going to the theater, Joyce Cowin walked up Broadway and across the park to the Upper East Side in a snowstorm. Ajit Jain, who is now a member of the Buffett Group, spent most meetings in his room, rushing through deals to please Buffett. Ron Olson, who had once been liked by almost everyone Buffett knew (except Judge Brieant), was now liked by the majority of people in greater Los Angeles. Then there were Bill Scott, Mike

Goldberg, and Chuck Rickershauser, all in various states of retirement after years of working under the nice, warm sun, and all in various stages of recovery from the effects of Rickershauser's Law of Thermodynamics.40 Bill Gates, unlike the others in so many ways, shared the group's intellectual interests and complete lack of pretense. Kay Graham, on the other hand, remained their only true connection to the upper echelons of society, titillating them even as she failed to seduce them. "Oh, Princess Diana," she would respond. "You are such a good friend. There is a lot more than meets the eye.

Buffett distributed copies of The Gospel of Wealth, a booklet written by Andrew Carnegie, a turn-of-the-century industrialist and philanthropist. As he celebrated his sixty-fifth birthday and reflected on his life thus far, he reread Carnegie. Now he led the group in a debate about Carnegie's premise that "He who dies rich dies disgraced." Carnegie had honored that philosophy by spending nearly his entire fortune, one of the greatest in history at the time, to establish libraries in towns and cities across the United States.41 Buffett had always planned to die rich and disgraced, as Carnegie would put it, so that there would be more to give away after he died. He insisted that the best use of his talents was to continue making more money until he died, and he had no desire to be personally involved in the foundation's activities. That would be Susie's project. But he wanted to hear what others thought and was clearly considering this question. They moved around the table. Bill Ruane, who had never cared about money and was poor compared to others, was about to embark on a project to transform New York's worst public schools. He would later collaborate with Columbia University to screen thousands of New York City schoolchildren for mood disorders and suicidal ideation.42 Fred and Alice Stanback were among the most significant donors to environmental causes in the US. Tom Murphy was the chairman of Save the Children. Ron's wife, Jane Olson, was chairman of Human Rights Watch's international board. Before Dan's death, the Cowins gave an important art collection to the American Folk Art Museum. Charlie Munger donated to Good Samaritan Hospital and Education. Walter and Suzanne Scott made large donations in Omaha. Ruth Gottesman sat on the Albert Einstein College of Medicine Board of Overseers. Marshall Weinberg gradually donated nearly all of his money to scholarships, global health, Middle East issues, and educational research. The others had their own causes.

When his turn in the conversation came, Bill Gates asked, "Shouldn't the measure of accomplishment be how many lives you can save with a given amount of money?" He agreed with Buffet that you had to make money first before giving it away. However, once he had made a certain amount, Gates stated that he would use it to save more lives in the present by giving the majority of it away.43

The Buffett Foundation spent very little money compared to Buffett's wealth. Buffett had chosen two major philanthropic issues: overpopulation and nuclear proliferation, which are nearly impossible to solve. Nuclear proliferation did not lend itself well to financial solutions, but Buffett would have given as much money as he could to his top priority, any plausible way to reduce the likelihood of nuclear war. His analysis of the problem was characteristically statistical.

"A nuclear attack is unavoidable." It is mankind's ultimate problem. If there is a 10% chance that something will happen in a year, there is a 99.5 percent chance that it will occur in fifty years. But if you can reduce that probability to three percent, it will drop to seventy-eight percent in fifty years. And if you can reduce it to one percent, there is only a forty percent chance in fifty years. That's a truly worthwhile goal; it could literally change the world."

The other major issue, in Buffett's opinion, was the strain placed on the already overburdened planet by an excessive population. Since the mid-1980s, the Buffett Foundation has spent most of its money on population control due to the lack of a solution to the nuclear problem. This, too, he approached mathematically. In 1950, the world's population was approximately 2.5 billion. A mere two decades later, shortly after Paul Ehrlich's The Population Bomb was published, the world population was approaching 3.7 billion.44 Ehrlich had predicted that the 1970s and 1980s would be periods of massive global starvation, with hundreds of millions of people dying. By 1990, the world's population had surpassed five billion, there had been no mass starvation, and many experts no longer took Ehrlich's ideas seriously—despite the fact that the population had increased dramatically. The debate centered on whether technology could outpace population growth, species extinction, and global warming. Buffett viewed the issue of population growth and diminishing resources through the lens of a "margin of safety."

"There is a carrying capacity for the Earth. It's far, far, far greater than [Thomas] Malthus ever imagined. On the other hand, there is some carrying capacity, and the one rule about carrying capacity is to err on the low side. If you were provisioning a large rocket ship for a trip to the moon and didn't know how long it would take, you probably wouldn't put more than 150 people on board. And we have a spaceship, but we don't know how long the supplies will last. It's difficult to argue that the world would be better off in terms of average happiness or livelihood with twelve billion people rather than six.45 There is a limit, and if you don't know what it is, you're better off erring on the side of caution. It is a margin of safety approach to the survival of the earth."

Since the 1970s, Buffett has focused on providing women with access to contraception and abortion—issues close to Susie's heart—as a solution to uncontrollable population growth. This was a common viewpoint among humanist organizations at the time.46 Munger, Tolles had gotten Buffett involved in supporting an important court case in California, People v. Belous, which was a major step toward the landmark abortion ruling in Roe v. Wade.47 Charlie Munger took up this case with zeal; the firm had chosen it out of concern for the way young women were being maimed and killed by illegal abortions. Buffett and Munger sponsored the Ecumenical Fellowship, a "church" that became part of the country's abortion underground railroad (48).

Buffett was particularly moved by Garrett Hardin's logic, which laid out how people who have no ownership stake in common goods—the air, the seas—overuse and destroy them.49 While Buffett adopted many principles conceived by Hardin, a leader of the "population control" movement, he rejected Hardin's solutions, which advocated authoritarian ideas and a eugenicist approach. Hardin had stated that the meek not only would inherit, but had already inherited the earth. He called it "genetic suicide": "Look around you. How many heroes do you have among your neighbors? Or your colleagues?...where are the heroes of yesterday? Where is Sparta today?"50

Buffett believed the Sparta revival idea had already been tried. Adolf Hitler tried it. The Spartans had genetically modified themselves by abandoning weak or "undesirable" babies on a mountainside. Sir Francis Galton developed modern eugenics, a social philosophy based on his cousin Charles Darwin's work, in which he proposed that selective breeding of the human race could improve population quality. This notion had received extremely widespread support in the early twentieth century, until it was discredited by Nazi Germany's experiments.51 There was no safe way to think along the lines that Hardin was pursuing, which led to a deadly division of humanity into competing groups.52 Buffett had renounced this view in favor of a civil-rights-based approach to the problems of spaceship Earth.

As a result, by 1994, Buffett's emphasis had shifted from "population control" to reproductive rights.53 This shift corresponded with a global evolution in thinking among the population control movement. Women "were no longer to be treated as a convenient means toward the 'end' of population control."54 Buffett had always believed that any method of solving the population problem that involved coercion was unacceptable.55 Now he went a step further. "I would not limit a woman's right to bear children even if the world was extremely overpopulated, and I would not prohibit the right to choose even if the planet had only two people and fertility was critical. I believe that the world should be limited to wanted people first. I don't think numbers should determine how many people are wanted. Even if everyone had seven children, I would not, as Garrett Hardin suggested, tie the right to the numbers." As a result, the Buffett Foundation supported reproductive rights.

The complexities and nuances of reproductive rights, civil rights, and population control were increasingly overshadowed by the abortion debate. Buffett's giving was ultimately based on what he dubbed the Ovarian Lottery.56 He had passed the concept on to a group called Responsible Wealth. Buffett found the idea very appealing.57

"I've had it pretty good in this world, you know. The odds were fifty-to-one against me being born in the United States in 1930. I won the lottery the day I was born by living in the United States rather than another country, where my chances would have been drastically different.

"Imagine there are two identical twins in the womb, both bright and energetic. And the genie tells them that one will be born in the United States and one in Bangladesh. And if you end up in Bangladesh, you won't have to pay taxes. What percentage of your income would you bid to be the one born in the US?It implies that society, rather than your innate qualities, influences your fate. People who say, 'I did it all myself,' and identify as Horatio Alger—believe me, they'd rather be in the United States than in Bangladesh. "That is the Ovarian Lottery."

The Ovarian Lottery had shaped all of Buffett's political and philanthropic views; Buffett's ideal was a world in which winners were free to pursue their dreams while helping losers. In his lifetime, he had witnessed extremes of inequality; he had grown up with the lynchings and beatings of the civil-rights era; and he had heard over and over about the Court House Riot, which saw authority shoved onto a scaffold with a noose around its neck at a time and place when one group of people felt more deserving than another. Buffett, perhaps unconsciously, had abandoned his father's libertarian leanings58 and spiritually circled back to the democratic idealism of Nebraska's William Jennings Bryan, who had written of "the class that the rest rested upon."

Buffett, one of the least peripatetic people in both philosophy and geography, could make a tectonic shift if he had enough conviction. After returning from Ireland, he and Susie met in Vancouver to embark on a seventeen-day trip to China, dubbed "Across Cathay." The Gateses inspired Buffett to embark on this round-the-world journey. Bill and Melinda went to great lengths to make the trip enjoyable for him. They sent him and the other guests a questionnaire in advance to find out what they enjoyed eating. Buffett was not taking any chances with an experience like the one he had at the Moritas'. "I don't eat any Chinese food," he explained. "If necessary, serve me rice, and I'll just move it around on my plate, then go back to my room and eat peanuts." Please get me a journal every day; it's really hard when I don't have one."

And so Buffett traveled to China.

After checking in at Beijing's grand old Palace Hotel on Goldfish Lane, the tour group met Dr. Robert Oxnam, president of the Asia Society, who would be their lecturer for the trip. Following a talk on modern China, they ate a magnificent Sichuanese dinner in the hotel's Emerald Room. Waiters served course after course on rotating platters, including tea-smoked duck, twice-cooked pork with chili sauce, spicy chicken, and Sichuan hot pot. However, the Gateses had arranged for the tour company, Abercrombie & Kent, to send people ahead to teach the chefs how to prepare hamburgers and french fries for Buffet. To his delight, he was served course after course of fries, including dessert.

The following morning, the group set out to visit the Forbidden City, Beijing University, and the National Palace Museum. Buffett was served hamburgers and french fries for lunch at Fangshan restaurant and again that evening at the Diaoyutai State Guesthouse, an imperial family fishing grounds and retreat, while the rest of the group dined on Chinese cuisine.

In Beijing, the group met with China's Premier, and Gates set up a Ping-Pong match between Buffett and a twelve-year-old champion. On the third day, Dr. Oxnam spoke about the Great Wall's history and folklore. When they reached the top, they were greeted with champagne—and Cherry Coke for Buffet. Everyone waited for Buffett to say something profound as they looked down on the world's largest structure, which represented eleven centuries of innovative engineering, human labor, and Chinese history. He would undoubtedly be moved by the sight.

"Boy, I sure would have liked to have been the company that got the brick contract for this thing," he told me.

He skipped his martial-arts lesson the next morning in favor of a tour of the local Coca-Cola plant. The next day, the group boarded a Chinese military transport plane bound for Ürümqi, a town in far northwestern China near Mongolia that was once a major stop on China's Silk Road. They would board a train, but not just any train, because the Gateses had arranged for the group to be the first Westerners to rent Chairman Mao's personal train for a trip across northwest China. The train followed the Old Silk Road route, stopping along the way to allow the group to ride camels in the desert, visit ancient cities and caves, see giant pandas in Xi'an, and tour the archaeological dig of the imperial Terra Cotta Warriors and Horses, which is believed to be the world's largest funerary site. The trip allowed for hours and hours of conversation, during which Buffett and Gates continued their discussions about why some banks are better than others, why retailing is such a difficult business, the value of Microsoft stock, and so on.61

On the tenth day, they visited the site of the Three Gorges Dam project before boarding the M.S. East Queen, a massive five-deck cruise ship with a ballroom, a barbershop, a masseuse, and a formally-dressed musician on the deck who performed "Turkey in the Straw."

The boat entered the first of three gorges, the Shennong Xi, where many of those on board donned orange life vests and climbed into longboats poled and pulled by river trackers along an upstream tributary of the river. A group of ten men dragged each boat against the current with ropes, while young, supposedly virginal girls sang to encourage the men in their difficult task.

Buffett made jokes about the virgins. But that night, during the Cantonese dinner, with his mind clearly focused on the implications of the Ovarian Lottery, he said, "There could have been another Bill Gates among those men pulling our boat." They were born here, and they were destined to spend their lives tugging those boats in the same way that we did. They did not have a chance. It was pure luck that we got a chance at the brass ring."

The boat continued its journey from Shennong Xi to Outang Gorge, passing through villages where schoolchildren came out to greet the strange Americans. The boat slowly made its way down the Yangtze, past a silk-reeling mill, between sheer, mist-shrouded peaks, and alongside a traditional cobblestone village. Finally, they arrived in Guilin for a private Li River barge cruise through one of the world's most scenically beautiful places, a pristine river lined with thousands of limestone pinnacles covered in green, "like jade hairpins," according to Tang poet Han Yu. Many members of the Gates party rode bicycles along the riverbank to see the long waterside parade of untouched prehistoric stone shafts that were two to three hundred feet high. Warren, Bill Sr., and Bill Jr. had obtained permission from their wives to perform an hour-long bridge orgy on the boat as the barge glided through the magnificent pine-forested scenery.

When they arrived in Hong Kong at the end of their journey, Buffett drove the Gateses directly to McDonald's to buy hamburgers in the middle of the night. "And all the way back from Hong Kong to San Francisco and then on to Omaha, I just read newspapers."

But even years after that journey through China, Buffett's mind kept returning to one of its moments. It wasn't the scenery, which he'd barely noticed, or the camel ride, which was captured in a photograph. Everyone else had enjoyed the endless meals of fries at Chinese banquets, but not me. He was thinking about the Three Gorges Dam and the longboats on the Shennong Xi river. But it wasn't the singing virgins who had seduced him. The fate of the men who spent their lives dragging the longboats upstream lingered with him, haunting his thoughts about personal destiny and fate.

TO HELL WITH THE BEAR
Omaha and Greenwich, Connecticut, 1994–1998

Buffett devoured the Wall Street Journal every day until 1994, looking for stocks to buy for Berkshire Hathaway. But it was getting harder to find a great business at a reasonable price. He continued to invest in Coca-Cola, eventually spending $1.3 billion on 100 million shares. He purchased another shoe company, Dexter. Here he was a little outside his "circle of competence," betting that demand for imported shoes would wane.1 A jeweler named Barnett Helzberg Jr., who knew about Borsheims, saw Buffett in New York in a conversation on Fifth Avenue and almost immediately sold him Helzberg Diamonds. Buffett was also purchasing American Express stock again.

He wanted the remainder of GEICO.

Since October 1993, GEICO had been led by two co-CEOs: Lou Simpson, the company's chief investment officer, and Tony Nicely, a soft-spoken, silver-haired teddy bear of a man who had worked there since he was eighteen and now oversaw the insurance operations. Nicely had stepped on the gas, and GEICO, after a period of dormancy, began adding half a million new customers per year. In August 1994, Buffett met with Nicely, Simpson, and Sam Butler, the chairman of the board's executive committee and the man who had found Jack Byrne many years before to save the company. Nicely, who disliked dealing with Wall Street, had believed since becoming co-CEO that GEICO should be privately owned.2 He would rather work for Buffett than a group of analysts and money managers.

Butler oversaw the negotiations. He wanted stock at a price in the $70s. Buffett found that outrageous. He wanted to pay cash and a price in the high $50s.3 They negotiated for a year. Buffett took out the circular saw. This was his strategy for undermining GEICO by giving Butler the impression that the company was weak and vulnerable. Buffett warned the market was out of control. This high-tech Internet stuff is going crazy, and it's going to hurt the entire industry—including GEICO. You have a significant advantage when selling over the phone, but the Internet is going to narrow that considerably. It was clear that by 1994, before the average person had an email address, Buffett, who claimed to know nothing about computers, had already predicted how the Internet would affect the auto-insurance industry in the coming decades—better than the auto-insurance industry itself.

Butler, however, was a tough and experienced lawyer who could not be Buffeted. Berkshire's stock price had doubled in two years. That April, with BRK trading at $22,000 per share, Money magazine cited the Overpriced Stock Service newsletter, which stated that the price of BRK "makes sense only if the company is run by God." Butler refused to lower his estimate. He wanted as many Berkshire shares as possible. The two had reached an impasse. Finally, Buffett used the ultimate weapon and hired Charlie Munger as the Appointed Bad Guy. This had been predictably successful at Salomon, but Sam Butler proved too tough to be Fingered.

After a year, it became clear that if Buffett wanted GEICO, he'd have to match Butler's price. Buffett wanted GEICO so badly he caved. In August 1995, he paid $2.3 billion for 52 percent of GEICO, after spending $46 million on the first 48 percent. And he paid with Berkshire stock rather than cash. Despite having fought so hard, Buffett saw the price as reasonable overall, given the bargain he had gotten on the first half of the stock.

The GEICO transaction signaled a turning point. The stock market had been on a tear, with new offerings of hot stocks unexpectedly popular in 1994, following a strong 1993.4 In February 1995, the Dow surpassed 4,000 for the first time. Microsoft released Windows 95 and sold $700 million on day one. Suddenly, everyone working in an office had a computer on their desk. People purchased computers for their children to complete homework after school. To stay up to date on carpool news, mothers of kindergarteners were given email addresses. Website designers were unable to meet the demand from businesses. Computer hackers made front-page headlines.

In August 1995, an Internet service provider called Netscape went public to raise funds for expansion. Many people were aware of Netscape's product, but the company had never made a dime. Morgan Stanley set up a toll-free number to handle the influx of calls requesting to buy stock. Orders for 100 million shares poured in for a company that had initially planned to sell 3.5 million shares.

Despite Buffett's use of a computer to play bridge and the Internet insights he demonstrated while negotiating for GEICO, his knowledge of technology was limited. He remained uninterested in computers despite the rest of the world could not get enough of them. Bill Gates accepted this as a challenge. He invited Buffett and Munger to a meeting at Microsoft to discuss technology. The night before, he and Melinda hosted a dinner at their home, and she seated Munger alongside Nathan Myhrvold, Microsoft's chief technology officer. The two quickly got into a lengthy conversation about naked mole rats. A naked mole rat resembles a boudin blanc—a French milk sausage—with teeth; it feels no pain when cut, scraped, or burned. Munger, a science buff, had some tangential knowledge about this subject. Sandy Gottesman had previously invested in laboratory mice, hoping to profit from the rising demand for experimental animals. But Gottesman's investment failed, leaving him with a building full of mice under a bridge in New York City. The naked mole rat was a superior beast, not only insensitive to pain but also parthenogenetic, meaning that the queen of the colony fertilizes and gives birth without the assistance of males. Munger and Myhrvold engaged in an animated discussion about the sex life of mole rats, while the others sat in numb disbelief.

The next morning, Gates brought Buffett and Munger to Microsoft so that his number two, Steve Ballmer, and a half-dozen engineers could interview them as anthropologists, given how strange it seemed to them that these two incredibly brilliant men were such latecomers to the computer world. They were like a couple of caveman savants discovered in the bush who saw an airplane but refused to take a ride. Despite his understanding of the Internet's importance, Buffett had not yet advised GEICO to hurry up and use the Internet to sell insurance. To Buffett, computers were simply tunnels that allowed him to connect with other bridge players.

"That piqued Bill's interest because he saw how an application could draw in someone who had no prior interest in computers. Everyone else was interested in the computer, but I was only interested in the application. You sell the computer first to computer enthusiasts, and then to people like me who don't give a damn about computers."

Buffett, who considered computers outside his "circle of competence," could have become the richest man in America instead of Gates if he had invested in Microsoft and Intel. Instead, he was now second. But he didn't care. Or, rather, he did care—a lot; he would rather be number one than anything else—but he cared far more about avoiding unnecessary risk. He had no idea which companies would become the next Microsoft or Intel, and which would fail. He would never abandon his margin of safety. He was aware that many technology businesses had a life cycle as short as that of a naked mole rat.

Buffett did not need to make risky bets, even if he had the temperament for it. He was still feeling the effects of decisions made years before. The hiring of Ajit Jain meant that when Hurricane

Andrew wiped out South Florida in 1992, Buffett was able to launch a new business, "catastrophe reinsurance," which charged a premium to stand by as an insurer of the unthinkable. Then the Northridge earthquake struck. Almost no one had the capital to take such a large risk. Berkshire Hathaway did.

Buffett's relationship with the Blumkins gave him the opportunity to acquire R. C. Willey is a Salt Lake City-based furniture retailer. The days of scouring Moody's Manuals for small businesses were over; instead, he played white knight once more to save FlightSafety from a corporate raider. This was a unique and profitable company that trained pilots and manufactured the massive flight simulators used in that training. He went on to acquire Star Furniture and International Dairy Queen. However, the majority of the ideas presented to him were what he referred to as "cocker spaniels," when he had requested "collies." In response to these proposals, he quipped in Berkshire's annual report, "If the phone doesn't ring, you'll know it's me."

Some may have assumed that if Buffett buys Dexter Shoes, he will buy anything. He was beginning to regret the deal. Dexter was being killed by foreign competition, and people were still interested in buying imported shoes. But the mistakes were few, and the home runs were plentiful: Cap Cities/ABC agreed to sell itself to Disney for $19 billion, and Berkshire made $2 billion, nearly four times its initial investment. Tom Murphy joined Disney's board, and Buffett became acquainted with Michael Eisner, the CEO of Disney, through Murphy. The Buffetts were now able to mingle with a crowd that included Coca-Cola executives and movie stars. He also returned to the board of the Washington Post, which was now led by Don Graham, one of his favorite people, allowing him to rejoin his favorite company in his favorite environment—newspapers.

In early 1996, Berkshire stock skyrocketed to $34,000 per share, valuing the company at $41 billion. An original partner who invested $1,000 in 1957 and left it alone now has $12 million in savings, more than doubling the amount just a few years ago. Buffett was worth $16 billion. Susie now owned $1.5 billion in Berkshire stock, which she had promised not to touch7. She and Charlie Munger were both billionaires on the Forbes 400 list. Berkshire was once invisible, but it was discovered by people who had never heard of it before. That year, 5,000 people from all 50 states attended the shareholder meeting/discount mall.

Buffett was proud to have never "split" the stock and vowed never to do so again. "My ego is wrapped up in Berkshire...." said the man. "I can gear my whole life by the price of Berkshire."8 However, it is now so expensive to buy a share of BRK that copycats have formed investment trusts. Their plan was to replicate Berkshire Hathaway's stock portfolio and allow people to buy in smaller increments, as if it were mutual funds. However, Berkshire was not a mutual fund; rather, it was a perpetual-motion vacuum cleaner that sucked up businesses and stocks before spitting out cash to buy more businesses and stocks. That could not be replicated by purchasing the stocks it held. Above all, you did not receive Buffett.

Furthermore, the copycat funds were buying Berkshire's stocks at much higher prices than Berkshire had paid, and charging high fees to do so. They cheated investors. The Buffett cop has now emerged.

"I don't want anyone buying Berkshire thinking they'll make a lot of money quickly. They won't do it in the first place. Some will blame themselves, others will blame me. They will all be disappointed. I don't want to disappoint anyone. From the moment I started selling stocks, I was terrified of setting unrealistic expectations for people.

To deter potential copycats, he decided to issue a new class of shares. Each B share—or "Baby B"—was worth 3.33 percent, or 1/30, of a pricey A share.

He had a lot of fun with the B shares, writing: "Neither Mr. Buffett nor Mr. Munger would currently buy Berkshire shares at that price, nor would they recommend that their families or friends do so." According to him, "current shareholders will not suffer any diminution in per-share intrinsic value, no matter how many Class B shares the Company decides it is necessary to sell." 9

By selling an unlimited amount of stock, they ensured that the price would not rise due to excess demand. "You don't want people to think of it as something that can double, you understand. You can also create your own market action for a while. I could have been a hero for a year as all the money flowed into a fixed supply of stock. Instead, we said we'd sell as much of this stuff as the world wanted, so it couldn't be a hot stock."

At the same time, Buffett was extremely pleased with the inverted logic of explicitly selling stock that he would not buy himself. Furthermore, issuing the B shares fulfilled a duty to his shareholder "partners." The cash inflow from the B shares would be a pretty good deal for them.

Never before had a CEO done something like this. Media coverage of Buffett's honesty felled a small forest of trees. Nonetheless, investors rushed to buy B shares. Buffett thought they were foolish and said so privately and frequently. However, there was no denying that it was extremely flattering that they did, as they were clearly buying solely for him. He would have been secretly disappointed if the B-share offering failed. The B shares were a no-risk deal for Buffet: his shareholders and he both profited regardless of how the offering turned out.

The Baby Bs forever altered the character of Buffett's "club." After May 1996, forty thousand new owners could call themselves shareholders. The following year, he relocated the meeting to the dilapidated old Ak-Sar-Ben Coliseum, where 7,500 people attended. They paid $5 million to Nebraska Furniture Mart. The meeting evolved into Woodstock for Capitalists, or BRKfest. The 1998 shareholder meeting drew 10,000 people. However, as the money, people, and fame poured in, an underlying shift occurred in the world in which Buffett worked, with far-reaching consequences for him and everyone else.

There was no such thing as "Wall Street" anymore. Now, financial markets were a network of blinking terminals linked by computers connected to the Internet that reached every corner of the globe. Mike Bloomberg, whom Salomon had been foolish enough to fire in the 1980s, had created a special computer that captured all the financial information anyone could possibly want. It generated graphs, tables, calculations, news, and quotes; it could perform historical comparisons and set up competitions between companies, bonds, currencies, commodities, and industries for those who were fortunate enough to have a Bloomberg terminal on their desk.

By the early 1990s, the Bloomberg terminal had become ubiquitous. The Bloomberg saleswoman had been calling Berkshire Hathaway three years in a row. "Nope" was the response every time. Buffett believed that following the market minute by minute and manipulating computers was not the way to invest. Even Buffett, who was computer-averse, realized that to trade bonds, a Bloomberg terminal was required. However, Bloomberg was located some distance from

Buffett's office, and he never looked at it; that was the responsibility of Mark Millard, the bond trader.

The introduction of the Bloomberg terminal, a symbol of new computerized trading, mirrored Salomon's internal struggle over its identity. Its laggard businesses had never recovered. Maughan attempted to realign pay at Salomon in 1994, arguing that employees should bear the same risk as shareholders. When times were good, they received bonuses; when times were bad, they suffered as well. There were those within the firm who agreed with him.11 However, this was not the case elsewhere on Wall Street, so thirty-five senior executives exited. The employees' refusal to share the risk disgusted Buffett.

The arbs fought for their share after losing Meriwether's bonus-pimping ability. Buffett was willing to pay them for results—the firm continued to make the majority of its money through arbitrage—but increased competition made it more difficult for them to produce.

Arbitrageurs bet that a temporary price gap between similar or related assets will eventually close. For example, the bet could be on whether two nearly identical bonds will trade at a similar price.12 With so much new competition, easy trades became scarce. The arbs took larger positions with higher risk. When they were losing, they doubled down and expanded the size of their trades. In both cases, they did so because trade margins were declining, and larger trades, often involving debt, helped to offset this.

The racetrack rules stated that you were not required to return it in the same manner in which you lost it. The reason is the math behind losing money, which works as follows: If someone has one dollar and loses fifty cents, she must double her money to make up the difference. That is difficult to do. It's tempting to borrow an additional fifty cents for the next bet. That way, you only need to make fifty percent (plus the interest on the loan) to break even—much easier to do. However, borrowing the money doubles your risk. If you lose 50% again, you're done. The loss has wiped out all of your capital. Hence Buffett's sayings: Rule number one, don't lose money. Rule number two: don't forget rule number one. Rule number three: don't get into debt.

However, the arbs' strategy was based on the assumption that their value estimate was accurate. As a result, when the market turned against them, all they had to do was wait to recoup their losses. However, defining "risk" in terms of volatility assumes the investor is patient and willing to wait. Of course, anyone who borrows to invest may not have that time. Furthermore, enlarging a losing trade necessitated having extra capital stashed somewhere that could be spent at a moment's notice if necessary. Capital has an opportunity cost.

Larry Hilibrand lost $400 million—a huge sum—arbitrating the difference in interest rates on mortgage-backed bonds. He was confident that if the firm doubled his bet, he would be able to recover his mortgage arbitrage losses. Buffett agreed with Hilibrand in this case and gave him the funds for the trade, which ultimately proved profitable.

The arbs had an almost supernatural belief in their own abilities, and as their market segment crowded, they wanted to expand into even more types of arbitrage involving more variables and less certainty. They relied heavily on computer models powered by complex mathematics, but they always claimed they were only guidelines. Buffett and Munger believed that using models to make investment decisions was like driving a car on cruise control. The driver may have thought he was fully alert and attentive, but he soon discovered otherwise when the road became winding, rain-slicked, and congested. What the arbs truly desired, more than capital to invest, was J.M. Meriwether initially remained on the sidelines during Salomon's recovery while the arbs begged him to return. Deryck Maughan made polite noises, but everyone knew he didn't want Meriwether back. Nonetheless, Buffett and Munger gave their approval, subject to certain conditions. Meriwether needed supervision. He could return to his old position, but he'd have to report to Maughan and have less control over his operation. Meriwether, unwilling to work on a shorter leash, ended negotiations in 1994 and went on to found his own hedge fund, Long-Term Capital Management. It would operate similarly to Salomon's bond arbitrage unit, except that Meriwether and his partners would retain the profits.

Meriwether's key lieutenants left Salomon one by one to join him at Long-Term Capital Management's new harborfront offices in Greenwich, Connecticut. Deryck Maughan, deprived of his most profitable assets, noticed the "for sale" sign on Buffett's block of stock and began planning for the day when Buffett would wash his hands of Salomon.

***

Warren Buffett had long been wary of market overvaluation, and the collapse of Long-Term Capital Management (LTCM) in 1998 reinforced his concerns. LTCM, led by John Meriwether, was a hedge fund that used extreme leverage and complex financial models to make small profits on vast numbers of trades. The fund's strategy was based on the assumption that financial markets would become more efficient over time, causing risky assets to converge in price with safer ones. However, when Russia defaulted on its ruble debt in August 1998, markets worldwide went into panic mode, and LTCM, which had bet on stability, suddenly found itself in free fall.

Buffett and his longtime business partner Charlie Munger had been skeptical of LTCM's approach from the beginning, believing the fund relied too much on leverage and mathematical models without fully accounting for catastrophic risk. When the crisis hit, LTCM found itself trapped—its high-risk positions lost value rapidly, and it was unable to raise additional capital. The fund, which had initially raised $1.25 billion and had grown to control over $129 billion in assets, suddenly faced insolvency. Desperate to avoid total collapse, Meriwether and his team reached out to investors and banks for a bailout.

Buffett, known for his aversion to high-risk investments, was initially uninterested in saving the fund. However, seeing an opportunity, he joined forces with Goldman Sachs and AIG to propose a buyout. Their consortium offered to purchase LTCM's entire portfolio for $250 million while injecting an additional $3.75 billion in capital, with Berkshire Hathaway providing most of the funding. However, the deal required Meriwether and his partners to retire. A drafting mistake in the offer and Meriwether's reluctance to relinquish control caused delays, and when LTCM attempted to negotiate, Buffett's satellite phone failed while he was traveling, preventing further communication.

Meanwhile, the Federal Reserve Bank of New York, fearing a broader financial crisis, convened a meeting of major banks. LTCM was so deeply entangled in the financial system that its collapse could trigger a domino effect, destabilizing global markets. The Fed brokered a rescue package in which 14 major financial institutions collectively injected $3.6 billion into the fund. Buffett's bid was ultimately rejected, and he later reflected that Meriwether and his team likely preferred not to sell to him, even though his offer could have been more favorable.

The LTCM debacle highlighted the dangers of unchecked leverage and the blind faith in financial models that assumed rare market shocks were nearly impossible. Buffett viewed the crisis as one of the greatest missed investment opportunities of his career. More broadly, the event raised concerns about "moral hazard"—the idea that if financial institutions believe they will always be bailed out, they will take on greater risks, assuming someone else will bear the consequences.

Following the bailout, the Federal Reserve lowered interest rates three times in quick succession to stabilize the economy. The stock market surged, reinforcing the perception that government intervention would always prevent financial disaster. For Buffett, the lesson was clear: no matter how sophisticated financial models seemed, risk was real, and extreme leverage always carried the potential for total loss. LTCM's failure was a stark reminder that markets are unpredictable, and even the smartest investors can be undone by overconfidence and excessive risk-taking.

Printed in Great Britain
by Amazon

62191143R00125